Maritime Container Port Security

Xufan Zhang · Michael Roe

Maritime Container Port Security

USA and European Perspectives

Xufan Zhang
Department of Logistics
Beijing WuZi University
Beijing, China

Michael Roe
Graduate School of Management
Plymouth University
Plymouth, UK

ISBN 978-3-030-03824-3   ISBN 978-3-030-03825-0   (eBook)
https://doi.org/10.1007/978-3-030-03825-0

Library of Congress Control Number: 2018960499

This Palgrave Macmillan imprint is published by the registered company Springer Nature Switzerland AG
The registered company address is: Gewerbestrasse 11, 6330 Cham, Switzerland

*This book is dedicated to Ms. Zheng Xu and Ms. Cuizhen Yang,
both of whom have been my guardian angels.*
Xufan Zhang

For Liz, Joe and Siân.
Michael Roe

Acknowledgements

First of all, I would like to express my sincere thanks to all of my Ph.D. supervisors Professor Michael Roe, Professor Jingjing Xu and Dr. Tuck, and my second supervisors Captain Syamantak Bhattacharya and Dr. Young Joon Seo, for their patience, encouragement, valuable advice and strict requirement regarding academic research. Professor Roe, who was my first director of supervision and supervised me for three years, has supported me with his warm heart throughout my entire Ph.D. process. He is more than an academic supervisor to me. He inspired me with his passion in life and coloured my dull Ph.D. journey. I also would like to give my special thanks to Dr. Tuck who took me in when I felt confused and helpless, and guided me through the very end of my Ph.D. with her sound academic ability.

Secondly, I would give my appreciation to the participants of my Delphi study, who took time out from their busy schedule and contributed their valuable knowledge to my research. This thesis would not be possible without their engagement and support.

My deepest gratitude and love go to my beloved family and friends. My mother, Ms. Zheng Xu, has always been an inspiration and the strongest backing of my life. She has been working so hard to provide me the opportunity of being educated in the UK. We have been through some ups and downs, and she is always there for me with great love. She is a marvellous, passionate and tough woman. I would not be me without her. My grandparents encourage me to pursue knowledge and support me with their selfless love. I also want to thank my beloved boyfriend Dawei and his lovely family for their encouragement and support. In addition, I would like to thank my dear friends who support me Teresa Zhu, David An, Daniel Shan, Jing Xing, my "old squad" members, Hanqing Zhao, Yanan Zhao, Xiaoyang Zhao, Dr. Chia-Hsun Chang, Safaa Sindi, Andy Wu, Xu Zhang, Dr. Seo, Yichen Jiang, "203" housemates, "No 8" friends and many other friends who shared life with me.

Last but not least, I would like to thank all of the academic and administration staff in Plymouth University, especially Professor John Dinwoodie and Ms. Ricky Lowes who provided me with the opportunity of working as a lecturer and personal tutor. Ms. Cher Cressey supported me throughout my study. In addition, I want to thank the academic team members Dr. Dave Jones, Kristin and Gemma from Plymouth University International College that accept me as a lecturer. I also want to thank Ms. Anna McKenna who helped me with my English writing in her tutorial.

Beijing, China   Xufan Zhang
West Hoe, Plymouth, UK   Michael Roe
October 2018

Contents

Abbreviations

ACI	Advanced Cargo Information
AEO	Authorized Economic Operator
AIS	Automatic Identification System
AMS	Automated Manifest System
ANOA	Advance Notice of Arrival
APEC	Asia-Pacific Economic Cooperation
APMO	Average Percentage of Majority Opinions
ASEAN	Association of Southeast Asian Nations
ATS	Automated Targeting System
BASC	Business Anti-Smuggling Coalition
CBP	US Customs and Border Protection
CBPIA	Customs and Border Protection Office of International Affairs
CSCL	China Shipping Container Line
CSI	Container Security Initiative
C-TPAT	Customer-Trade Partnership Against Terrorism
DEA	Data Envelopment Analysis
DHS	US Department of Homeland Security
EC	European Committee
EDI	Electronic Data Interchange
EESC	European Economic and Social Committee
ERP	Enterprise Resource Planning

EU	European Union
FAST	Free and Secure Trade
FBI	Federal Bureau of Investigation
GAO	US Government Accountability Office
GIS	Geographic Information System
GMPH	Gantry Moves Per Hour
HLH	Hamburg-Le Havre
ILO	International Labour Organisation
IMO	International Maritime Organisation
IQR	Interquartile Range
ISO	International Organisation for Standardisation
ISO/PAS	International Standards Organisation Publicly Available Specifications
ISO28000	International security program originated from ISO Technical Committee
ISPS	The International Ship and Port Facility Security
LTTE	Liberation Tigers of Tamil Eelam
MARSEC	Maritime Security
MTSA	Maritime Transportation Security Act
NII	Non-Intrusive Inspection
NISAC	National Infrastructure Simulation and Analysis Centre
NTC-C	National Targeting Centre-Cargo
OCS	Outer Continental Shelf
OECD	Organisation for Economic Co-operation and Development
OSC	Operation Safe Commerce
PIP	Partnership in Protection
ROPMIS	Resources, Outcomes, Process, Management, Image, Social responsibility
RPM	Radiation Portal Monitor
SAFE	Framework of Standards to Secure and facilitate Global Trade
SCS	Supply Chain Security
SD	System Dynamics
SEP	Secured Export Partnership
SFI	Secure Freight Initiative
SOLAS	Convention on the Safety of Life at Sea
SST	Smart and Secure Trade-lanes
STAR	Secure Trade in the APEC Region
TAPA	Transport Asset Protection Association

TEU	Twenty-foot Equivalent Unit
THC	Terminal Handling Cost
UNCTAD	United Nations Conference on Trade and Development
USCG	US Coast Guard
VTS	Vessel Traffic System
WCO	World Customs Organisation
WMD	Weapon of Mass Destruction
WSC	World Shipping Council
WTO	World Trade Organisation

List of Figures

List of Tables

List of Equations

1

Introduction

The 9/11 events in 2001 caused worldwide concern about global safety and security. World commerce depends heavily on maritime transport, so its security has attracted great attention (UNCTAD 2004). Several major international organisations reacted swiftly to enhance maritime transport safety by strengthening security measures. They produced both voluntary and compulsory rules and programmes, which have been implemented internationally.

In the academic field, there has been considerable research undertaken on maritime safety and security. Roach (2004) studied security management of terrorism threats in shipping companies. Håvold (2005) discussed safety climate and culture in the shipping industry and revealed 11 risk factors. Thai (2007) examined the effects of security improvements in maritime transport with an empirical study of Vietnam. Lun et al. (2008) discussed how technology could enhance container transportation security.

Most non-bulk cargoes are transported within standardised containers. The container shipping system is efficient and economical, but also vulnerable to illegal intrusion and misuse. Weapons of mass destruction (WMD), illegal goods and human trafficking can be concealed within

© The Author(s) 2019
X. Zhang and M. Roe, *Maritime Container Port Security*,
https://doi.org/10.1007/978-3-030-03825-0_1

containers by terrorists and criminals. Vessels themselves can be used as a weapon in a terrorist attack. In addition, terrorists can operate vessels to finance and support their logistics operations (OECD 2003).

The Container Security Initiative (CSI) was established in 2002 by US Customs and Border Protection (CBP) to cope with '*the threat to border security and global trade posed by the potential terrorist using a maritime container*' (Donner and Kruk 2009, p. 27). Participating states cooperate with the US CBP to ensure all high-risk containers are identified and inspected before loading onto vessels destined for US ports. Currently, the CSI has been operated in 58 ports worldwide. It is labelled as voluntary since the regulations are not mandated by a law or international convention.

Despite the positive implications of conducting security initiatives for global trade safety and security, arguments arise from the potential issues caused by compliance with the CSI. Additional costs and operational inefficiency are the two major issues raised by many studies (OECD 2003; Dekker and Stevens 2007; Bennett and Chin 2008; Bichou and Evans 2007; UNCTAD 2007; Kruk and Donner 2008; Bichou 2011). A major part of the cost burden comes from the container scanning required by the new security regime. In order to comply with the regime, initialisation costs occur for purchasing, installation, initial training and civil engineering works. Moreover, there are extra costs for operating the container scanning equipment. The cost estimation varies, but the results of past research conclude that the additional cost could cause problems for both low-volume and high-volume container ports (OECD 2003; Miller 2007; Bichou and Evans 2007; UNCTAD 2007; Dekker and Stevens 2007). In addition, stakeholders argued that procedural requirements act against operational and logistical efficiency. Both the direct functional redundancies and the indirect supply chain disruptions that arise out of the longer lead times could lead to less reliable demand and supply scenarios (Bichou 2011).

On the other hand, advocates of maritime security measures argue that the total cost and time of cargo inspection can be lower than conventional random physical inspections since '*detailed data recording, electronic reporting and other procedural requirements*' by the new security regulations make pre-screening and targeting suspicious containers possible (Bichou 2008, p. 30). A shipment through a CSI port will undergo zero inspections upon arrival except for an occasional random examination (Bichou 2011). Productivity of the entire supply chain can be improved because of better procedural arrangements. Moreover, security regime compliance is commercially rewarding. Much research focuses on positive impacts regarding logistical efficiency (Crutch 2006; Gutiérrez et al. 2007; Thai 2007). Positive impacts include reduced transit time and improvements of lead-time predictability (Thai 2007; Bichou 2011), a reduction in stowaways (Timlen 2007), improved manpower utilisation (Thai 2007), better document processing and cargo handling (Thai 2007), and improved customer satisfaction and enhanced branding (Gutiérrez et al. 2007; Thai 2007; Bichou 2011).

Nonetheless, to date, there is little data and empirical analysis to support either the positive or negative operational and financial impacts of maritime security regime compliance. There are some studies that examine the existence of these impacts, based on conceptual work, economic situation or anecdotal evidence (Babione et al. 2003; Lee and Whang 2005; Thai 2007; Rabadi et al. 2007; Gutiérrez et al. 2007; Bennett and Chin 2008; Yang 2010; Urciuoli et al. 2010; Voss et al. 2009; Talas and Menachof 2009).

Dekker and Stevens (2007, p. 499) conducted an explorative empirical study of maritime security-related costs and financing in European Union (EU) states and in addition suggested three topics for further study on maritime security costs and financing and associated regulations: (i) *'assessment of a harmonised (legal) system of best practice'*; (ii) *'long-term analysis on the effects of security measures on the competitive positions of seaports'*; and (iii) *'provision of empirical evidence for the answer to the question whether security measures should be more (port) administration-based than industry-based'*.

There are a number of benefits from complying with the CSI, mainly focused on trade facilitation. However, some effects still remain controversial. According to the earlier discussion, two major debates over the CSI are compliance cost and operational inefficiency. Moreover, CSI has been introduced as a voluntary bilateral arrangement between US Customs and container export ports overseas; therefore, a concern of port competition distortion was expressed by some stakeholders.

Theoretically, trade and transport operators can still operate with or without participating in those programmes (Donner and Kruk 2009). However, implications in terms of port competition distortion have emerged. First of all, financial problems have become a major concern since the CSI was introduced, such as the financial cost for carrying out both the non-intrusive inspections (NII) and physical inspections. The CSI member ports could ultimately transfer these extra costs to the US importers as their cost-recovery measures; however, these costs may be significant enough to cause importers to consider cheaper alternatives (Parliament of Australia 2003). Although not joining the CSI does not cease a country's container movement to the USA, the shipment processing from non-CSI ports may be less efficient than CSI-affiliated countries. Longer processing time from a non-CSI port may affect the export port's efficiency, which will influence the customer decision towards port choice.

Port competition is becoming increasingly complex and is affected by various factors within logistics (Haezendonck and Notteboom 2002). The competitive position of a container port is affected by '*its competitive offering to the host of shippers and shipping lines for specific trade routes, geographical regions and other ports to which the container port is connected*' (Notteboom and Yap 2012, p. 551). Parola et al. (2017, p. 117) defined competitiveness as '*the skill or talent resulting from acquired knowledge, able to generate and sustain a superior performance as well as face competitive dynamics*'. Port competitiveness is decided by the competitive advantages created or acquired by a port (Haezendonck and Notteboom 2002). Much port competitiveness analysis highlighted port selection criteria (Pearson 1980; Willingale 1981; Brooks 1984, 1985; Slack 1985; Murphy et al. 1988, 1989, 1991; Peters 1990; Murphy and Daley 1994; UNCTAD 1992; Jeon et al. 1993; McCalla 1994; Malchow and Kanafani 2001, 2004; Haezendonck and Notteboom 2002; Lirn et al. 2003; Bichou and Gray 2005). Yeo (2007) summarised 38 port competitiveness determinants based on existing research. Port efficiency and charges remain the most significant factors for port competitiveness. Port service is another factor that differentiates a port from its competitors (Bennathan and Walters 1979). Apart from the factors mentioned above, issues such as port policy and port management are also related to port competitiveness.

Port competition varies in different locations depending on how port competition forces affect the port environment. Therefore, factors that influence EU container seaport competition need to be identified and used to analyse how the CSI affects the EU container port market.

This suggests the following research objectives:

O1: To review previous work on maritime security and EU container seaport competition.

O2: To review the various port security regulations of the USA, focusing on the CSI programme and the existing debates over its implications.

O3: To identify the determinants of EU container port competitiveness.

O4: To investigate the effects of the CSI on EU container seaport competition.

O5: To propose a sustainable solution to existing issues of maritime security.

A qualitative approach was applied in order to address the research gap identified above. The Delphi technique was chosen to gather and analyse the primary qualitative data required to assess the conceptual model. Delphi was chosen because it can stimulate participant discussion without the necessity of gathering subjects into one place and without the risk of 'group think' (De Meyrick 2003; Rowe et al. 2005; Iqbal and Pipon-Young 2009). It provides rich qualitative information (Clayton 1997; Hsu and Sandford 2007; Cottam 2012).

Regarding this research, the term 'security' refers to terrorism since the research is designed to investigate measures against terrorism. Therefore, maritime security is related to maritime terrorism. A literature review on various maritime security initiatives, including the CSI and their impacts on port competition, was carried out. Following the literature review, a conceptual model that included five conceptual assumptions was developed. From each of these conceptual assumptions, a set of statements was derived, which formed the basis for the Delphi study.

The Delphi survey consisted of three rounds, and the Delphi statements were formed based on the conceptual assumptions. Three groups of experts comprised the Delphi panel: (i) academics who have the opinions and expertise of scholars researching maritime security and container port competition; (ii) industry users, having the opinions and industry experience of EU container port management and CSI implementation; and (iii) administrators, occupying the positions and experience of major organisations involved in maritime security regulation and maritime governance on international, supranational and national levels. All participants remained anonymous to protect their identity and the integrity of the companies and organisations involved. The Average Percentage of Majority Opinions (APMO) cut-off rate was used as a consensus measure.

Clearly, there were some limitations beyond the researchers' control. Firstly, due to the nature of the research topic and time factor, the primary data were collected based on a small panel size. Keeping participants' momentum and interests in the survey is also very difficult. Therefore, a larger panel size would be better for data collection. The second limitation stems from the nature of the Delphi technique. As one of the survey methods, the results showed inconsistency among participants (Bichou 2008). Three groups of experts with different backgrounds were included in the Delphi, and their understanding of statements was influenced by their backgrounds. Lastly, due to the varying port competition environments in different regions, this research focused only upon the EU port region rather than the globe. In order to obtain a more comprehensive understanding of how CSI affects the port industry, other port regions such as Asia and the Americas should be considered for future research.

The structure of this book consists of the following ten chapters:

Chapter 1: Introduction: An overview of this research including the research background, aim and objectives and research methods is explained in this section. It also provides an outline of the overall structure.

Chapter 2: Maritime Security Measures and the Container Security Initiative (CSI): This chapter presents and discusses issues regarding maritime security and the relevant framework, including major compulsory and voluntary measures. The CSI and its controversial implications are included as well.

Chapter 3: Port Competition: In order to fulfil the research aim and objectives, port competition and competitiveness determinants are discussed in this chapter. Theories on political economics are introduced additionally as the foundation of this abductive research.

Chapter 4: Models of Container Port Security: This chapter demonstrates a conceptual model by developing five conceptual assumptions. These conceptual assumptions form the basis of this research.

Chapter 5: Research Methodology for Container Port Security: This chapter describes and explains the research philosophy, strategy and approach, data collection method, Delphi design and data analysis techniques.

Chapter 6: The Delphi Research Process: This chapter presents the Delphi survey. It begins with a discussion of the panel selection process, followed by description and presentation of the pilot study. The chapter then outlines the process of each round of Delphi. The results of the three rounds, including the response rate and consensus level, are presented.

Chapter 7: The Delphi Results: This chapter presents discussions of statements that reached consensus for each round. The conceptual assumptions of the model developed in Chapter 4 are revised as well.

Chapter 8: The Implications for Container Port Security: This chapter starts with a discussion of quality criteria of this Delphi research and critically analyses the Delphi implementation. The rest of this chapter discusses and analyses the primary and secondary data collected from the Delphi study and the literature review, based on the conceptual model and assumptions developed in Chapter 4.

Chapter 9: Maritime Governance, Security Measures and Port Competition in the EU: A new model is developed in this chapter to provide explanations of the research gap revealed in Chapter 2 and results of the Delphi. Since this research is shaped within an abductive approach, this research attempts to explain the incomplete observation specified in Chapter 2. The model built in this chapter provides an insight into the current maritime security initiatives and how they have affected EU container seaport operations and competition.

Chapter 10: Conclusions for Container Port Security: This chapter provides a summary of the realisation of the research aim and objectives, contribution and limitations. It also gives suggestions to the issues discovered from this research and recommendations for further study.

References

Babione, R., Kim, C. K., Phone, E., & Sanjaya, E. (2003). *Post 9/11 Security Cost Impact on Port of Seattle Import/Export Container Traffic* (Working Paper GTTL 502). The University of Washington.

Bennathan, E., & Walters, A. A. (1979). *Port Pricing and Investment Policy for Developing Countries*. Oxford: Oxford University Press.

Bennett, A. C., & Chin, Y. Z. (2008). *100% Container Scanning: Security Policy Implications for Global Supply Chains* (Master of Science Dissertation). Massachusetts Institute of Technology.

Bichou, K. (2008). *Security and Risk-Based Models in Shipping and Ports: Review and Critical Analysis, in ITF, Terrorism and International Transport: Towards Risk-Based Security Policy*. Paris: OECD Publishing.

Bichou, K. (2011). Assessing the impact of procedural security on container port efficiency. *Maritime Economics and Logistics, 13*(1), 1–28.

Bichou, K., & Evans, A. (2007). Maritime security and regulatory risk-based models: Review and critical analysis. In K. Bichou, M. G. H. Bell, & A. Evans (Eds.), *Risk Management in Port Operations, Logistics and Supply Chain Security* (pp. 265–280). London: Informa.

Bichou, K., & Gray, R. (2005). A critical review of conventional terminology for classifying seaports. *Transportation Research A, 39*, 75–92.

Brooks, M. (1984). An alternative theoretical approach to the evaluation of liner shipping—Part 1: Situational factors. *Maritime Policy and Management, 11*(1), 35–43.

Brooks, M. (1985). An alternative theoretical approach to the evaluation of liner shipping—Part 2: Choice criteria. *Maritime Policy and Management, 12*(2), 145–155.

Clayton, M. J. (1997). Delphi: A technique to harness expert opinion for critical decision-making tasks in education. *Educational Psychology: An International Journal of Experimental Educational Psychology, 17*(4), 373–386.

Cottam, H. (2012). *An Analysis of Eastern European Liner Shipping During the Period of Transition* (PhD thesis). Plymouth University, UK.

Crutch, M. (2006). *The Benefits of Investing in Global Supply Chain Security: Executive Summary from the DVDR 2006 Roundtable Meeting.* Lehigh University Centre for Value Chain Research.

Dekker, S., & Stevens, H. (2007). Maritime security in the European Union-empirical findings on financial implications for port facilities. *Maritime Policy and Management, 34*(5), 458–499.

De Meyrick, J. (2003). The Delphi method and health research. *Health Education, 103,* 7–16.

Donner, M., & Kruk, C. (2009). *Supply Chain Security Guide* (pp. 1–107). The World Bank/DFID. Available at http://siteresources.worldbank.org/INTPRAL/Resources/SCS_Guide_Final.pdf. Accessed 20 April 2016.

Gutiérrez, X., Hintsa, J., Wieser, P., & Hameri, A. P. (2007). Voluntary supply chain security program impacts: An empirical study with BASC member companies. *World Customs Journal, 1*(2), 31–48.

Haezendonck, E., & Notteboom, T. (2002). The competitive advantage of seaports. In M. Huybrechts, et al. (Eds.), *Port Competitiveness: An Economic and Legal Analysis of the Factors Determining the Competitiveness of Seaports* (pp. 67–87). Antwerp: De Boeck.

Håvold, J. I. (2005). Safety-culture in Norwegian shipping company. *Journal of Safety Research, 36*(5), 441–458.

Hsu, C. C., & Sandford, B. A. (2007). The Delphi technique: Making sense of consensus. *Practical Assessment Research and Evaluation, 12*(10), 2.

Iqbal, S., & Pipon-Young, L. (2009). The Delphi method. *Psychologist, 22*(7), 598–601.

Jeon, I.-S., Kim, H.-S., & Kim, B.-J. (1993). *Strategy for Improvement of Competitive Power in Korea Container Port.* Seoul: Korea Maritime Institute.

Kruk, C., & Donner, M. (2008). *Review of Cost of Compliance with the New International Freight Transport Security Requirements.* Washington, DC: The World Bank.

Lee, H. L., & Whang, S. (2005). Higher supply chain security with lower cost: Lessons from total quality management. *International Journal of Production Economies, 96*(3), 289–300.

Lirn, T. C., Thanopoulou, H. A., & Beresford, A. K. C. (2003). Transhipment port selection and decision-making behaviour: Analysing the Taiwanese case. *International Journal of Logistics: Research and Applications, 6*(4), 229–244.

Lun, Y. H. V., Wong, C. W. Y., Lai, K. H., & Cheng, T. C. E. (2008). Institutional perspective on the adoption of technology for the security enhancement of container transport. *Transport Reviews, 28*(1), 21–33.

Malchow, M., & Kanafani, A. (2001). A disaggregate analysis of factors influencing port selection. *Maritime Policy and Management, 28*(3), 265–277.

Malchow, M. B., & Kanafani, A. (2004). A disaggregate analysis of port selection. *Transportation Research Part E, 40,* 317–337.

McCalla, R. (1994). Canadian container: How have they fared? How will they do? *Maritime Policy and Management, 21*(3), 207–217.

Miller, J. (2007, October 25). New Shipping Law Makes Big Waves in Foreign Ports. *Wall Street Journal.*

Murphy, P. R., & Daley, J. M. (1994). A framework for applying logistical segmentation. *International Journal of Physical Distribution and Logistics Management, 24*(10), 13–19.

Murphy, P., Dalenberg, D., & Daley, J. (1988). A contemporary perspective on international port operations. *Transportation Journal, 28*(1), 23–32.

Murphy, P., Dalenberg, D., & Daley, J. (1989). Assessing international port operations. *International Journal of Physical Distribution and Materials Management, 19*(9), 3–10.

Murphy, P., Dalenberg, D., & Daley, J. (1991). Analysing international water transportation: The perspectives of large U.S. industrial corporations. *Journal of Business Logistics, 12*(1), 169–190.

Notteboom, T., & Yap, W. Y. (2012). Port competition and competitiveness. In W. Talley (Ed.), *The Blackwell Companion to Maritime Economics* (pp. 549–570). Malden: Blackwell.

OECD. (2003). *Maritime Transport Committee Security in Maritime Transport: Risk Factors and Economic Impact.* Available at https://www.oecd.org/news-room/4375896.pdf.

Parliament of Australia. (2003). *The US Container Security Initiative and Its Implications for Australia.* Available at http://www.aph.gov.au/About_Parliament/Parliamentary_Departments/Parliamentary_Library/Publications_Archive/CIB/cib0203/03cib27.

Parola, F., Risitano, M., Ferretti, M., & Panetti, E. (2017). The drivers of port competitiveness: A critical review. *Transport Reviews, 37*(1), 116–138.

Pearson, R. (1980). *Containerline Performance and Service Quality*. Liverpool, UK: University of Liverpool.

Peters, H. J. (1990). *Structural Changes in International Trade and Transport Markets: The Importance of Markets*. The 2nd KMI International Symposium, Seoul.

Rabadi, G., PintoI, C. A., Talley, W., & Arnaout, J. P. (2007). Port recovery from security incidents: A simulation approach. In K. Bichou, M. Bell, & A. Evans (Eds.), *Risk Management in Port Operations, Logistics and Supply Chain Security* (pp. 83–94). London: Informa.

Roach, A. (2004). Initiatives to enhance maritime security at sea. *Marine Policy, 28*(1), 41–66.

Rowe, G., Wright, G., & McColl, A. (2005). Judgment change during Delphi-like procedures: The role of majority influence, expertise and confidence. *Technological Forecasting and Social Change, 72,* 377–399.

Slack, B. (1985). Containerisation inter-port competition and port selection. *Maritime Policy and Management, 12*(4), 293–303.

Talas, R., & Menachof, D. (2009). The efficient tradeoff between security and cost for seaports: A conceptual model. *International Journal of Risk Assessment and Management, 13*(1), 46–59.

Thai, V. V. (2007). Impacts of security improvements on service quality in maritime transport: An empirical study of Vietnam. *Maritime Economics and Logistics, 9*(4), 335–356.

Timlen, T. (2007, April/May). The ISPS Code: Where are we now? *Cargo Security International, 5*(3), 14–15.

UNCTAD. (1992). *Port Marketing and the Challenge of the Third Generation Port* (pp. 358–361). Geneva.

UNCTAD. (2004, February 26). *Container Security: Major Initiatives and Related International Developments*. Report by the UCTAD Secretariat, Geneva.

UNCTAD. (2007). *Maritime Security: ISPS Code Implementation, Costs and Related Financing UNCTAD/SDTE/TLB/2007*. Available at http://unctad. org/en/Docs/sdtetlb20071_en.pdf.

Urciuoli, L., Sternberg, H., & Ekwall, D. (2010, July 11–15). *The Effects of Security on Transport Performances*. Paper Presented at the 12th World Conference on Transport Research, Lisbon, Portugal.

Voss, M., Whipple, J., & Closs, D. (2009). The role of strategic security: Internal and external security measures with security performance implications. *Transportation Journal, 48*(2), 5–23.

Willingale, M. (1981). The port routing behaviour of short sea ship operator theory and practices. *Maritime Policy and Management, 8*(2), 109–120.

Yang, Y. C. (2010). Impact of the container security initiative on Taiwan's shipping industry. *Maritime Policy and Management, 37*(7), 699–722.

Yeo, G. T. (2007). *Port Competitiveness in North East Asia: An Integrated Fuzzy Approach to Expert Evaluations* (PhD thesis). Plymouth University, UK.

2

Maritime Security Measures and the Container Security Initiative (CSI)

This chapter begins by introducing the background to implementation of maritime security regimes. Various risk factors and the potential vulnerability posed in global supply chains are identified and discussed. With the growing concern about seaborne trade safety and security, compulsory and voluntary frameworks have been introduced at international, supranational, national and regional level. These frameworks and measures are in relation to the relevant regulatory body. This chapter provides a comprehensive description of the Container Security Initiative (CSI), including its background, regulatory body, strategic goals and elements, criteria for membership and implementation during different phases. Its controversial benefits and negativity are discussed critically, particularly focusing on the aspects of financing, operational efficiency and trade facilitation.

© The Author(s) 2019
X. Zhang and M. Roe, *Maritime Container Port Security*,
https://doi.org/10.1007/978-3-030-03825-0_2

Development of Maritime Security

The world economy depends on global trade. Seaborne trade carries over 90% of global commerce by economic value, mainly via containerised cargo. Great efforts have been made to develop and improve this system in order to boost the global economy. Nevertheless, the vulnerability of maritime transport has posed a variety of risks. One significant risk arises from terrorist groups and in particular containerised shipping. '*The stakes are extremely high, as any important breakdown in the maritime transport system would fundamentally cripple the world economy*' (Organisation for Economic Co-operation and Development [OECD] 2003, p. 2).

The events of 11 September 2001 caused international concerns in terms of safety and security. Worldwide governments and relevant authorities started assessing their vulnerabilities to highly organised terrorist groups right after the devastating attack, and evidence has shown that the threat of terrorism is growing (Sandler 2014). Based on statistics from RAND (2012), in the 2000s, there were 23,000 terrorism cases growing from around 4700 in the 1990s and 3400 in the 1980s. Based on the threat imposed by seaborne trade, a series of actions have been set in place to enhance maritime trade security and minimise the threat of terrorism.

Several major international organisations such as the World Customs Organisation (WCO), International Maritime Organisation (IMO), International Organisation for Standardisation (ISO) and International Labour Organisation (ILO) immediately reacted to the need to enhance safety and security in the maritime sector. A wide variety of rules and measures have been introduced and implemented at the level of international, supranational, national and regional (Bichou 2008). They can also be categorised as mandatory regulations and voluntary initiatives. In 2009, the World Bank and DFID jointly produced the supply chain security guide to address topics of supply chain security (Donner and Kruk 2009). The guide included a brief overview of the current compulsory and voluntary supply chain security (SCS) (Tables 2.1 and 2.2). However, many requirements of these regulations have overlaps and inconsistency that have caused confusion for both the shipping

Table 2.1 Summary of main compulsory SCS programmes

Name/year implemented	Origin country/institute	Regulatory body	Route covered	Mode	Participation/status	Category	Goal
US 24-hour rule, 2003	USA	Customs	From any country to US import	Sea	US ports	Govt. Mand.	Advanced information
ISPS Part A, 2004	IMO	IMO	Global	Ship/port	167 member states	International/Mand.	Standardisation and consistency framework for evaluating risk
Pre-arrival and Pre-departure EU, 2009–2011	EC	Member state Customs	With EU, and any country to EU	Sea	All EU member states	EU—will become Mand. on 1-1-2011	Advanced information
Japan ACI, 2007	Japan	Customs	From any country to Japan	Sea/air	Japan ports and airports	Govt. Mand.	Advanced information
Mexico 24-hour rule, 2007	Mexico Customs	Customs	From any country to Mexico	Sea	Mexico ports	Govt. Mand.	Advanced information
US10+2, 2009	USA	CBP	From any country to USA	All	US ports	Govt. Mand.	Advanced information
China 24-hour advanced Manifest Rule, 2009	China	Customs	From any country to China	Sea	China ports, except for Hong Kong and Macau	Govt. Mand.	Advanced information
100% scanning, 2012 (delayed)	USA	CBP	Global to USA	Ship/Port	Pilot phase, 5 ports operating	International Mand. in 2012	Comprehensive SCS

Source The authors adapted from Donner and Kruk (2009, p. 25)
ISPS—The International Ship and Port Facility Security, ACI—Advance Cargo Information, IMO—International Maritime Organisation, EC—European Committee, Mand.—Mandatory, Govt.—Government

Table 2.2 Summary of major voluntary SCS programmes

Name/year implemented	Origin country/ institute	Regulatory body	Route covered	Mode	Participation status	Category	Goal
TAPA, 1997	USA	Body	Only truck transport routes in USA, ME, AF and Asia	Truck	207 members	Private voluntary	Crime incident reporting/ identify solutions/share information
C-TPAT	USA	CBP	From any country to USA	All	6375 certified and 3916 validated companies	Govt. voluntary	SCS
CSI, 2002	USA	CBP	Applied to US imports	Sea	58 ports	Govt. voluntary	SCS
WCO SAFE FoS, 2005	WCO	WCO	Worldwide	All	156 member states	Intl.-Voluntary	Standards for SCS and trade facilitation
ISO 28000 Series, 2005	ISO Technical Committee	ISO	All	All	157 member states	Intl.-Voluntary	Improve SCS
EU-AEO, 2008	European Commission	EC Directorate General Taxation and Customs Union	Any country to EU (Imp. & Exp.)	All	192 companies	Govt. voluntary	Trade facilitation and SCS

Source The authors adapted from Donner and Kruk (2009, p. 31)
TAPA—Transport Asset Protection Association, C-TPAT—Customs-Trade Partnership Against Terrorism, WCO SAFE—World Customs Organisation SAFE Framework of Standards, CBP—US Customs and Border Protection, ME—Middle East, AF—Africa, ISO—International Organisation for Standardization, EU-AEO—EU Authorized Economic Operator

industry and relevant authorities (Chang and Thai 2016). This issue has also been the focus of Thibault et al. (2006), Sarathy (2006), Hintsa et al. (2009), Yang (2010) and Sadovaya and Thai (2012). For instance, the International Ship and Port Facility Security (ISPS) Code, the Regulation No 725/2004 of the EU, Advance Notice of Arrival (ANOA) of the USA and Singapore regulations all require vessels to submit ship security information before entering port. According to Chang and Thai (2016, p. 722), Sadovaya and Thai (2012) classified maritime security requirements for carriers and ports into four categories, namely '*security onboard a ship and/or in port facility, personnel-related security, cooperation with authorities regarding security issues, and security of overall company management*'.

Maritime Security

It is difficult to provide a comprehensive definition of maritime security. Bueger (2014, p. 159) critically reviewed various existing maritime security definitions, and he concluded that '*no international consensus over the definition of maritime security has emerged*'. Nevertheless, he explained that discussions of maritime security are frequently related to various threats which could jeopardise seaborne trade. These threats are '*maritime inter-state disputes, maritime terrorism, piracy, trafficking of narcotics, people and illicit goods, arms proliferation, illegal fishing, environmental crimes, or maritime accidents and disasters*' (Bueger 2014, p. 159). The concept of marine safety differs from maritime security. Bueger (2014) indicated that 'marine safety' emphasises vessel safety, protection of seafarers and the marine environment. To be more specific, marine safety implies regulations of, *inter alia*, vessel construction, maritime installations, safety procedures and maritime professionals' education. Despite the differences, safety is the core of maritime security, and maritime security and marine safety are increasingly linked since the vessel herself, carriers and seafarers could be the targets or perpetrators of terrorist and other crimes. Therefore, in order to be inclusive, it is important to adopt the concept of 'maritime safety and security' which combines maritime security (terrorist acts, illicit cargo) and marine safety (vessel safety and seafarer protection). In a similar vein, port safety and security is also an umbrella term that consists of two aspects: port safety issues (safety and health of persons, safety of vessel and environmental aspects) (Kristiansen 2005) and port security issues. European Council Directive 2005/65/EC (2005) defined security incidents as resulting from terrorism activities. Port security refers to measures and actions against terrorist acts, while the term 'security' standalone refers to actions against terrorism.

Terrorism Threats

According to the definition given by the US Federal Bureau of Investigation (FBI), terrorism can be categorised as international and domestic terrorism. International terrorism is defined by the FBI (2013, n.p.) with three characteristics:

- Involve violent acts or acts dangerous to human life that violate federal or state law.
- Appear to be intended (i) to intimidate or coerce a civilian population; (ii) to influence the policy of a government by intimidation or coercion; or (iii) to affect the conduct of a government by mass destruction, assassination, or kidnapping.
- Occur primarily outside the territorial jurisdiction of the US, or transcend national boundaries in terms of the means by which they are accomplished, the persons they appear intended to intimidate or coerce, or the locale in which their perpetrators operate or seek asylum.

Transportation is critical to terrorism. Various transportation modes have been used by terrorists to transport weapons. The terrorists of 9/11 used an aeroplane to conduct the attack, while the 'Madrid train bombings' in 2004 occurred on a commuter train. In addition, transportation systems have become a target because of their vulnerabilities which could lead to economic damage and human casualties. The significance of cost to the local economy caused by a terrorist attack has been estimated. For example, GAO (2003, p. 8) referred to work by O'Hanlon (2002) that a US port closure due to a detonated WMD could reach

US$1 trillion. Gerencser et al. (2003) noted that discovering an undetonated WMD at a US seaport could cause a 12-day closure, which would cost about US$58 billion. Hall (2004, p. 354) stated that '*a 10-day shutdown of port facilities would cost the U.S. economy US$1.94 billion a day*'. Saywell and Borsuk (2002) estimated this disruption would cause a loss as much as 1.1% of the combined GDP of Hong Kong, Singapore and Malaysia.

Maritime transport is exposed to security challenges because it is a complex international transportation network. One of the challenges is the multiplicity of terrorist risk factors related to shipping. Objects for terrorism attacks include logistics infrastructure such as ports and operational aspects of transport and cargo. According to Parfomak and Frittelli (2007), maritime terrorism contains varying potential attack scenarios. They argued that although individual scenarios could be distinctive from each other, they may be characterised by five common dimensions: perpetrators, objectives, locations, targets and tactics. The OECD also identified a variety of risk factors within the maritime sector in terms of terrorism, which are cargo, vessels, people, finance and logistics support (OECD 2003).

Container Cargo

Containerised shipping transports most of the world's non-bulk cargoes. These standardised boxes have become dominant since their first introduction in the 1950s (OECD 2003). According to Rodrigue et al. (2009), the early stage of container shipping development can be divided into two phases: introduction (1958–1970) and adoption (1970–1990). During the period of growth which was from 1990 to 2008, containerisation began to significantly influence global trade patterns and manufacturing strategies, particularly with China's entry in the global economy. It has been playing an increasingly significant role in the process, largely due to its numerous economic and technical advantages. According to Drewry (2015), the share of container trade in the total cargo trade volume has steadily increased from 11% in 2000 (236.6 million TEU) to 14% in 2010 (541.8 million TEU). The key drivers behind this global container trade volume growth were the *'sustained global trade growth, increased global sourcing and manufacturing, a shift from transporting cargo in bulk to transporting cargo in containers and growth in transhipment volumes'* (Drewry 2015, p. 98).

In order to lower the cost and achieve economies of scale, container vessel size has increased after 1956, when the first container ship with a capacity of 58 containers completed her first voyage. In 2006, the 14,770 TEU *Emma Maersk* with dimensions of 397 metres long, and draught equal to 15.5 metres, started her first voyage (Maersk Line 2011). In 2011, Maersk Line put eight PS-class vessels, sized like *Emma Maersk* into services across the world. Maersk's *Triple-E* which is 400 metres long, 59 metres wide and 73 metres high is deployed on the Asia to Europe trade (Maersk Line 2013). China Shipping Container Lines (CSCL) launched its *CSCL Globe* ship with a maximum capacity of 19,000 TEU in 2014 (OECD 2015). Both the maximum and average size of container ships have grown over recent years. Many shipping lines that had no container ships of over 18,000 TEU capacity have ordered new ships. In April 2015, the order book included 52 ships with capacity larger than 18,000 TEU. With the current record in terms of TEU capacity, Samsung Heavy Industries OOCL's vessel with 21,000 TEU broke new capacity records when it was delivered in 2017.

In 2002, it was claimed that an average cargo ship can carry 6000 Twenty-Foot Equivalent (TEU) containers (*The Economist* 2002). One container may involve as many as 25 different parties and 30–40 documents since a container can carry goods from many different customers. Therefore, it has been estimated that even by 2002, an average container ship voyage involved up to 40,000 documents such as bills of lading and container manifests, and by 2006, the estimate was 98,000 such documents (Allen 2006).

There are serious security challenges caused by the sheer volume of container movements as well as the uniformity of containers and their relatively high speed of movement. First of all, the containerised system is porous so that it can be used for illegitimate purpose. Terrorists could use containers to deliver Weapons of Mass Destruction (WMD). One worst case could be where a terrorist organisation smuggles a global positioning satellite-enabled WMD into a container and then sends it into the international transport network in a legitimate way and remotely detonates the weapon when it arrives at a population centre. Besides terrorism, drugs and illegal goods can be concealed within containers by criminals. From 1996 to 1998, 950 seizures of narcotic drugs in commercial ocean cargo shipments were reported, accounting for 223,502 kilos of drugs (OECD 2003). When comparing the figures to other transport modes, it is obvious that maritime transportation is the preferred option for drug smugglers. Containers are also the target of high-value cargo theft.

Various hazardous cargos, such as explosive compounds, munitions and dangerous chemicals are shipped by containers (OECD 2003). The explosion that occurred on *Hanjin Pennsylvania* in 2002 near Sri Lanka was caused by improperly stored fireworks and calcium hypochlorite containers (Smeele 2010). Other explosions and fires on container vessels include the *Sea-Land Mariner* near Crete in April 1998 and the *Zim Haifa* in 2007 (Ellis 2010). Since the events of 9/11, two separate terrorism cases that used containers to enter another country occurred in Italy and Israel (Allen 2006). Ten civilians were killed in the latter case (Coleman and Levin 2006). All these examples have shown the potential risks posed by container shipping.

Vessels

Vessels can be used as a weapon in a terrorist attack against a population area located near a port or shipping channel to damage port facilities or vessels and cause blocked access to a port facility (UNCTAD 2004). According to the OECD (2003), previous terrorism attacks involving vessels have tended to target the ships instead of using them. For example, the boarding of the cruise vessel *Achille Lauro* in 1985, the oil tanker *Limburg* in 2000 and the suicide attacks against the *USS Cole* in 2000 all reveal the vulnerability of marine vessels (Parfomak and Frittelli 2007).

It appears that a boat laden with explosives rammed the *MV Limburg* causing 90,000 barrels of oil to be spilled in 2002 (GlobalSecurity. org, no date). As a result, ships were diverted from Yemeni ports such as Aden and insurance premiums for those still calling at ports in the

Yemen tripled (Richardson 2004). Ships could also be the facilitator of other attacks. The terrorist group named the Liberation Tigers of Tamil Eelam (LTTE) developed its own forwarders and seaborne transport network (OECD 2003). LTTE funded ships to carry weapons for a possible war against the Sri Lankan government. In addition, there are many cases with the cargo itself being targeted, such as in the case of *Hanjin Pennsylvania* (Smeele 2010). Most container cargoes and the ship were seriously damaged.

People

Seafarers are often directly targeted and indirectly suffer from terrorist attacks on vessels, such as the case of the *Limburg*. Another risk factor is that some seafarers could actually work for terrorist groups. The latter should be especially notable, considering that seafarers normally travel around with the ships, which could bring significant difficulties on detecting terrorism activities (OECD 2003).

Financing and Logistics Support

The OECD explained that terrorist groups can operate vessels to generate funds, furthermore, to support their logistics operations. The aforementioned case of LTTE is extensively documented. The LTTE has developed freight forwarders and shipping lines since the mid-1980s. Their legitimate operations have carried cargoes such as wood and tea, and the vessels operate openly in the world seaborne market. They have carried weapons and ammunition for other terrorist groups for money (OECD 2003). The funds generated from their operations have been used to support their fight against the Sri Lankan government.

Overview of Maritime Security Programmes

With the growing concern about international shipping security of goods and passengers, several compulsory and voluntary frameworks have been introduced at international, supranational, national and regional level in order to enhance maritime security and safety. These programmes could help to form a multi-layer regulatory system to fill the potential security gaps (Willis and Ortiz 2004). Bichou (2008, p. 21) provided a model illustrating the hierarchy of current regulatory programmes by level of security and supply chain converge was illustrated in Bichou (2008).

International regulatory measures that have been implemented and endorsed are the ISPS Code, the IMO/ILO code of practice on security in ports and the WCO 'Framework of Standards to Secure and facilitate Global Trade' ('SAFE Framework') (WCO 2007; OECD 2009). The ISPS Code drafted and developed by the IMO is the most important and influential security initiative that affects more than the international shipping industry (Bichou 2004). The ISPS Code contains Part A (see Table 2.1) and Part B. As Table 2.1 shows, Part A is mandatory, while Part B guidelines are voluntary, but some countries have incorporated them in their national security regulations as mandatory requirements (Bichou 2011). As to various national levels, the USA has developed many significant initiatives. Bichou (2008) listed several US-led: (1) the Maritime Transportation Security Act (MTSA) of 2002 that includes both mandatory and voluntary ISPS provisions; (2) a range of security programmes targeting specific maritime operations, including the CSI, the 24-hour Advanced Manifest Rule (the 24-hour rule), the Customs and Trade Partnership against Terrorism (C-TPAT), the Operation Safe Commerce (OSC), the megaport initiative and the Secure Freight Initiative (SFI). These programmes, except the 24-hour rule, have been codified into the US Security and Accountability for Every Port Act of 2006. There are also other national programmes, including Canada's and Mexico's own 24-hour rules and the Swedish Stair-sec programme.

Various initiatives are set and implemented at supranational level. Bichou (2008, 2011) provided a comprehensive review of supply chain and maritime security measures. For instance, in the EU, Council Regulation (EC) No 725/2004 (2004) was aimed at enhancing ship and port facility security. Commission Regulation (EC) No 884/2005 (2005) laid down procedures for carrying out Commission inspections in maritime security; however, it ended validity at 29 April 2008. Commission Regulation (EC) No 324/2008 (2008) laying down revised procedures for conducting Commission inspections in the field of maritime security repealed Commission Regulation (EC) No 884/2005. Council Directive 2005/65/EC (2005) enhanced port security. The Authorised Economic Operator (AEO) which was part of the EU Custom Security Programme came into force on 1 January 2008 and can be seen as the EU response to the US C-TAPAT programme. Bichou (2008) also mentioned several regional initiatives such as the US-Canada-Mexico Free and Secure Trade (FAST) initiative, the Association of Southeast Asian Nations (ASEAN)/Japan Maritime Transport Security, the Secure Trade in the APEC Region (STAR) for Asia Pacific and the Secured Export Partnership (SIP).

Last but not least, Bichou (2008, p. 3) stated that there is a set of industrial led and voluntary security programmes worth mentioned, including '*Secured Export Partnership (SEP) programme, the ISO/PAS 28000:2005 standard (Specification for security management systems for the supply chain), the Business Anti-Smuggling Coalition (BASC) scheme, the Technology Asset Protection Association (TAPA) initiative, and a series of Partnership in Protection (PIP) arrangements*'. The ISO/PAS 28000:2005 was applicable to all sizes of organisations in a supply chain and was revised by ISO 28000:2007 (ISO 2007). Bichou (2008) believed that these measures would form a more effective framework and a higher level of security assurance across the shipping network. However, voluntary programmes are not imposed by a law or international code like compulsory programmes (Donner and Kruk 2009). Theoretically, trader and transport operators could operate although possibly at a competitive disadvantage without joining in one of those programmes.

The Introduction of the CSI

US Customs and Border Protection (CBP)

The vision of the Department of Homeland Security's (DHS) is to '*ensure a homeland that is safe, secure, and resilient against terrorism and other hazards*' (DHS 2016, n.p.). It has 16 operational and support components.

The US Coast Guard (USCG) is one of the five armed forces of the USA and the only military department of the DHS to protect the maritime economy and the environment. The CBP is one of the DHS's largest and most complex components with a priority to keep terrorists and their weapons out of the USA (DHS 2016). The CBP has made great progress to ensure that US-bound supply chains are more secure against potential terrorist acts and keep away from the delivery of weapons of mass effect. The CBP uses a multi-layered approach to ensure the completion of the supply chain from the point of loading through arrival at a US port of entry (Fig. 2.1). The DHS (2009, n.p.) explained the multi-layered approach which includes:

- Advanced information under the 24 Hour Rule and Trade Act of 2002 (supplemented now by Imported Security Filing requirements).
- Screening the information through the Automated Targeting System (ATS), the 10+2 Program and National Targeting Centre-Cargo (NTC-C).

The figure illustrates the container delivery system from cargo origin, through packing and loading onto a container ship, and through arrival at a US port and delivery to the final customer.

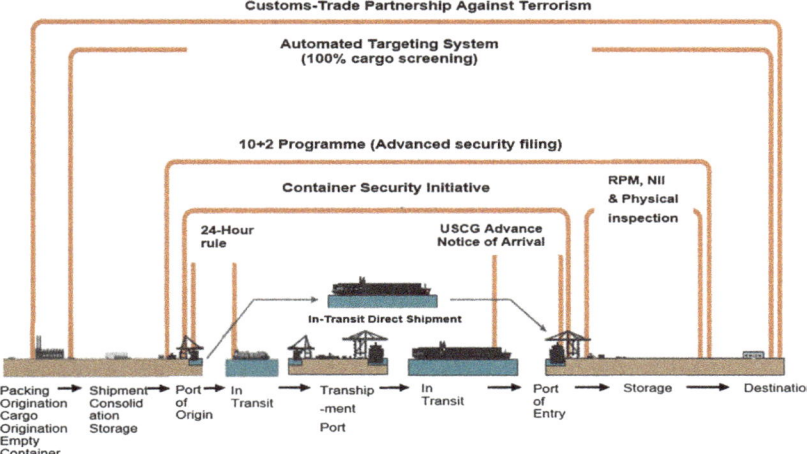

Fig. 2.1 US CBP Layered Defence Strategy. NII—Non-intrusive imaging, RPM—Radiation portal monitor, USCG—US Coast Guard (*Source* The authors adapted from Congressional Budget Office [2016, p. 10])

- Partnerships with industry and the private sector such as the C-TPAT.
- Partnerships with foreign governments, such as the CSI and the Secure Freight Initiative (SFI).
- Use of Non-Intrusive Inspection (NII) technology and mandatory examinations for all high-risk shipments.
- Radiation portal monitoring and Secondary radiation monitoring systems.

The layered approach helps the CBP to receive, process and act swiftly upon commercial information to target suspect shipments without interfering with cargo movements through ports (DHS 2009). Various inspection equipment and technologies are utilised during this process to ensure the safety and security of container movements (Table 2.3). The NII system is the most common inspection system to give a reasonably accurate image of a container's contents. It has two types of imaging systems: large

Table 2.3 A list of major scanning systems and container sealing technologies

System/technology	Description
Non-Intrusive Inspection (NII)	Imaging system consists of various technologies (gamma-ray, x-ray) with different capabilities (large scale, small scale) to identify specific materials with different kinds of equipment (mobile, crane mounted, hand-held)
Radiation Portal Monitors (RPMs)	Passive radiation detection for screening. It detects traces of radiation emitted from an object passing through a RPM. Gamma radiation is detected and in some cases complemented by neutron detection when sensitivity for nuclear material is desired
Mechanical seals: Indicative seals	The seals are affixed either on the handle mechanism directly or to the door superstructure. It indicates when unauthorised entry into the container has occurred
Mechanical seals: Security seals	Similar to indicative seals but it only indicates whether the seal has been compromised. It has a unique identification number and is marked by the seal owner's stamp
Mechanical seals: High-security seals	In addition to the same functions of the above two seals, it also serves to physically prevent or delay entry into the container. It has stronger materials and more strategic locations. The most common forms are the bolt seal and cable seal
'Smart' seals: Electronic seals	It integrated physical security and information management capabilities. It has a physical sealing device with a data chip and a mechanism for information reading

Source The authors adapted from European Conference of Ministers of Transport (2005), Donner and Kruk (2009), and DHS (2014)

scale (portal gamma-ray, mobile truck gamma-ray, rail, etc.) and small scale. It inspects and screens conveyances or cars, trucks, railcars, containers and personal luggage, packages through either gamma-ray imaging systems or x-ray. The total time for inspection is about 2–5 minutes per object (DHS 2014). The Radiation Portal Monitors (RPMs) serve a similar goal as the NII, using gamma-ray and neutron detection. It is considered to be the first measure to prevent the illicit trafficking of radioactive and nuclear materials (Congressional Budget Office 2016). In addition to scanning systems, different technologies are used to prevent the container from interception and being tampered with. Technical specifications on secure containers and sealing have been set out (Table 2.3).

The Establishment of the CSI

The CSI was established in 2002 to cope with the threat to border security and global trade caused by potential terrorists using a sea container to deliver a weapon. The main aim of the CSI, as Donner and Kruk (2009, p. 27) quoted from the words of the CBP, was '*to extend the zone of security outward so that American borders are the last line of defence, not the first*'.

The CSI was proposed to ensure all containers that pose potential risks for terrorism were screened and inspected at foreign ports before they were loaded on vessels importing to the USA. Over 80% of all waterborne cargo shipping to the USA is subject to pre-screening (CBP 2011). A foreign member port agrees to inspect the US-bound containers thoroughly at its own ports.

According to the CBP (2011), the CSI was firstly conducted in ports which have the highest volume of container shipments to the USA. Currently, the programme has been implemented in 58 ports around the world, including North, Central and South America, the Caribbean, Europe, Africa, the Middle East and throughout Asia (Fig. 2.2).

Before the introduction of the CSI, less than 5% of the 17,000 containers entering the USA each day were examined, accounting for approximately US$1.3 billion worth of goods (Lenain et al. 2002; Allen 2006). These container cargos were inspected with drive-by imaging

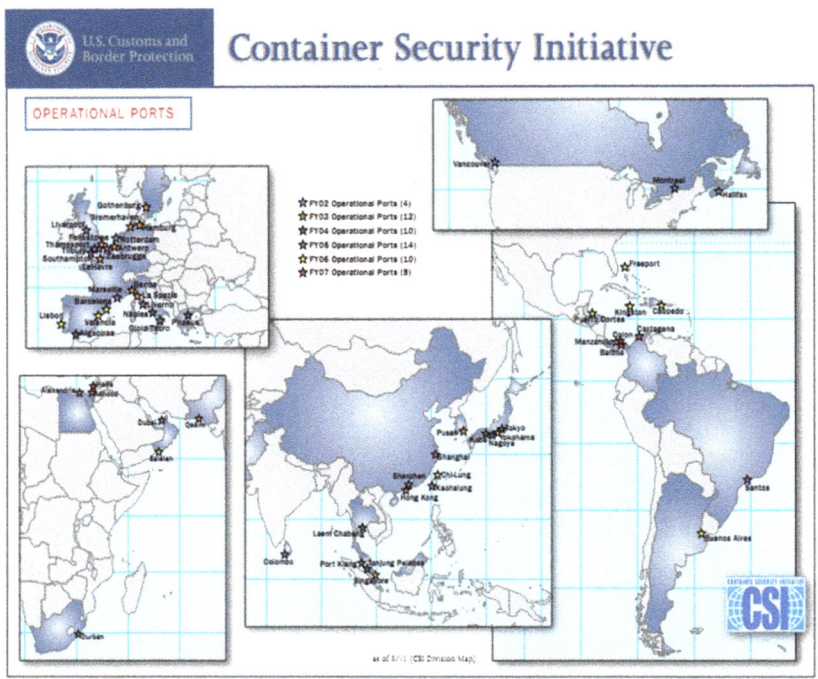

Fig. 2.2 CSI Current Operational Ports (*Source* CBP [2011, p. 5])

equipment and the vast majority of that activity occurred at the port of entry in the USA (Koch 2002). In the fiscal year 2010, more than 10.1 million maritime shipments were screened at CSI ports before leaving for US ports, an average of 27,600 a day (CBP 2011). In 2013, US ports handled 18 million TEUs of cargo. Selection for inspections is mostly triggered by data mining shipping information and intelligence to identify suspicious container contents (American Shipper 2014). In fiscal year 2013, the DHS's fiscal year 2015 budget request to Congress revealed that CSI teams reviewed more than 11.2 million bills of lading prior to container loading and conducted 104,000 examinations of high-risk shipments in cooperation with host country CSI teams. About 94% of examination requests are granted by foreign authorities, which left 6% of cases where further scrutiny is denied, according to the CBP.

The CSI Strategic Goals and Core Elements

The CSI itself has adopted a multi-layered approach in a similar way to the USA overall, which consists of three strategic goals and their associated objectives (Table 2.4).

Table 2.4 CSI three strategic goals

Strategic Goal 1	Secure US Borders	**Objective 1.1**: Enhance the process for identifying high-risk cargo by receiving and making full use of advance trade data
		Objective 1.2: Improve the process of screening and examining containers by developing and fully utilizing state-of-art technology
		Objective 1.3: Promote parity through increased examinations of high-risk containers prior to entering the USA
Strategic Goal 2	Build a Robust CSI Cargo Security System	**Objective 2.1**: Advance security of all world nations by promoting an international framework of standards covering data elements, host country examinations, risk management and detection technology
		Objective 2.2: Enhance cargo security and trade facilitation by strategically identifying the optimal trade lanes and ports for inclusion into CSI
		Objective 2.3: Expedite the movement of low-risk shipments through the global supply chain
		Objective 2.4: Continue to work with other agencies on maritime contingency and recovery plans and efforts
Strategic Goal 3	Protect and Facilitate Trade	**Objective 3.1**: Increase the effectiveness of CSI by negotiating with host countries to review and request examination of all-risk shipments identified by CBP through the Automated Targeting System (ATS)
		Objective 3.2: Ensure effective coordination with host countries by conducting periodic risk evaluations of ports to assess the level of staffing and other resource needs
		Objective 3.3: Encourage interagency cooperation by developing a capacity to collect and share information and trade data gathered from CSI ports
		Objective 3.4: Present CSI standards and promote greater participation by international governments, international organisations, trade communities and other organisations engaged in maritime security
		Objective 3.5: Improve CSI operations by evaluating the feasibility of regionalizing management of CSI teams

Source The authors adapted from CBP (2006)

Holmes (2004) stated that the CSI is the umbrella term for security initiatives that include C-TPAT, the 24-hour rule and the CSI itself. The CSI discussed in this project includes the proper specific port-to-port shipping element and the 24-hour rule which is a primary aspect of the CSI. Table 2.5 gives an outline of the CSI and the 24-hour rule. According to the CBP (2006, n.p.), the CSI has three core elements:

- Using intelligence and automated advance targeting information to identify and target containers that pose a risk for terrorism.
- Pre-screening those containers that pose a risk at the port of departure before they arrive at the port of entry.
- Using state-of-the-art detection technology to scan containers that pose a risk.

Joining the CSI

Three main criteria, trade volume, terrorism connections and geographical interest, are set up for participation in the CSI. Certain steps need to be implemented once a port has been selected. The steps include *'negotiating and executing a Declaration of Principles document with the host country; conducting an operational assessment of the proposed port; determining CSI facility possibilities and conducting surveys and estimates of requirements to establish a CSI office; staffing the CSI office; and building-out all facilities, support and IT infrastructure necessary for the CSI team to be operational'* (CBP 2006, n.p.). In addition, Allen (2006, p. 440) listed four basic requirements for CSI candidates: *'(1) determine criteria for establishing if a container represents a 'high risk'; (2) have local customs officials work with US Customs agents, who are posted at these ports, to identify 'high risk' containers; (3) pre-screen these containers before they are loaded onto US bound ships with non-intrusive inspection (NII) equipment (including gamma or X-ray imaging capabilities) and radiation detection equipment; (4) the port must implement the use of 'smart' or tamper proof container-seals in order to secure the containers once they are en route to the US'*. Additionally, the host port authorities need to *'implement an 'automated risk management system' and share intelligence on potential security threats from within the country with U.S. Customs*

Table 2.5 Outline of the CSI and the 24-hour rule

	Arrangement	Targets/participants	Requirements and responsibility	Inspection and certification	Observation
CSI	Bilateral agreement/partnership between the USA and foreign-trade country/port partners	Foreign ports (US ports under reciprocity) with substantial and direct waterborne container traffic to the USA	Establish security procedures to identify high-risk container cargo. Work with deployed CBP officers to target containers at risk. Provide NII equipment for container screening and inspection	Validation process and risk assessment mechanism (updated regularly)	CBP offers CSI reciprocity (As of April 2005, Canada and Japan customs personnel are already deployed in US ports)
24-hour rule	Compulsory regulation, not applicable to bulk cargo	Ocean carriers or their agents. Licensed or registered NVOCCs	Electronic reporting to CBP, via AMS and 24-hour before loading at foreign ports, of complete manifest information for all cargo on board ships calling in US ports, even if the cargo is being transhipped or continues on the ship to a third country after it departs the USA	CBP identification/clearance of trans-mitted information Non-issuance or delay of permits to unload suspected cargo, or cargo with incomplete/late advance manifest. Penalties may also apply	Exception may be made for break-bulk cargo shipments. Importers may request confidentiality of their identity and the identity of their shippers Generic descriptions are not accepted

Source Bichou (2011)

Table 2.6 Minimum standard for CSI candidate ports

1	The availability of NII equipment and radiation detection equipment in order to meet the objective of quickly screening containers without disrupting the flow of legitimate trade. The ability to inspect cargo originating, transiting, exiting or being transhipped through a country
2	The seaport must have regular, direct and substantial container traffic to ports in the USA
3	Commit to establishing a risk management system to identify potentially high-risk containers and automating that system. This system should include a mechanism for validating threat assessments and targeting decisions and identifying best practices
4	Commit to sharing critical data, intelligence and risk management information with the US CBP in order to do collaborative targeting and developing an automated mechanism for these exchanges
5	Conduct a thorough port assessment to ascertain vulnerable links in a port's infrastructure and commit to resolving those vulnerabilities
6	Commit to maintaining integrity programs to prevent lapses in employee integrity and to identify and combat breaches in integrity

Source The authors adapted from CBP (2006)

agents, and identify and resolve security breaches in the port area'. The minimum standards for the candidate countries are listed in Table 2.6.

According to the US Government Accountability Office (GAO) (2003, p. 10), the bilateral agreement of the CSI stated that the US Customs *'sends an assessment team to the CSI port to collect information about the port's physical, informational infrastructure and the host country's customs operations'*. Then a CSI team of Customs personnel will assist the host country's customs officials to identify high-risk containers departing from a CSI port. A typical CSI team is made up of four to five team members. This team is structured as: *'two to three inspectors from Customs' Office of Field Operations, one intelligence research analyst, and one agent as a CSI team leader representing the Office of Investigations'* (GAO 2003, p. 11). The team utilises Customs' Automated Targeting System to screen containers that pose risks for inspection. To improve its screening capabilities, the team further analyses these containers by using data provided by the host nation's customs administration. Then host countries' customs inspect containers identified by both the USA and host customs as high risk. One key tenet of the CSI is that the US Customs inspectors are able to *'observe and verify the inspections'* (GAO 2003, p. 10).

CSI Three Phases Implementation

There are three phases for global implementation of the CSI. During the first year of the CSI, US Customs quickly achieved active participation among the nations, respectively, which applied to enrol in the CSI. Phase I included international 'megaports' and strategic ports (CBP 2003). Firstly, Canada agreed to place US Customs officials at three seaports under the Smart Border Declaration that preceded the announcement of the CSI. Between January 2002 and January 2003, bilateral agreements with 12 governments were concluded, including 18 of the 20 'megaports' which have the highest shipment volume of containers to the USA, as well as two other governments representing three strategic ports (Table 2.7).

US Customs soon deployed CSI teams to five of these ports.

These initial ports were chosen based on the criteria of '*regular, direct and substantial container traffic, originating, transiting, exiting or being trans-shipped through their facilities to the US*' (Allen 2006, p. 440). Approximately, 70% of all goods entering US ports depart from these 'megaports'. As the CSI progressed, Customs adjusted its provisions as it met challenges. For instance, the first CSI team in Europe found that manifest data which was required from the host customs was not readily available. Consequently, the CSI team was not able to thoroughly screen containers overseas. To resolve this issue, Customs implemented the 24-hour rule requiring carriers to submit key information directly to Customs. Additionally, to develop an adequate survey instrument, Customs embedded additional expertise into the teams and developed

Table 2.7 Phase I CSI ports

Phase I ports		
Hong Kong, China	Shanghai, China	Singapore, Singapore
Kaohsiung, Taiwan	Rotterdam, The Netherlands	Pusan, Korea
Bremerhaven, Germany	Tokyo, Japan	Genoa, Italy
Shenzhen, China	Antwerp, Belgium	Nagoya, Japan
Le Havre, France	Hamburg, Germany	La Spezia, Italy
Felixstowe, UK	Algeciras, Spain	Kobe, Japan
Yokohama, Japan	Laem Chabang, Thailand	Montreal, Canada
Vancouver, Canada	Halifax, Canada	

Source The authors adapted from Allen (2006)

comprehensive and standardised port surveys (GAO, 2003). US Customs claimed that the CSI teams conducted manifest data screening for more than 606,000 containers and identified 2091 which were considered as high risk between the time of initial deployments for the first five CSI ports (Halifax, Montreal, Vancouver, Le Havre, Rotterdam) and May 2003 (26 CSI ports in total including two of China's ports). These containers then were inspected by host customs administrations. However, at the early stage of the programme, '*Customs has not taken adequate steps to incorporate factors crucial to the programme's long-term success and accountability*' (GAO 2003, p. 4). A systematic human capital recruitment plan, to train and assign relevant programme staff, was still absent after one year of implementation. Customs also lacked '*performance measures that demonstrate programme achievements and establish accountability*', although they were tracking number of countries which participated in the CSI (GAO 2003, p. 4). Without indicators that measure programme outcomes, Customs could not accurately assess the programme's success or establish an oversight basis. The US Customs only focused on short-term operational planning to quickly roll out the programme without considering its long-term success Chan (2005).

During Phase II, the CSI was extended to ports in 'middle-income' developing countries: Argentina, Brazil, Panama, Sri Lanka, Malaysia and South Africa (Allen 2006). None of the least developed countries were included in Phase II since most of these regions are landlocked and rely on exporting unprocessed and raw commodities which are transported by bulk carriers rather than containers. During Phase II, the strategic importance of the port and if it had expressed willingness to meet the CSI requirements were considered as eligible standards (CBPIA 2002). There were 23 ports in this phase, including Marseilles, Naples, Barcelona, Valencia, Southampton, Thamesport, Lisbon, Buenos Aires, Santos and Colon (Table 2.8).

According to the last published official information of the CBP (2014), the CSI is in Phase III at the moment. There are 58 ports that have joined the programme (Table 2.9). It targets ports which did not qualify under Phase I and Phase II. Table 2.9 presents the foreign ports participating in the CSI, which account for 85% of container traffic destined for the USA.

Table 2.8   Phase II CSI ports

Phase II ports		
Port Klang, Malaysia	Tanjung Pelepas, Malaysia	Gothenburg, Sweden
Marseilles/Fos, France	Livorno, Italy	Gioia Tauro, Italy
Naples, Italy	Barcelona, Spain	Valencia, Spain
Southampton, UK	Thamesport, UK	Zeebrugge, Belgium
Osaka, Japan	Piraeus, Greece	Lisbon, Portugal
Buenos Aires, Argentina	Santos, Brazil	Colon, Panama
Balboa, Panama	Durban, South Africa	Colombo, Sri Lanka
Izmir, Turkey	Dubai, UAE	

Source The authors adapted from Allen (2006)

Table 2.9   Current CSI operation ports (2018)

In the Americas and Caribbean	**In Asia and the East**
Montreal, Vancouver and Halifax, Canada	Singapore, Singapore
Santos, Brazil	Yokohama, Tokyo, Nagoya and Kobe, Japan
Buenos Aires, Argentina	Hong Kong, China
Puerto Cortes, Honduras	Pusan, South Korea
Caucedo, Dominican Republic	Port Kiang and Tanjung Pelepas, Malaysia
Kingston, Jamaica	Laem Chabang, Thailand
Freeport, The Bahamas	Dubai, United Arab Emirates (UAE)
Balboa, Colon and Manzanillo, Panama	Shenzhen and Shanghai, China
Cartagena, Colombia	Kaohsiung and Chi-Lung, Taiwan
	Colombo, Sri Lanka
In Europe	Port Salalah, Oman
Rotterdam, The Netherlands	Port Qasim, Pakistan
Bremerhaven and Hamburg, Germany	Port of Ashdod, Israel
Antwerp and Zeebrugge, Belgium	Port in Haifa, Israel
Le Havre and Marseille, France	
Gothenburg, Sweden	**In Africa**
La Spezia, Genoa, Naples, Gioia Tauro, and Livorno, Italy	Durban, South Africa
Felixstowe, Liverpool, Thamsport, Tilbury, and Southampton, UK	Alexandra, Egypt
Piraeus, Greece	
Algeciras, Barcelona, and Valencia, Spain	
Lisbon, Portugal	

Source Adapted by Authors from CBP (2014)

Phase III included more ports in 'middle income' developed countries. Pakistan is considered as a high-risk nation for potential terrorist tampering of containers. Hence, Port Qasim is the only port in the world that inspects every US-bound container prior to loading (American Shipper 2014). The agency reached an arrangement with

Pakistan Customs to go through all sea containers with x-ray imaging equipment and radiation portal monitors. The scanning results are uploaded in real time to a secure website for CBP analysts to observe. Pakistani authorities will open to inspect any containers that are identified as suspicious and CBP can supervise the process by video. During 2013, more than 44,700 containers were scanned at port Qasim (DHS 2014). This programme was named as the SFI by the CBP and conducted as a pilot programme at six ports to test the idea of 100% container scanning prior to vessel loading. However, the rest of the pilot ceased after proving too difficult to replicate. The reason why the programme is made possible in Qasim is the low container volume from Qasim to the USA, limiting logistical challenges and strong Pakistani government support in order to maintain trade with the largest consumer market in the world (American Shipper 2014). Moreover, the region is considered too dangerous for US personnel work at the site overseas. Therefore, the process is carried out remotely. The long-term goal of the US Customs is to screen all US-bound containers and if necessary scan them at the port of origin (CBP 2014).

The CSI Positive Implications for Seaborne Trade

Trade Facilitation

There are a number of benefits of the CSI programme that have been highlighted by the CBP, mainly focused on trade facilitation. The WTO (2017, n.p.) defined trade facilitation as '*removing obstacles to the movement of goods across borders (e.g. simplification of customs procedures)*'. It is about the simplification, modernisation and harmonisation of international trade procedures (WTO 2017) meaning '*activities, practices and formalities involved in collecting, presenting, communicating and processing data required for the movement of goods in international trade*' (WTO 2017, n.p.). Trade facilitation involves activities related to financing, insurance, import/export procedures and the actual movement of goods (Allen 2006).

First of all, the CSI could increase the level of awareness for securing global trade (CBP 2014). The programme contributes to the development of world supply chain security standards. International organisations, such as the WCO, World Bank, the IMO as well as other domestic outreach forums, allow the CSI to be an integral part of the supply chain security system. It adds protection to the primary system of international trade on which the worldwide economy depends. Besides the intended benefits arising from improved security, there have been discussions that seaborne trade could be facilitated indirectly or directly by the CSI implementation.

The international collaboration between Customs could improve the capabilities and the overall effectiveness of the targeting process (CBP 2006). The CSI offers opportunities to expand and take advantage of technological resources, and the use of additional cargo information from the trade community could improve the opportunities to obtain advance information on potential threats and identify high-risk containers. Carriers could also benefit from the kind of investment required to meet the US container screening requirements. Overall, supply chain performance will be enhanced by quicker clearance of containers and more efficient and effective administrative tools. From this perspective, supply chain performance can be improved in the medium term. Furthermore, Allen (2006) pointed out that the CSI compliance required customs modernisation, port facilities investment and the streamlining of regulations to remove technical barriers, and these measures could potentially increase the competitiveness of developing country exporters.

To fulfil Objective 2.3 (see Table 2.4), CSI participating countries, sea carriers and the importing and exporting parties must commit to effectively using the cargo loading time at a foreign port (CBP 2006). The CSI transfers the container examinations from unloading ports in the USA to loading ports overseas, utilising the normal downtime for a container awaiting loading to speed up customs clearance at US ports of entry. However, the cargo movement at the export ports could be interfered with. In order to identify high-risk containers, CBP officers cooperate with host customs administrations to set up security criteria. NII technology and other methods like radiation checks are used at the leaving port (CBP 2011). High-security Mechanical Seals (see Table 2.3) and Tamper Evident Tape are applied after container examination to maintain the integrity of the container during transit to the USA (Donner and Kruk 2009). All the checks are carried out in the host countries which bear the equipment cost for such checks. Costs caused by this examination transfer to foreign ports may have more significant effects on less developed country exporters' competitiveness than developed countries. Apart from cost aspect, there are other obstacles at the participation ports. These issues include '*the frequency of reloading of goods, congestion at ports, complex customs-clearance regulations, non-transparent requirements, documentation costs due to lack of automation, and the uncertainty about whether bills of lading or letters of credit are enforceable*' (Allen 2006, p. 444). Notwithstanding the possible disruption at export ports, cooperation between Customs authorities helps to increase the communication between terminal operators and carriers, reduce delays in vessel departure and mitigate corruption in ports (Donner and Kruk 2009). Additionally, foreign customs officials physically presenting themselves could help to diminish certain obstacles.

Establishment of a Collaborative Network

The CSI programme is voluntary and aims at fostering '*a collaborative working relationship with the participating foreign governments, promoting, among other things, the sharing of intelligence, local trends, and best practices*' (Donner and Kruk 2009, p. 27). This collaborative work plays a crucial role when there is increased risk, heightened threat levels and re-establishing the flow of commerce in the event of a terrorist attack. The CSI ports could get special continuity considerations, and their cargo could enjoy facilitated handling at ports of entry in the USA during the recovery process after a domestic or international terrorist attack (Donner and Kruk 2009). The CBP claimed the most important benefits brought by this CSI collaborative work is cooperation enhancement and intelligence sharing. Nevertheless, the establishment of this collaborative work around the world has triggered certain concerns.

Firstly, the European Commission (EC) started legal proceedings against those EU states which have individually reached bilateral agreements with the USA. The EC expressed their concern that European ports would '*become divided into those which are approved by US Customs and those which are not, resulting in the erosion of fair and genuine competition between ports*'. In response to the legal action by the EC, US Customs claimed that the CSI builds on certain existing WCO concepts and has gained some endorsements from the WCO and the G-8 group. Dallimore (2008, p. 192) stated that the CSI contravenes '*the freedom of transit because it makes a distinction between cargo containers (including those in transit) based on the port of departure*'. It could create discrimination against cargo departing from a non-CSI port. Although it is claimed that non-CSI ports would still be able to transport containers to the USA under normal circumstances, the processing may be less efficient than the affiliated ports (CBP 2006). On the one hand, shippers and carriers may be forced to route through a CSI port to avoid cargo delay at US ports of arrival, therefore, preventing them from choosing more efficient routes through non-CSI ports. The CBP could disrupt the most efficient transit route available because of '*the competitive distortion that expedited clearance creates between seaports*' (Dallimore 2008, p. 192). On the other hand, smaller ports may not be qualified to join the programme and reduce their US-inbound business since they cannot bear the compliance requirements (UNCTAD 2003). In a terrorist event, the USA has the right to refuse ships from non-CSI ports altogether. Larger ports may gain new business from non-CSI ports.

Secondly, the CSI sets up a reciprocal system of arrangements between the US coastguard and a foreign country port. Under this system, there could be sensitive information exchange, which may be considered necessary to ensure safety and security of any ports involved (CBP 2011). This bilateral system of information exchange requires a host country to execute security checks on US-bound containers. In return, the host country can send its officers to any US port to inspect ocean container shipments being shipped to their country (CBP 2011). Under the CSI framework, US Customs officials present themselves to 'observe' screening of cargo shipped to the USA and participation in the CSI could be counted as 'supervision' of the foreign nation practices in foreign ports by US authorities. It has been pointed out that there could be potentially significant sovereignty issues under the CSI system (Metaparti 2010). Moreover, in a fully CSI compliant cooperative network, the substantial liability issue under the CSI in the event of a terrorist attack utilising shipping or sea containers remained unaddressed.

Maritime Security Measure's Implications for the Maritime Sector

Many maritime security studies have stressed the importance of security measures like the ISPS Code, the 24-hour rule and their impacts on assessment (Stasinopoulos 2003; Bichou et al. 2007; Park 2013). The ISPS Code has two parts: Part A introduces mandatory provisions to establish the new international framework to enhance maritime security (Bichou 2004); Part B involves voluntary guidance, consisting of detailed procedures to be implemented to comply with the provisions of ChapterXI-2 of the SOLAS convention and of Part A of the code. Although Part B is non-mandatory, the USA is already implementing it on a mandatory basis. Based on the argument of Goulielmos and Anastasakos (2005), measures such as the ISPS should be viewed as policies which facilitate international trade instead of hindering cargo movements in the global supply chain. Thibault et al. (2006) reported on how companies involved in US containerised trade have responded to the new maritime container security programmes through interviewing senior container line executives, port officers and marine terminal security officers. They found that the most significant benefit is the cooperative security relationship between industry and government formed under the new initiatives. Thai (2007) conducted an empirical study of Vietnam with a group of shipping, port and freight forwarding companies. He found that security improvements resulting from maritime security requirements could enhance service quality as a result of the increased reliability of service, social responsibility awareness, and operation and management efficiency improvement and hence enhance the market image.

Park (2013) mentioned a survey undertaken by the Korea Maritime Institution in 2008, where both the port group and users agreed that balancing port security and efficiency is a critical factor. To obtain the minimum required compliance level, port and shipping companies need to undertake technical and organisational measures that would create additional costs for shipping industries (Dekker and Stevens 2007, p. 499). They suggested three topics for further study: *(i) 'assessment of a harmonised (legal) system of best practice', (ii) 'long-term analysis on the effects of security measures on the competitive positions of seaports' and (iii) 'provision of empirical evidence for the answer on the question whether security measures should be more (port) administration-based than industry-based'.*

Financing and Costs Associated with Maritime Security Measures

In order to comply with the new security regime, maritime operators are frequently required to invest in security equipment, procedures and human capital recruitment and training. Additionally, Bichou (2008, p. 22) mentioned extra costs are generated to cover *'provisions for detailed reporting, further inspections and other operational requirements'*. Regarding non-ISPS initiatives, he referred to DNV Consulting (2005) who noted that voluntary security programmes would cost port and terminal operators in the EU around €5 million just for auditing. He also mentioned there are two major kinds of maritime security costs: compliance costs, and procedural and operational costs.

Ex-Ante Costs Assessment

Various studies have assessed the compliance cost of port security at a very early stage of new security regulations. The data and methods used for these *ex-ante* assessments emerged mostly from national regulatory risk assessment models. These models are ad hoc programmes conducted by governmental agencies for new initiatives costs and benefits assessment. Bichou (2008) provided a summary of aggregate *ex-ante* estimates for ISPS compliance cost (Table 2.10).

Table 2.10 A summary of ISPS *Ex-Ante* cost estimations by various regulatory risk assessment impacts

Source of estimates	Cost items	Scope	Initial costs	Annual costs	10 years total cost (2003–2013) @7% DFC
US Coast Guard (USCG)	Total ISPS US ports	226 port authorities, of which 5000 facilities are computed (ISPS Parts A and B MARSEC Level 1)	1125	656	5399
	Total ISPS US-SOLAS and non-SOLAS vessels subject to the regulation	3500 US-flag vessels, as well as domestic and foreign non-SOLAS vessels (operating in US waters) (ISPS Parts A and B MARSEC Level 1)	218	176	1368
	Automated Identification System (AIS)	47 Captain of the port US zones	30	1	50
	Maritime Area (contracting government)	40 US OCS Facilities under US jurisdiction	120	46	477
	Outer Continental Shelf facility (OCS) (offshore installations)		3	5	37
	US cost for ISPS implementation	ISPS parts A and B	115	884	7331
	Aggregate cost of elevating MARSEC level from 1 to 2	Based on a twice Maritime Security Level (MARSEC level) 2 per annum, each for 21 days	16 per day		
UK	Total ISPS UK port facilities	430 facilities (ISPS Part A MARSEC Level 1)	26	2.5	
	Total ISPS UK-flagged ships and company related costs	620 UK-flag vessels (ISPS Parts A, MARSEC Level 1) (Assumed UK£1 = 1.6 US$)	7.4	5.2	
OECD	AIS	Based on 43,291 international commercial fleet of more than 1000 GT (excluding passenger and cruise vessels), MARSEC Level 1, ISPS Part A only	649.3	Undetermined(UD)	
	Other vessel measures		115.11	14.6	
	Ship operating companies		1163.89	715.4	
	Total ships and shipping companies		1279	730	
	Port Facility Security Assessment, Port Facility Security Officer, Port Facility Security Plan	2180 port authorities worldwide, of which 6500 facilities are computed (from Fairplay) (ISPS Part A only MARSEC Level 1)	390.8	336.6	
	Total ISPS ports		UD		
	Global cost for ISPS implementation		UD		
Australian Government	• Total costs for Australia	MARESC level 1, ISPS part A only; 70 Australian flag ships and 70 ports, of which 300 port facilities	240AUD	74AUD	UD
Shipowners' Association	• Total costs for vessels	47 Australian vessels	2965SAUD	UD	

All cost figures are expressed in 2003 US$ million, except for Australia where costs are expressed in 2002 AUD $ million
Source The authors adapted from Bichou (2008, p. 24)

Table 2.10 illustrates that the USCG estimated the initial costs of ISPS compliance for the US ports could reach US$1.1 billion, and the annual cost was US$656 million thereafter up to 2012 (DHS 2003). Bichou and Evans (2007) included data on *ex-ante* estimates of port security in the UK and Australia. Within the UK, the initial cost for ISPS Code compliance for 430 port facilities was US$26 million and the annual cost was US$2.5 million; while in Australia, the cost of ISPS compliance for 300 port facilities was US$240 million initially with an annual cost at US$74 million. The OECD (2003) reported comprehensively on the global economic influence of maritime security measures. They estimated the ISPS implementation costs for ports were around US$2 billion for the initial investment and US$1 billion for annual expenditure for developing country ports alone.

Ex-Post Costs Assessment

Following the new measures entering into force, researchers adopted varying methods ranging from surveys and economic impact analysis to financial assessment and insurance risk modelling for *ex-post* compliance cost assessment. A survey by UNCTAD (2007) suggested that the average cost for ISPS compliance would be US$0.08 for each ton handled and US$3.6 for each TEU handled, of which US$0.03 and US$2 was for recurrent costs, respectively. A World Bank survey conducted by Kruk and Donner (2008) pointed out that the average ISPS compliance costs amounted to US$0.22 per ton and US$4.95 per TEU handled. Bichou (2004, 2008) and Bosk (2006) explained that such contradictory findings may be explained by two reasons: the diverse approaches used to calculate the ISPS costs and different interpretations of the code across ports and terminals worldwide. As to economic impact studies, Damas (2001) estimated the cost of the new security measures introduced in response to the 9/11 event would be US$151 billion annually for the USA, of which US$65 billion only accounted for logistical changes to supply chains. The other costs were for workplace security, IT security and contingency operations, insurance and liability and employee absenteeism (Russell and Saldanha 2003). The International Monetary Fund (IMF) estimated the monetary costs owing to higher security amounted to about US$1.6 billion annually, with an extra financing burden of maintaining 10% higher inventories at US$7.5 billion per year (IMF 2001). Dekker and Stevens (2007) undertook another exploratory empirical study on maritime security-related costs and their financing in European member states. A survey which covered the EU27 and the European Economic Area (EEA) countries with a cross section of 30 'top seaports' was conducted. The chosen seaports were located in Northern, Central and Southern Europe. According to the results, the port facilities had to make a relatively limited effort to achieve 100% compliance. The results also revealed that 44% of the investment costs were on 'landside-accesses and entrances' and accounted for the largest share in the total investment. The second and third largest part was electronic systems (34%) and seaside access (14%). The categories 'landside-railways and roads' and 'inspections and insurance' rated 4 and 3%, respectively (Dekker and Stevens 2007). The category 'personnel' accounted for only 1% of the investment costs. Personnel costs accounted for 57% of total running costs and inspections and insurance for a further 2%.

The Implications of CSI Compliance Cost for Different Stakeholders

Every stakeholder involved in the global supply chain would be affected by the compliance costs of the CSI. These stakeholders are identified by Allen (2006, p. 441) as '*exporters, port authorities, carriers, US manufacturers who rely on foreign inputs, retailers who sell goods with imported components, and finally US consumers*'. Moreover, these entities must recognise the monetary costs are necessary and could be offset by the more cost-effective facilitated cargo processing and increased security (CBP 2006). The initial costs would fall on ports for investing in required capital. They would likely charge carriers who then recover this cost by charging exporters (Allen 2006; Bichou 2008). Allen (2006) focused on port authorities, carriers and exporters who would experience the most observable CSI-related cost increase.

Port Authorities

In order to maximise the security of cargo shipping into the US ports and ensure the safety of the global supply chain, cargoes need to be scanned before coming into US ports. Port authorities are responsible for investing in new security equipment and technologies such as the NII and RPMs (Table 2.3), developing relevant security plans, implementing formal security procedures, recruiting security personnel and carrying out regular training and security drills (Bichou 2011).

As to the compliance cost of the CSI, DHS (2009) pointed out that few additional costs are incurred. However, much research implies a different story. Various cost assessments on ISPS compliance have already been discussed, and the CSI cost estimation mainly focused on infrastructure-related investment and running costs. According to Miller (2007), analysts believed that each port would have to purchase 1–10 scanners. Allen (2006) stated that purchasing or upgrading container-scanning devices would cost between US$1 and US$5 million per device although this figure varied considerably. The expenditure for a container scanner for the port of Rotterdam was EUR€14 million, while the Singapore Ministry of Trade spent US$1.9 million on purchasing the scanners. The port authority of Buenos Aires approved a US$33 million budget for equipping the port with four container scanners, reserving US$20 million for device acquisition and the rest for upgrading existing infrastructure (Ceriotto 2004). Besides the investment in purchasing scanners, the other compliance costs such as developing IT systems and personnel training were too high to be overlooked. It would cost as much as two to three times the initial investment for device upgrading in the actual scanner. Yet these costs are set by the divergent labour costs in different countries and different infrastructure investment requirements.

The CSI-related costs are not limited to initial investments in port upgrading. It would be difficult and costly for some countries to meet the advance notification requirements of both the CSI and the 24-hour rule since their customs officials may not have the required skills (Allen 2006). The EU estimated the average initialisation cost for one port to be about US$100 million, and there would be billions of Euros in extra spending (Miller 2007). Some smaller ports from which only very few containers are shipped to the USA may find this cost is too large to be justifiable, and they lacked resources for purchasing NII scanning devices. Small ports still faced other problems such as space constraints, even if they are capable of purchasing the scanners.

Depending on the port nature and ownership, the capital and human resource investments would be borne either by the public/private port management, state customs or commercial terminal operators (OECD 2003). Therefore, how these costs are covered will depend on the body that is responsible for the initial capital cost. This will directly influence how the fees are passed onto shippers, carriers and final consumers.

Carriers

Carriers initially bear the costs of 24-hour rule compliance cost stemming from new IT systems investment, personnel training and working hours (UNCTAD 2003). Thibault et al. (2006) found that small shipping companies generally bear lesser initial compliance costs but higher running costs due to the complexity of spreading fixed costs across a small business base. Moreover, ports would also pass security compliance costs onto carriers. The Port Klang Authority in Malaysia had announced that it would start charging carriers the 'extra movement charges' between US$30 and US$150 for containers picked for scanning (The Star 2004). However, the Singapore Port Authority declared that carriers would not be charged any extra fees for CSI-related infrastructure expenses, nor for scanning. Anyhow, these costs would most likely be passed onto the exporters as documentation fees charged by carriers. Based on Allen (2006), most carriers had started to charge between US$25 and US$35 per bill of lading for administrative expenses recovery. For small container lines, they normally bear less initial compliance cost but higher running costs because of their small business base (Thibault et al. 2006)

Exporters

According to Allen (2006), exporters would be most likely to bear the cost passed on by the CSI ports and carriers, under the category of documentation fees or specific fees on containers picked for screening. Nevertheless, these extra charges do not appear excessive when compared to overall costs of moving a container throughout the supply chain. According to Felixstowe Port Authority (2004), supposing the cost of shipping a container is US$1000, a US$20 movement fee only accounts for 2% of total transport costs. These containers can also benefit from US 'green lanes' to avoid costs associated with delays. For shipments from non-CSI ports, the CBP may delay cargo release or deny the carrier's preliminary entry permit to unload at the US port (Dallimore 2008). This would take a considerable amount of time due to required container physical inspections. By routing through a CSI port, this situation could be avoided.

Allen (2006) also believed that exporters located near a CSI port would bear the least costs among all possible exporters, while exporters located further away from a CSI port would bear a considerably higher cost regardless of their adopted strategy. Normally, these exporters located in a non-CSI port may choose not to reroute their containers through a CSI port and bear the risks of cargo delay when entering the USA. Based on Machalaba (2001), in some cases, containers are delayed up to two weeks at US ports because of security screening and average delays represent between 3 and 4 days. Spending one extra day in Customs adds almost 1% to the total transport costs. Exporters could choose to alter their direct route to the USA through a CSI port; however, this would lead to an increase in both the length of the haul and the associated cost by affecting '*supply and demand of a particular route, freight insurance, the value and commodity category of the goods shipped, and the distance of the route*' (Allen 2006, p. 442). Furthermore, the cost of shipping the containers is very different in different regions. These charges account for 3% of the market price in the USA but 12% in Africa (Limao and Venables 2001). The latter argued that transportation costs may be more critical to many developing countries than developed countries. For companies in Bangladesh which export finished clothing to the USA, the most significant cost factor is the transportation cost of the final merchandise to the buyer rather than the labour or capital cost (Bradsher 2004). Therefore, the increase in transportation costs can cause heavy losses in developing countries, noted by Walkenhorst and Dihel (2002) and also that every 1% increase in transport cost would cause sub-Saharan African countries to suffer a decrease of 0.3% in their GDP, while South Asian countries would experience a reduction of approximately 0.6%. A fall of 10% in transport costs could increase trade by 25% in some African areas. To remain competitive in the export-oriented sector, developing country exporters may have to lower wages or lay off employees, leading to higher unemployment and lower welfare. Therefore, the decision whether an exporter chooses to reroute through a CSI port is largely determined by how much risk they are willing to take and is much more critical for developing country exporters.

Operational and Logistical Efficiency

Although cargo scanning can maximise supply chain security, Bennett and Chin (2008, p. 28) quoted Zin (2007, p. 13): '*it slows down cargo and causes a gridlock at ports*'. Opponents of the 100% scanning measures quoted a cost-benefit analysis conducted by Martonosi et al. (2005) to express their concerns about cargo delay and congestion where the estimated delay would increase from 0.5 hours per TEU under current operations to 5.5 hours per TEU under the 100% scanning measures. The World Shipping Council (WSC) (2007) estimated that the 100% scanning requirement would influence US$500 billion of commerce. The WSC also mentioned the possibility of ceasing US imports to minimise costs. Asian port operations were predicted to suffer the largest impact of a range of US supply chain security initiatives, since over 50% of US imports are loaded in China.

According to Bichou (2011), there were two major debates over port efficiency due to security initiative implementation. While port security measures enhance port security, many argued that procedural requirements of the new security measures would lower operational and logistical efficiency (Lenain et al. 2002; Bichou 2008; Thai 2009). Supply chain disruption could arise as an indirect result of the additional lengthy procedure.

Implementation of the security regulations could potentially bring negative and/or positive impacts on extra costs, delaying cargo transit times and port efficiency (Yeo et al. 2013). Bichou (2011) found that under the 24-hour rule, the vessel waiting time can be extended to three days or even more for carriers due to their failure in connecting electronically to the US CBP Automated Manifest System (AMS). As a result, shippers and receivers would have to make adjustments to their production plan, distribution and inventory management. Additionally, ports are affected by the documentation requirement which could lead to congestion and possible delays in both ships' departures and arrivals. Shippers also need to spend extra time and resources for carriers to complete documentation procedures. Although higher security quality is gained from the stricter security procedures, port efficiency and timeliness may be jeopardised (Chang and Thai 2016). Shipping companies have already begun passing the direct and indirect cost impacts of the 24-hour rule to shippers and cargo owners (Bichou 2008).

Some studies advocate that security initiatives bring positive effects on port efficiency and performance owing to better procedural arrangements (Banomyong 2005). Donner and Kruk (2009) stated that the 24-hour rule has improved the self-discipline of both the export shipping and maritime logistics industry, which in turn improves the efficiency of port operation. Bichou (2011) explained that measures such as the CSI and the 24-hour rule are prevention oriented that would be more cost-effective and less time-consuming than traditional random physical inspections. Clark et al. (2004) and Yeo et al. (2013) argued that having an appropriate level of regulation at port can improve port efficiency. Proponents of the new security regime argued that its implementation is also commercially rewarding (Bichou 2011). Moreover, compliant participants would gain commercial benefits from '*access certification and fast-lane treatment*', '*reduced insurance costs, penalties and risk exposure*' (Bichou 2008, pp. 30–31). Conventional security screening at the unloading port could lead to containers being delayed for up to two weeks at US ports (Machalaba 2001). In addition, new security regimes also bring benefits such as '*support of legitimate commerce, reduced risk of cargo theft and pilferage, stronger protection against illegal drugs and human trafficking, and improved lead-time predictability and supply chain visibility*' (Bichou 2011, p. 6).

However, Bichou (2008) stated that there is little empirical analysis to support both arguments and noted that much maritime security research is based on mathematical modelling, conceptual work, the economic situation or anecdotal evidence. Erera et al. (2003) included the mathematical modelling in their heuristic method to estimate the delays caused by container scanning. Babione et al. (2003) used simulation to analyse the impacts of post 9/11 security initiatives on the container traffic flow in Seattle Port. Lee and Whang (2005) used a simple quantitative model to assess how supply chain security could be assured with a total quality management approach. Bennett and Chin (2008) used port statistics, field study data and industry insights and adopted Monte Carlo simulation and queuing models to quantify the financial and operational implications of 100% export US-bound container scanning. There are also simulators specifically designed for '*pre-defined disruption scenarios and to predict their impacts on port efficiency*' (Bichou 2008, p. 31), such as NISAC's two port simulators (NISAC 2005). Talas and Menachof (2009) developed a conceptual model to calculate a port facility's remaining security risk after the risk treatment implementation decisions (such as regulatory measures).

In the next chapter, we move on to a detailed consideration of port competition.

References

Allen, N. H. (2006). The container security initiative costs, implications and relevance to developing countries. *Public Administration and Development, 26*(5), 439–447.

American Shipper. (2014). *CSI's Evolution*. Available at http://www.americanshipper.com/main/news/csis-evolution57536.aspx?taxonomy=Security. Accessed 10 December 2016.

Babione, R., Kim, C. K., Phone, E., & Sanjaya, E. (2003). *Post 9/11 Security Cost Impact on Port of Seattle Import/Export Container Traffic* (Working Paper GTTL 502). The University of Washington.

Banomyong, R. (2005). The impact of port and trade security initiatives on maritime supply chain management. *Maritime Policy and Management, 32*(1), 3–13.

Bennett, A. C., & Chin, Y. Z. (2008). *100% Container Scanning: Security Policy Implications for Global Supply Chains* (Master of Science Dissertation). MIT Press, Cambridge.

Bichou, K. (2004). The ISPS code and the cost of port compliance: An initial logistics and supply chain framework for port security assessment and management. *Maritime Economics and Logistics, 6,* 322–348.

Bichou, K. (2008). *Security and risk-based models in shipping and ports: Review and critical analysis.* ITF, Terrorism and International Transport: Towards Risk-based Security Policy. Paris: OECD.

Bichou, K. (2011). Assessing the impact of procedural security on container port efficiency. *Maritime Economics and Logistics, 13*(1), 1–28.

Bichou, K., & Evans, A. (2007). Maritime security and regulatory risk-based models: Review and critical analysis. In K. Bichou, M. G. H. Bell, & A. Evans (Eds.), *Risk Management in Port Operations, Logistics and Supply Chain Security* (pp. 265–280). London: Informa.

Bichou, K., Lai, K. H., Lun, V. Y. H., & Cheng, T. C. E. (2007). A quality management framework for liner shipping companies to implement the 24-hour advance vessel manifest rule. *Transportation Journal, 46*(1), 5–21.

Bosk, L. B. (2006). *Port and Supply Chain Security Initiatives in the United States and Abroad* (Policy Research Report, 150). Austin, TX: The University of Texas at Austin, pp. 1–192.

Bradsher, K. (2004, December 14). Bangladesh is Surviving to Export Another Day. *The New York Times.*

Bueger, C. (2014). What is maritime security? *Marine Policy, 53,* 159–164.

CBP. (2003). *Container Security Initiative: Update. United States Department of Homeland Security 2003.* Available at http://www.whitehouse.gov/homeland/. Accessed 17 October 2014.

CBP. (2006). *Container Security Initiative: Strategic Plan 2006–2011.* Available at http://www.cbp.gov/linkhandler/cgov/trade/cargo_security/csi/csi_strategic_plan.ctt/csi_strategic_plan.pdf. Accessed 30 July 2013.

CBP. (2011). *Container Security Initiatives in Summary.* Available at https://www.cbp.gov/sites/default/files/documents/csi_brochure_2011_3.pdf. Accessed 7 August 2016.

CBP. (2014). *CSI: Container Security Initiatives.* Available at https://www.cbp.gov/border-security/ports-entry/cargo-security/csi/csi-brief. Accessed 27 August 2016.

CBPIA. (2002). *Container Security Initiative Fact Sheet. 2002*, pp. 1–5.

Ceriotto, L. (2004). *Buscantecnologia china para la aduana.* Available at www.clarin.com. Accessed 30 October 2014.

Chan, Y. (2005). A statistical study of intrastate vs. interstate regulatory reforms. *Journal of Geography, 13*, 165–171.

Chang, C., & Thai, V. (2016). Do port security quality and service quality influence customer satisfaction and loyalty? *Maritime Policy and Management, 43*(6), 720–736.

Clark, X., Dollar, D., & Micco, D. (2004). *Port Efficiency, Maritime Transport Costs and Bilateral Trade* (NBER Working Paper No. 10353). Available at http://www.nber.org/papers/w10353.pdf. Accessed 4 January 2017.

Coleman, N., & Levin, C. (2006). *An Assessment of US Efforts to Secure the Global Supply Chain: Prepared by the Majority & Minority staffs of the Permanent Subcommittee on Investigations*. Available at https://www.hsdl.org/?view&did=464168.

Congressional Budget Office. (2016). *Scanning and Imaging Shipping Containers Overseas: Costs and Alternatives*. Available at http://www.cbo.gov/sites/default/files/114th-congress-2015-2016/reports/51478-Shipping-Containers.pdf. Accessed 10 March 2017.

Dallimore, C. (2008). *Securing the Supply Chain: Does the Container Security Initiative comply with WTO Law?* (Dissertation). University of Münster, Münster, Germany.

Damas, P. (2001, November). Supply chains at war. *American Shipper*, pp. 17–18.

Dekker, S., & Stevens, H. (2007). Maritime security in the European Union-empirical findings on financial implications for port facilities. *Maritime Policy and Management, 34*(5), 458–499.

DHS. (2003). *N-RAT Assessment Exercise Part II: Implementation of National Maritime Security Initiatives*. The Federal Register: 68/204.

DHS. (2009). *Testimony of Acting Commissioner Jayson P. Ahern, U.S. Customs and Border Protection, before the House Appropriations Committee, Subcommittee on Homeland Security, on Cargo and Container Security*. Available at https://www.dhs.gov/news/2009/04/01/us-customs-and-border-protection-acting-commissioner-jason-aherns-testimony-cargo. Accessed 15 June 2016.

DHS. (2014). *Privacy Impact Assessment for the Non-Intrusive Inspection Systems Programme*. Available at https://www.dhs.gov/sites/default/files/publications/privacy_pia_cbp_nii_jan2014.pdf. Accessed 2 May 2016.

DHS. (2016). *Operational and Support Components*. DHS. Available at https://www.dhs.gov/operational-and-support-components. Accessed 30 March 2017.

DNV Consulting. (2005). *Study on the Impacts of Possible European Legislation to Improve Transport Security* (European Commission Report 40008032-6-2, pp. 1–236).

Donner, M., & Kruk, C. (2009). *Supply Chain Security Guide* (The World Bank and DFID, 1), pp. 1–107. Available at http://siteresources.worldbank.org/INTPRAL/Resources/SCS_Guide_Final.pdf. Accessed 20 April 2016.

Drewry. (2015, January). Analysis of the shipping markets. *Shipping Insight Monthly*.

Ellis, J. (2010). Undeclared dangerous goods-risk implications for maritime transport. *WMU Journal of Maritime Affairs, 9*(1), 5–27.

Erera, A, Lewis, B., & White, C. (2003). *Optimisation Approaches for Efficient Container Security Operations at Transhipment Seaports* (Transportation Research Record, No. 1822), pp. 1–8.

European Conference of Ministers of Transport. (2005). *Container Transport Security Across Modes*. Available at http://www.itf-oecd.org/sites/default/files/docs/05containersec.pdf. Accessed 10 May 2016.

Federal Bureau of Investigation (FBI). (2013). *Terrorism 2000/2001*. Available at https://www.fbi.gov/stats-services/publications/terror. Accessed 15 November 2016.

Felixstowe Port Authority. (2004). *Security Charge—Q&A*. Available at http://www.phoenixcargo.com/news/documents/Security%20Charge%20QA.pdf. Accessed 15 November 2016.

GAO. (2003). *Container Security: Expansion of Key Customs Programs Will Require Greater Attention to Critical Success Factors 2003*. United States Government Accountability Office (GAO) Reports, p. 1.

Gerencser, M., Weinberg, J., & Vincent, D. (2003). *Port Security War Game: Implications for US Supply Chains*. Washington, DC: Booz Allen Hamilton.

GlobalSecurity.org. (no date). *Homeland Security: Limburg Oil Tanker Attacked*. Available at https://www.globalsecurity.org/security/profiles/limburg_oil_tanker_attacked.htm. Accessed 26 April 2018.

Goulielmos, A. M., & Anastasakos, A. A. (2005). Worldwide security measures for shipping, seafarers and ports: An impact assessment of ISPS Code. *Disaster Prevention and Management, 14,* 462–478.

Hall, P. V. (2004). "We'd have to sink the ships": Impact studies and the 2002 West Coast port lockout. *Economic Development Quarterly, 18*(4), 354–367.

Hintsa, J., Gutierrez, X., Wieser, P., & Hameri, A. P. (2009). Supply chain security management: An overview. *International Journal of Logistics Systems and Management, 5*(3/4), 344–355.

Holmes, J. L. (2004). The container security initiative. *Fleet Equipment, 30*, 15.

IMF. (2001). *World Economic Outlook: The Global Economy after September 11*. Available at http://www.imf.org/external/pubs/ft/weo/2001/03. Accessed 20 December 2015.

International Organisation for Standardisation (ISO). (2007). *ISO 28000:2007: Specification for Security Management Systems for the Supply Chain*. Available at https://www.iso.org/standard/44641.html. Accessed 20 March 2016.

Koch, C. (2002). *Testimony Before the House Transportation and Infrastructure Committee*. Available at http://www.house.gov/transportation/cgmt/03-13-02/koch.html. Accessed 13 March 2016.

Kristiansen, S. (2005). *Maritime Transportation: Safety Management and Risk Analysis*. New York: Routledge.

Kruk, C., & Donner, M. (2008). *Review of Cost of Compliance with the New International Freight Transport Security Requirements*. Washington, DC: The World Bank.

Lee, H. L., & Whang, S. (2005). Higher supply chain security with lower cost: Lessons from total quality management. *International Journal of Production Economies, 96*(3), 289–300.

Lenain, P., Bonturi, M., & Vincent, K. (2002). *The Economic Consequences of Terrorism* (Economics Department Working Paper, 334). Organisation for Economic Co-Operation and Development, pp. 23–32.

Limao, N., & Venables, A. J. (2001). Infrastructure, geographical disadvantage, transport costs and trade. *The World Bank Economic Review, 15*(3), 451–479.

Machalaba, D. (2001, July 9). US ports are losing the battle to keep up with overseas trade. *The Wall Street Journal*. Available at http://www.nc.gsu.edu/_ecojxm/7030/notes/articles/w070901.htm. Accessed 2 December 2016.

Maersk Line. (2011). *Emma Maersk/The Largest Container Ship*. Available at http://www.emma-maersk.com/. Accessed 10 January 2015.

Maersk Line. (2013). *The World's Largest Ship*. Available at https://www.maersk.com/en/explore/fleet/triple-e. Accessed 15 January 2015.

Martonosi, S. E., Ortiz, D. S., & Willis, H. H. (2005). Evaluating the viability of 100 percent container inspections at America's ports. In H. W. Richardson, P. Gordon, & J. E. II Moore (Eds.), *The Economic Impacts of Terrorist Attacks*. Cheltenham: Edward Elgar Publishing.

Metaparti, P. (2010). Rhetoric, rationality and reality in post-9/11 maritime security. *Maritime Policy and Management, 37*(7), 723–736.

Miller, J. (2007, October 25). New shipping law makes big waves in foreign ports. *Wall Street Journal*.

NISAC. (2005). *Port Operations and Economic Conditions Simulators* (pp. 1–15). Washington, DC: NISAC.

O'Hanlon, M. E. (2002). *Protecting the American Homeland: A Preliminary Analysis*. Washington, DC: Brookings Institution.

OECD. (2003). *Maritime Transport Committee Security in Maritime Transport: Risk Factors and Economic Impact*. Available at https://www.oecd.org/newsroom/4375896.pdf.

OECD. (2009). *Terrorism and International Transport: Towards Risk-Based Security Policy*. Round Table 144.

OECD. (2015). *International Transport Forum: The Impact of Mega-Ships*. Available at http://www.itf-oecd.org/sites/default/files/docs/15cspa_mega-ships.pdf.

Parfomak, P., & Frittelli, J. (2007). *CRS Report for Congress. Maritime Security: Potential Attacks and Protection Priorities*. Available at http://www.fas.org/sgp/crs/homesec/RL33787.pdf.

Park, H. G. (2013). *Impact of Supply Chain Security Orientation on Port Performance* (PhD thesis). Cardiff University, UK.

RAND. (2012). *RAND Database of Worldwide Terrorism Incidents*. Available at http://www.rand.org/nsrd/projects/terrorismincidents.html. Accessed 19 April 2013.

Richardson, M. (2004). *Growing Vulnerability of Seaports from Terror Attacks, to Protect Ports While Allowing Global Flow of Trade Is a New Challenge*. Viewpoint, Institute of South East Asian Studies.

Rodrigue, J. P., Comtois, C., & Slack, B. (2009). *The Geography of Transport Systems*. New York: Routledge.

Russell, D. M., & Saldanha, J. P. (2003). Five tenets of security-aware logistics and supply chain operation. *Transportation Journal, 42*(4), 44–54.

Sadovaya, E., & Thai, V. V. (2012, May 27–30). *Maritime Security Requirements for Shipping Companies and Ports: Implementation, Importance and Effectiveness*. Paper presented at International Forum on Shipping, Ports and Airports (IFSPA) 2012, Hong Kong.

Sandler, T. (2014). The analytical study of terrorism: Taking stock. *Journal of Peace Research, 51*(2), 257–271.

Sarathy, R. (2006). Security and the global supply chain. *Transportation Journal, 45*(4), 28.

Saywell, T., & Borsuk, R. (2002, October 24). The fallout of the Bali bombings on regional economies: The neighbourhood takes a hit. *Far Eastern Economic Review*, Hong Kong.

Smeele, F. (2010). International civil litigation and the pollution of the marine environment. In J. Basedow, U. Magnus, & R. Wolfrum (Eds.), *The Hamburg Lectures on Maritime Affairs 2007 and 2008* (pp. 77–118). Berlin: Springer.

Stasinopoulos, D. (2003). Maritime security: The need for a global agreement. *Maritime Economics and Logistics, 5*(3), 311–320.

Talas, R., & Menachof, D. (2009). The efficient tradeoff between security and cost for seaports: A conceptual model. *International Journal of Risk Assessment and Management, 13*(1), 46–59.

Thai, V. V. (2007). Impacts of security improvements on service quality in maritime transport: An empirical study of Vietnam. *Maritime Economics and Logistics, 9*(4), 335–356.

Thai, V. V. (2009). Effective maritime security: Conceptual model and empirical evidence. *Maritime Policy and Management, 36*(2), 147–163.

The Economist. (2002, April 6). *Special Report: When Trade and Security Clash-Container Trade.* London.

The Star. (2004). *Temporary Reprieve from CSI-Related Charges.* Available at http://thestar.com.my/. Accessed 5 April 2015.

Thibault, M., Brooks, M., & Button, K. (2006). The response of the US maritime industry to the new container security initiatives. *Transportation Journal, 45*(1), 5–15.

UNCTAD. (2003, February 24–28). *Report on the Expert Meeting on Efficient Transport and Trade Facilitation to Improve Participation by Developing Countries in International Trade: Problems and Potential for the Application of Current Trade Facilitation Measures by Developing Countries.* Trade and Development Board. Commission on Enterprise, Business Facilitation and Development Seventh session, Geneva, pp. 2–9.

UNCTAD. (2004, February 26). *Container Security: Major Initiatives and Related International Developments.* Geneva: Report by the UCTAD Secretariat.

UNCTAD. (2007). *Maritime Security: ISPS Code Implementation, Costs and Related Financing. UNCTAD/SDTE/TLB/2007.* Available at http://unctad.org/en/Docs/sdtetlb20071_en.pdf.

WCO. (2007). *SAFE Framework Standards.* http://www.wcoomd.org/files/1.%20Public%20files/PDFandDocuments/SAFE%2.

Walkenhorst, P., & Dihel, N. (2002). *Trade Impacts of the Terrorist Attacks of 11 September 2001: A Quantitative Assessment.* Paper presented to the Institute of Global Research (DIW) workshop on The Economic Consequences of Global Terrorism, Berlin. Available at http://www.diw.de/documents/dokumentenarchiv/17/diw_01.c.39105.de/diw_ws_consequences200206_walkenhorst.pdf.

Willis, H. H., & Ortiz, D. (2004). *Evaluating the Security of the Global Containerised Supply Chain.* RAND Technical Report Series.

WSC. (2007). *Statement Regarding Legislation to Require 100% Container Scanning.* http://www.worldshipping.org/pdf/wsc_legislation_statement.pdf.

WTO. (2017). *Trade Facilitation.* https://www.wto.org/english/tratop_e/tradfa_e/tradfa_e.htm#I.

Yang, Y. C. (2010). Impact of the container security initiative on Taiwan's shipping industry. *Maritime Policy and Management, 37*(7), 699–722.

Yeo, G., Pak, J., & Yang, Z. (2013). Analysis of dynamic effects on seaports adopting port security policy. *Transportation Research Part A, 49,* 285–301.

Zin, C. T. (2007). US container screening bill slammed. *Bunker World.* http://www.bunkerworld.com/news/2007/08/68737.

3

Port Competition

In this chapter, port competition and various competitiveness determinants will be presented and discussed, including port selection, port efficiency, port service and other related issues. Moreover, maritime transportation is fundamental to global trade which is influenced by political activities. The shipping industry is closely affected by the political economy which will be assessed to lay a foundation for this abductive research and its interpretation to follow.

Port Competition

The phenomena of globalisation and liberalisation have had a positive effect on international trade. Demand for freight transport is a derived demand and a port's basic activity is maritime trade, which is in turn driven by international commerce and economic activity (Estache and Trujillo 2009). The position and function of a port has become a crucial node in the logistics chain which connects the origin and the

© The Author(s) 2019
X. Zhang and M. Roe, *Maritime Container Port Security*,
https://doi.org/10.1007/978-3-030-03825-0_3

destination of goods. Various stakeholders with conflicting interests are involved in this logistics process, which leads to difficulty in giving an unequivocal definition of port competition. Many different parties are involved in global supply chains, and therefore, the competitive position of a seaport is determined by many other factors than its own infrastructure and organisation (Meersman et al. 2010). According to Van de Voorde and Winkelmans (2002), defining port competition takes every aspect relevant to ports and competition into consideration. As a result, the following definition is provided:

> Sea port competition refers to competition between port undertakings, or as the case may be, terminal operators in relation to specific transactions. Each operator is driven by the objective to achieve maximum growth in relation to goods handling, in terms of value added or otherwise. Port competition is influenced by (1) specific demand from consumers, (2) specific factors of production, (3) supporting industries connected with each operator, and (4) the specific competencies of each operator and their rivals. Finally, port competition is also affected by port authorities and other public bodies'. (Van de Voorde and Winkelmans 2002, p. 11)

Heaver (1995) argued that a competitive strategy mainly focuses on terminals rather than ports. Notteboom and Yap (2012) explained that the nature and characteristics of port competition depend upon the type of port and the commodity. Haezendonck and Notteboom (2002) argued that port competition is affected by a combination of factors within the whole logistics chain. Merkel (2017) also believed that port competition is affected by not only the port itself but also by modes of traffic within a logistics chain. Notteboom and Yap (2012, p. 549) outlined port competition. It:

> essentially involves a competition for trades, with terminals as the competing physical units, transport concerns and/or industrial enterprises as the chain managers and representatives of the respective trades, and port authorities and port policy makers as representatives and defenders of the port sector at a higher level, engaged in offering good working conditions (e.g. infrastructure) to this sector.

Container Port Competition and Port Competitiveness

There has been an increasing attention on the container port industry in recent years as containerised transportation evolves (Cullinane et al. 2005). Notteboom and Yap (2012) suggested container port competition includes three levels, namely intra-port competition, inter-port competition at the national and regional levels and inter-port competition between terminal operators in different port ranges.

The length of Europe's coastline is 100,000 km, and more than 1200 ports are located along it (OECD 2011). In addition, there are several hundred ports that lie along its 36,000 km of inland waterways. These ports handle 90% of Europe's international trade by volume, acting as the key points of modal transfer. According to Notteboom (2012), the total European port throughput was 4.26 billion tons in 2008, 3.76 billion tons in 2009 and 4.04 billion tons in 2010. There are about 130 container seaports in Europe, and 40 of them provide intercontinental container services; container throughput was 900 million tons in 2010. With total sea container volumes handled by the world's top 100 container ports amounting to 545.6 million TEUs in 2015, the European container port system is one of the busiest worldwide. It features established large ports and medium to smaller-sized ports each with specific features in hinterland markets and geographic locations (Lloyd's List 2016). Smaller ports contribute to Europe's economy because they are fundamental to short sea shipping and inland waterways traffic. They also provide ferry services that freely move people and goods within the EU.

The contemporary containerised transportation and container port industries play vital roles in the world economy, and the container port industry market structure has changed greatly over recent years. Cullinane et al. (2006, p. 355) highlighted two main challenges for the contemporary container port industry:

1. 'the complicated nature of its operations; this is a consequence of the number of different agents involved in importing and exporting containers and the complex operational interactions between the different service processes taking place at a port';

2. 'the increasingly competitive commercial environment that has arisen in recent years'.

Many container ports have lost their monopoly control over cargo from their hinterland. Competition within certain regions is becoming more intensive (Yap and Lam 2006a). Ports not only compete with their neighbours within a hinterland, but also compete with other ports located in the wider region (Notteboom and Yap 2012). Wan and Zhang (2013) investigated the relations between port competition and urban road congestion and noted that port competition has changed to competition between alternative intermodal systems. Ishii et al. (2013) used a game theory approach to analyse inter-port competition and the incentives for ports to engage in competitive behaviour. According to Marcadon (1999), ports started extending their hinterland into areas which were neglected to cope with rising competition. At policy level, Cui and Notteboom (2018) mentioned that many governments consider privatising public ports as an option to increase port competitiveness.

With the development of advanced infrastructure and equipment, container ports are concerned if they can successfully compete for cargoes from within their hinterlands, as well as their capacity to physically handle cargoes (Cullinane et al. 2006). This is because liner companies have more than one port choice when designing their cargo movement routes. Therefore, in such a competitive environment, a port has to obtain a suitable economic scale to cement their customer base because economies of scale are always chosen by customers. Various strategies have been introduced to make them more profitable and attractive. It was pointed out by Perez-Labajos and Blanco (2004) that commercial seaports are faced with the loss in customer loyalty and need to establish new strategies to secure container traffic. They suggested two 'factor groups' for strategy development: (1) a commercial factor group that includes '*develop their infrastructure, integrate themselves in the transport networks, increase their offer of logistics services, encourage improvement in the operators, regulate services and offer something different as regards price and/or quality*' (Perez-Labajos and Blanco 2004, p. 554) and (2) a technological factor group, including electronic data interchange (EDI), vessel traffic system (VTS) and geographic information system (GIS).

Veldman and Buckmann (2003, p. 10) adopted two major factors (cost and quality of service) to analyse port competition and choice. The cost factors are '*the costs of transporting a container between the stack in a seaport and the centre of a hinterland region by road, rail or barge*'. The service factors included the frequency and quality of service and probability of choosing a route. They suggested that competition in the Antwerp–Hamburg range is intense since there are many alternative routings that the customer can choose, and there are substantial overlaps between hinterlands of seaports. Cost and service quality were also cited by Ohashia et al. (2005) in the study of airport competition. However, they detailed cost and service quality based on airline services which were slightly different from Veldman and Buckmann (2003). Cost factors include port charges and cargo transport cost. Service quality factors include '*cruising/flight time, loading/unloading time, and customs clearance time, and waiting time caused by schedule delay*' and waiting time for the next available flight (Ohashia et al. 2005, p. 151).

According to Yeo (2007), multidimensional factors were used by varying scholars for evaluating port competition. Others used a single or simple measure for calculating the competition phenomenon. Rimmer (1998) concluded that port competitive position was affected by the port's location and throughput to a great extent. Heaver et al. (2001) also proposed port location as one of the two critical factors for port competitive position. The other influential factor was network strategies and '*initially, such new competitors may not pose much of a threat, but some gain a critical mass of traffic and establish effective hinterland connections. Monitoring the effectiveness of new ports requires careful attention to the success of their network strategies, even at the level of agencies and forwarding firms*' (Heaver et al. 2001, p. 300). Figueiredo et al. (2015) noted that ports have integrated inland transportation into their services to address rapid development in the shipping industry. A better access to intermodal facilities can attract more traffic for a port from its neighbour.

Robinson (1998) added the number of port calls by shipping companies as an evaluation factor of port competition. McCalla (1999) believed that concentration of port services was the most effective way to maintain and increase port traffic. Chang (2000) claimed that transhipment and intermodal cargo were closely related to improving port competitive position. As an important node of an intermodal system, a port in a smooth intermodal system can attract more containers than a congested one (Wan and Zhang 2013). The Ports of Hong Kong and Singapore were analysed as examples to illustrate that transhipment cargoes could make container ports increasingly larger. The importance of transhipment cargo was also mentioned and related to the success of ports of Singapore and Hong Kong by Fung (2001).

The concept of port competition was outlined by Van de Voorde and Winkelmans (2002) and Notteboom and Yap (2012, pp. 85–86). Port competitiveness is different from port competition. Parola et al. (2017, p. 117) gave the definition of competitiveness as '*the skill or talent resulting from acquired knowledge, able to generate and sustain a superior performance as well as face competitive dynamics*', based on their interpretation of Porter (1990). Notteboom and Yap (2012, p. 551) explained that the competitive position of a container port depends upon '*its competitive offering to the host of shippers and shipping lines for specific trade routes, geographical regions and other ports to which the container port is connected*'. Parola et al. (2017) considered port competitiveness as a multidimensional concept which stems from the ability of port authorities and operators to execute value-added activities. Broadly speaking, port competitiveness is decided by the competitive advantages created or acquired by a port (Haezendonck and Notteboom 2002). Notteboom and Yap (2012) listed factors that could bring port competitive advantages, and they explained the complexity and difficulties in defining competitiveness. Two major areas were addressed by varying scholars, namely identification of port competitiveness drivers and identification of port competitiveness measurements (Parola et al. 2017). Yeo (2007) reviewed and summarised six categories of aspects regarding port competitiveness—efficiency, service, performance, competition, selection and the somewhat vague 'port related issues'.

Various research studies have ascertained the characteristics of container port competitiveness. Notteboom and Yap (2012) summarised studies that have utilised quantitative techniques (Table 3.1) and others that are descriptive in nature (Table 3.2).

Table 3.1 Port competitiveness quantitative research

Quantitative method	Studies
Integer linear programming	Aversa et al. (2005)
Dynamic programming	Zeng and Yang (2002)
Analytical hierarchy process	Guy and Urli (2006) and Lirn et al. (2004)
Stochastic frontier analysis	Notteboom et al. (2000) and Tongzon and Heng (2005)
Data envelopment analysis	Garcia-Alonso and Martin-Bofarull (2007) and Trujillo and Tovar (2007)
The logit model	Veldman et al. (2005)
Structural equation model	Bichou and Bell (2007)
Cointegration test and error correction model	Yap and Lam (2006a)
Transport cost model	Jara-Diaz et al. (2001)
Transport demand model	Luo and Grigalunas (2003)
Cluster analysis	De Langen (2002)
Shipping networks	Yap et al. (2006)
Oligopolistic model	Yap and Lam (2006b)

Source The authors adapted from Notteboom and Yap (2012, p. 552)

Table 3.2 Port competitiveness descriptive research

Areas discussed	Studies
Container port development	Cullinane et al. (2004), Notteboom and Rodrigue (2005), and Slack and Fremont (2005)
Container port competition	Notteboom (2002), Robinson (2002), Van de Voorde and Winkelmans (2002), and Yap and Lam (2004)
Container shipping lines	Heaver et al. (2000) and Slack et al. (2002)
The supply chain	Notteboom and Winkelmans (2001)

Source The authors adapted from Notteboom and Yap (2012, p. 553)

Port Selection

Port selection criteria have been highlighted by many port competitiveness studies (Parola et al. 2017) and summarised by Yeo et al. (2008). The key port competitiveness components included geographical factors, port facilities, port tariffs, frequency of port callings, port reputation, port services and the safe handling of cargoes. Malchow and Kanafani (2004) conducted research on major US ports, and they identified port location as the most significant port characteristic. As to container ports, Yap and Lam (2006a, p. 37) noted the influential factors as '*hinterland accessibility, productivity, quality, cargo generating effect, reputation and reliability*'.

Ha (2003, p. 134) evaluated the service quality factors of 15 ports that handle containers worldwide and categorised these factors into seven groups: '*ready Information availability of port-related activities, port location, port turnaround time, facilities available, port management, port costs and customer convenience*'. The importance of these factors was ranked by respondents (shipping lines) and service quality was evaluated through scoring. The survey suggested that besides monetary factors and efficiency, many ports should improve their service quality by improving '*the quantity and quality of information flows and data availability*' (Ha 2003, p. 137). Lirn et al. (2003) studied the criteria and sub-criteria for transhipment ports. Forty-seven relevant criteria were identified through interviews. Using a Delphi method, they grouped these criteria into four main service criteria and 16 sub-criteria. The four major factors were '*port basic physical characteristics, port geographical location, port management perspective, carriers' cost perspective*' (Lirn et al. 2003, p. 237). Lirn et al. (2004) conducted another round of Delphi and reduced the criteria from 16 to 12. Using the AHP method, they suggested that the most important factors were container handling cost, proximity to main navigation routes, proximity to import/export areas, basic infrastructure condition and existing feeder networks.

Port Competition and Port Selection at Regional Level

Tongzon and Heng (2005) argued that port competition has generally become more intense, and the port competition environment varies between regions and places. The port-regional relationship topic has been overlooked after the 1990s (Ng 2013), and few systematic studies on the implications of regional transformation on a port's competitiveness are available (Homosombat et al. 2016). Regional research on the competition among ports has been undertaken by several researchers, particularly in Asia (Hoshino 2010). Yeo (2007, p. 71) noted the work by Kim (1993) that investigated port choice by Korean shippers, consignees and shipping companies. In descending order of significance, the selection criteria of export ports identified were '*distance between origin and destination, annual cargo handling volume, loading hours, average detention hours at port, goods value per tonne and inland trucking cost per kilometre affected*'. Import port selection depends on '*sea transportation distance, number of liners calling-in, annual volume imported and inland transportation charges per unit distance*'. Yeo et al. (2008, p. 916) referred to the work by Jeon et al. (1993), noting that port selection depends on '*navigation facilities and equipment holding status, port productivity, price competition, and port service quality*'. Nir et al. (2003, p. 168) analysed shippers' port choice behaviour in Taiwan, using four variables that are '*travel time, travel cost, route and frequency*' in a linear multiple port selection model. They found that travel time and cost were the most significant attributes. Tiwari et al. (2003), using China as case study, used conventional transport mode choice models to assess how shippers select liner companies and ports. They concluded that the most influential factors were distance of the shipper from port, distance to destination (for exports) and distance from origin (for imports), port congestion and vessel size. Huybrechts et al. (2002) used a survey to investigate the attractiveness of the port of Antwerp, based on respondents' perspective on port choice determinants. They found that port accessibility mainly due to the restrictions of the River Scheldt prevented Antwerp from becoming a market leader within North Europe. Tongzon and Sawant (2007) investigated port choice determinants from the perspective of the shipping lines from Southeast Asia, using a survey questionnaire. In descending order of significance, efficiency, port charges and connectivity, location, infrastructure, wide range of port services and cargo size were identified as the 'stated preference' of the shipping lines (Tongzon and Sawant 2007). However, the 'revealed preference' approach they adopted showed that port charges and a wide range of port service were the only significant factors in shipping lines' port choice.

Regarding regional port competitiveness research, Cullinane et al. (2004) analysed the container terminal development process in China and its impact on the competitiveness of Hong Kong and other neighbouring ports. Cullinane and Song (2007) focused on Northern Asian ports and applied a variety of models to assess factors relevant to port competitiveness. Song and Yeo (2004) identified cargo volume, port facilities, port location, service level and port expenses as the five most influential criteria for the competitiveness of Asian ports. Fleming and Baird (1999) focused on the UK, the USA and North-Western Europe and found that six sets of key factors were affecting port competitiveness. Valentine (2002, p. 8) summarised them as '*port tradition and organisation, port accessibility, by land and sea, state aid and their influence on port costs, port productivity, port selection preferences of carriers and shippers, and comparative locational advantage*'. In the study by Malchow and Kanafani (2001), they tried to find criteria for port selection in the USA by using the discrete choice model. They found out that in addition to port location, efficiency could increase port competitiveness.

Determinants of Port Competitiveness

Aronietis et al. (2010) stated that it is essential to identify the criteria that determine port competitiveness so that the strengths and weaknesses of the ports can be evaluated. In this research, the criteria and factors that determine port competitiveness are referred to as 'port competitiveness determinants'. Haezendonck and Notteboom (2002) categorised these criteria into quantitative (hinterland accessibility, productivity, cargo generating) and qualitative (quality, reputation and reliability). Yeo (2007) summarised 38 port competitiveness determinants after eliminating overlaps of previous research. He concluded cost was considered as a very important port competitiveness determinant. Port geographic location and service factor were other vital attributes. Parola et al. (2017) conducted a critical review of 170 papers to explore the nature of port competitiveness, covering a 32-year period (1983–2014).

The key drivers of port competitiveness they found were in hierarchical order. Port cost is the most-cited driver. Besides port costs, in the order of ranking, other drivers are hinterland proximity, hinterland connectivity, port geographical location and port infrastructure. Operational efficiency and service quality are two other notable determinants. De Martino and Morvillo (2008) categorised port competitiveness components as hardware and software. Hardware components are related to infrastructure and link to the transport system. They include port location, infrastructure and supra-structures and equipment, and inland logistics (De Martino and Morvillo 2008; Parola et al. 2017). Software components are related to port service quality. They include efficiency factors, service factors, IT systems, safety and security that are vital to maintain customer loyalty (Bichou and Gray 2004). Huybrechts et al. (2002) and De Martino and Morvillo (2008) believed that the software component is the most significant determining factor in port competitiveness. Parola et al. (2017) also grouped port competitiveness components into three categories, supporting the views of Notteboom (2008), namely hinterland-related, maritime-related and endogenous factors. Endogenous factors are *constituted by a number of attributes that strictly originate from the port itself* and *have been traditionally considered as the main drivers of port competitiveness*' (Parola et al. 2017, p. 125). The components of port competitiveness that Yeo (2007) selected are presented in Table 3.3 based on three categories from Parola et al. (2017). The components include port location, port facilities including superstructure (berth, depth, channel length), terminal efficiency, hinterland networks, value-added logistics; and port services, safe handling of cargoes, confidence in port schedules, operational efficiency, electronic data interchange, IT, integration, simplification of procedures, incentives, operational transparency, and port labour and skills.

Based on Table 3.3, the endogenous factors, including cost factor (price), efficiency factor and service factor, together with safety and security (component of software drivers) are chosen to analyse and test for port competitiveness in the EU.

Port Efficiency

Port efficiency is one of the important elements of port competitiveness (Clark et al. 2001). A variety of research projects on port competitiveness looked into port efficiency factors. Figueiredo et al. (2015) undertook a Data Envelopment Analysis (DEA) to investigate the role played by inter-port competition. Cullinane et al. (2006) concluded that the container port industry is characterised by intense competition. They also suggested that the intense competition has stimulated container ports to have an overt interest in resource utilisation efficiency. Therefore, port industrial players must undertake a container port or terminal performance analysis to survive and compete. Such analysis *'not only provides a powerful management tool for port operators, but also constitutes an important variable for informing regional and national transport/port planning and operations'* (Cullinane et al. 2006, p. 355).

Table 3.3 Summarised port competitiveness components

Component categories	Components
Hinterland-related: attributes affect the capacity of the port to expand its commercial influence on-shore, e.g. inland transportation	• Deviation from main trunk routes • Efficient inland logistics network • Inland transportation cost • Intermodal link • Land distance and connectivity to major shippers • Size and activity of Free Trade Zone (FTZ) in port hinterland • Size of contiguous city's economy
Maritime-related: dimensions regarding maritime cargo demand and shipping service connectivity	• Cargo proportion of transhipment cargo • Frequency of cargo loss and damage • Frequency of ship's calling and diversity of ship's route • Frequency of large container ships calling • Level of ship's entrance and departure navigation aids system • Number of direct calls of ocean-going vessel • Port congestion • Volume of inducing cargoes by your company • Volume of total container cargoes

(continued)

Table 3.3 (continued)

Component categories	Components
Endogenous: attributes that strictly originate from the port itself	• Cost for cargo handling, transfer and storage • Cost-related vessel and cargo entering • Government, local autonomous entity, private sectors • Level of service for fresh water, bunkering and ship's products • Promptness of issue document handling • Professionals and skilled labours in port operation • Prompt response • Port sales: port promotion • Port's safety and security • Real working time • Recognition and reputation of port • Reliability of schedules in port • Service capacity for ship's size • Sophistication level of port information and its application scope • Free dwell time on the terminal • Availability of vessel berth on arrival in port • Stability of port's labour • Terminal productivity • Water depth in approach channel and at berth • Zero waiting time service • 24 hours a day, seven days a week service • Port accessibility

Source The authors adapted from Yeo (2007, p. 72) and Parola et al. (2017, p. 125)

Cullinane et al. (2006) also conducted a critical review of port competitiveness studies from the 1970s to 2002 and concluded that a great number of studies sought to evaluate the performance of ports and optimise cargo-handling operational productivity. Nevertheless, among the studies they reviewed, they found that only a few tried to derive a summary evaluation of port productivity. For example, at an early stage, De Monie (1987) tried to measure single factor productivity, and in 1998, Talley compared actual with optimum throughput over a specific time period. Research on the measurement of productivity activities efficiency has gained significant progress over the years.

Blonigen and Wilson (2006) stated that surveys are a common method to measure port efficiency. Gonzalez and Trujillo (2009) conducted a systematic analysis of the existing parametric and non-parametric approaches to economic efficiency and productivity analysis as applied to the port sector. Cullinane and Wang (2010) mentioned that non-parametric frontier methods have been developed for transport productivity and efficiency measurement. Cullinane et al. (2006), Cullinane and Wang (2010), and Nguyen et al. (2016) suggested DEA and Stochastic Frontier Analysis (SFA) as more holistic and complex methods to measure port performance. Blonigen and Wilson (2006) adopted a simple econometric-based method using US Census data on imports into US ports to measure port efficiency.

With the development of logistics and supply chain management, the port has become a vital node in the overall trading chain and port privatisation has been one of the most obvious industry phenomena (Tongzon and Heng 2005). Port competitive position and operations efficiency are vital for a nation to gain competitive position in world trade (Tongzon 1989; Chin and Tongzon 1998). Therefore, it is essential to identify the relationship between port efficiency and port ownership.

Port Ownership Structure and Port Efficiency

Tongzon and Heng (2005) reviewed early empirical research and suggested that much seemed to show there is a lack of clear-cut relationship between ownership and port efficiency. For example, based on the observation of output and inputs for 28 UK ports, Liu (1995) used SFA to assess the impact of port ownership structure on inter-port efficiency. However, the results did not show that port ownership significantly influences port performance. Notteboom et al. (2000) studied the efficiency of a sample of 36 European container terminals and four Asian container ports, using the Bayesian Stochastic Frontier Model. No relationship was discovered between the type of ownership and the efficiency level. In contrast to these studies, some argued that port ownership affected port efficiency. Estache et al. (2002) analysed how Mexico's 1993 port reform affected port efficiency through analysing 44 observations from 11 independent port administrations' panel data. The study showed that the reform of decentralisation and privatisation undertaken at Mexican ports stimulated significant improvements in the average port performance in the short term. Cullinane et al. (2002) applied a 'port function matrix' to major Asian container ports for analysing port ownership structure and its impacts on port efficiency. The results suggested that privatisation improves port economic efficiency. Song (2003) studied the administrative and ownership structure of ports and found that the Hutchison Port Holding Group invested largely in both the ports of Hong Kong and Shenzhen. These two ports are rivals of each other. He concluded that competition and cooperation could exist in the same region at the same time. Hence, a strategy called coopetition is needed by terminal operators to deal with both situations. Cullinane and Song (2003) applied SFA to selected Korean container ports and analysed the effects of privatisation on port efficiency, using both the cross-sectional and panel data versions of the stochastic frontier model. The results suggested some evidence for supporting the opinion that privatisation and deregulation improve port productive efficiency. Barros and Athanassiou (2004) used DEA to estimate the efficiency of Portuguese and Greek seaports, and the results indicated that privatisation helps to improve efficiency. Baird (2000) applied a 'port privatisation matrix' to study the UK situation. He argued that since the primary objective of a port is to facilitate trade, hence seaport property rights transfer would not necessarily improve the operational efficiency or may even be counterproductive (Baird 2000). Tongzon and Heng (2005) looked at the relationship between port ownership structure and port efficiency as well as port competitiveness determinants from a quantitative angle. They found that the participation of the private sector in the port industry can improve port operation efficiency. Cui and Notteboom (2018) argued that port privatisation can positively affect cost-effectiveness and technical efficiency. However, full port privatisation is not an effective way to increase port operation efficiency, which indicates that it is not a linear relationship (Tongzon and Heng 2005).

Port Size and Port Efficiency

Apart from research on ownership, some empirical research also examined the relationship between port size and port efficiency. Liu (1995) found that port efficiency could be explained by port size to a limited degree. Martinez-Budría et al. (1999) illustrated the results of DEA on the relative efficiency of 26 Spanish Port Authorities during 1993–1997. The results showed that ports with larger size were more efficient than the smaller ones. The work of Barros and Athanassiou (2004) also indicated that the scale of port operation could improve port efficiency level. In the study of Notteboom et al. (2000), a positive relationship was found between port size and port efficiency level. The results of the 'port function matrix' analysis conducted by Cullinane et al. (2002) indicated that larger port terminals have certain efficiency advantages over smaller rivals. Nevertheless, Coto-Millan et al. (2000) adopted SFA to investigate the efficiency level of 27 Spanish ports during 1985–1989. The results suggested that relatively larger ports tend to be less efficient. Tongzon (2001) also applied DEA to compare four ports' efficiency levels in Australia and 12 other international container ports, showing that there is no clear relationship between a port's efficiency and its size and function (hub or feeder).

Port Service

In addition to port efficiency, port managers also need to differentiate their services from competitors (Bennathan and Walters 1979). McCalla (1999) mentioned that many ports were facing '*global issues and the local responses*' in terms of port service. The global issues included world shipping alliances and increasing vessel size, and local responses were services from port towards customers' needs, i.e. increasing draught, terminal capacity, port cost and labour productivity. Foster (1978) determined that the priority of service quality was over that of the monetary factor, from the shipper's perspective. Foster (1979) also targeted shippers. However, he argued that service cost and port charges were still the most important determinants. Haralambides (2002) argued that port charges, including port dues and cargo-handling charges, were one of the most important port service factors. In a survey by Ha (2003), a questionnaire was used to investigate service quality and the criteria and sub-criteria in broad terms. '*Ready information availability of port-related activities (operation and quality of customs clearance, EDI system, provisions of online port-related information, provision of cargo tracking system), location, port turnaround time (ship congestion in port, free dwell time for containers, on-dock container handling), available facilities, port management (labour performance, safety rules, authority marketing activities, worker's foreign language skills), monetary cost (charges, terminal charges, pilotage, towage) and customers' convenience (ready procedure for port use, reflection on port user's opinions and requirements, settlement of accident claims in port, benefits to the regular shipping operators, immediate handling of container port users' dissatisfaction)*', were identified as the major factors (Ha 2003, pp. 131–137). The survey collected viewpoints of ship operators and logistics managers. They were asked to give scores to these service quality factors. Ha (2003) found that, in addition to monetary costs and time efficiency, ports need to improve their service quality, especially by improving the quantity and quality of information flows and data availability. Moreover, perceptive factors like available information (from various sources like experience and port marketing) and the port's reputation could be equally important as monetary cost (Ng 2006). Chang and Thai (2016) suggested that corporate quality, interactive quality, physical quality and port security are the elements of port service quality. Thai (2008) proposed the 'resources, outcomes, process, management, image, social responsibility' (ROPMIS) model to measure service quality in maritime transport. Thai (2015) proposed that the ROPMIS model could be used to measure maritime transport services and specific sub-sectors, such as ports. Pallis and Vaggelas (2005, p. 4) argued that a port should have more than two providers to ensure better port service. Port service was categorised as '*echno-navigational services regarding: (a) pilotage, (b) towage, and (c) mooring*' and '*cargo-handling services including: (a) stevedoring, stowage, transhipment and other intra-terminal transport, (b) storage, depot, and warehousing, depending on cargo categories, and (c) cargo consolidation*' and '*passenger services, including embarkation and disembarkation*'.

Other Issues

Apart from port efficiency, port service, port selection and port performance discussed above, Yeo (2007) also mentioned that issues such as port policy, construction of container terminals and port functions are related to port competitiveness.

Clark et al. (2004) mentioned that in the case of transport cost, the determinants of port efficiency not only consisted of infrastructure variables, but also policy variables and management. Their research also suggested that the effect of regulations on port efficiency is an inverted U-shape. Some level of regulations can increase port efficiency; however, an excess of it would reverse these gains (Clark et al. 2004).

Pallis and Vaggelas (2005) suggested that each port should have at least two service providers so that port users would have choice. The EC heavily promoted common competitive standards across ports in the EU as an indispensable move to achieve a European market for port services. The port policy attempted to enforce a competitive regime in large ports in the EU, which required a port to have at least two providers of services. Although the EC believed this regime would intensify competition, improve service quality and reduce costs, it has experienced protracted and largely ineffectual attempts at implementation (Roe 2009). Wang et al. (2004) looked at China's port governance and analysed the ports of Shenzhen and Shanghai as two sub-models. The port of Shenzhen was managed by a port authority following the principles of commercial operation. Wang et al. (2004) called this form of governance a 'hands-off' policy, while the port of Shanghai was managed by central government. The latter model is more common in the older major ports in China that mainly rely on institutional resources (Yeo 2007). Wang et al. (2004) suggested the former 'hands-off' model as a better policy. Wang and Slack (2000) stated that port policy was one of the most important factors that influenced port competitiveness in the Pearl River Delta in China. The other factors included the impact of globalisation, container standardisation, multimodal accessibility and connectivity and port cost (Wang and Slack 2000). Another example of political influence on port competitiveness can be found in Seabrooke et al. (2003) who emphasised similar important factors for Hong

Kong. The factors were macro-economic conditions, regional competition, the direct trade between China and Taiwan and China joining the WTO.

Tsai and Su (2005) used a Delphi method to construct political risk factors for container ports. They suggested 19 factors under five main categories, namely port development policy, port management policy, foreign enterprise policy, political and social systems and macroeconomic factors. They concluded that low political risk could help to create a better business environment and attract more container traffic. They also studied how various port stakeholders would react to different political risks. Chan (2005) came to a similar conclusion that regulation influenced logistics activities through looking at state policy and regulations in the USA.

In the next chapter, we turn to the conceptual basis of our analysis of the maritime container security sector before moving on to the design and application of the Delphi approach.

References

Aronietis, R., Van de Voorde, E., & Vanelslander, T. (2010). *Port Competitiveness Determinants of Selected European Ports in the Containerised Cargo Market.* International Association of Maritime Economists Conference IAME (Vol. 10), Lisbon, Portugal.

Aversa, R., Botter, R. C., Haralambides, H. E., & Yoshizaki, H. T. Y. (2005). A mixed integer programming model on the location of a hub port in the east coast of South America. *Maritime Economics and Logistics, 7*(1), 1–18.

Baird, A. J. (2000). Port privatisation: Objectives, extent, process, and the UK experience. *International Journal of Maritime Economics, 2*(3), 177–194.

Barros, C. P., & Athanassiou, M. (2004). Efficiency in European seaports with DEA: Evidence from Greece and Portugal. *Maritime Economics and Logistics, 6,* 122–140.

Bennathan, E., & Walters, A. A. (1979). *Port Pricing and Investment Policy for Developing Countries.* Oxford: Oxford University Press.

Bichou, K., & Bell, M. G. H. (2007). Internationalisation and consolidation of the container port industry: Assessment of channel structure and relationships. *Maritime Economics and Logistics, 9*(1), 35–51.

Bichou, K., & Gray, R. (2004). A logistics and supply chain management approach to port performance measurement. *Maritime Policy and Management, 31,* 47–67.

Blonigen, B., & Wilson, W. (2006). *New Measures of Port Efficiency Using International Trade Data* (NBER Working Paper 12052). New York: National Bureau of Economic Research.

Chan, Y. (2005). A statistical study of intrastate vs. interstate regulatory reforms. *Journal of Geography, 13,* 165–171.

Chang, S. (2000). Disasters and transport systems: Loss, recovery and competition at the port of Kobe after the 1995 earthquake. *Journal of Transport Geography, 8*(8), 53–65.

Chang, C., & Thai, V. (2016). Do port security quality and service quality influence customer satisfaction and loyalty? *Maritime Policy and Management, 43*(6), 720–736.

Chin, A., & Tongzon, K. (1998). Maintaining Singapore as a major shipping and air transport hub. In T. Toh (Ed.), *Competitiveness of the Singapore Economy* (pp. 83–114). Singapore: Singapore University Press.

Clark, X., Dollar, D., & Micco, A. (2001). *Maritime Transport Costs and Port Efficiency.* Available at http://documents.worldbank.org/curated/en/451431 468766755364/122522322_20041117184549/additional/multi0page.pdf. Accessed 9 March, 2016.

Clark, X., Dollar, D., & Micco, D. (2004). *Port Efficiency, Maritime Transport Costs and Bilateral Trade* (NBER Working Paper No. 10353). Available at http://www.nber.org/papers/w10353.pdf. Accessed 4 January 2017.

Coto-Millan, P., Banos-Pino, J., & Rodriguez-Alvarez, A. (2000). Economic efficiency in Spanish ports: Some empirical evidence. *Maritime Policy and Management, 27*(2), 169–174.

Cui, H., & Notteboom, T. (2018). A game theoretical approach to the effects of port objective orientation and service differentiation on port authorities' willingness to cooperate. *Research in Transportation Business and Management, 26,* 75–86.

Cullinane, K., & Song, D. W. (2003). A stochastic frontier model of the productive efficiency of Korean Container Terminals. *Applied Economics, 35*(3), 251–267.

Cullinane, K., & Song, D. W. (Eds.). (2007). *Asian Container Ports: Development, Competition and Co-operation.* New York: Palgrave Macmillan.

Cullinane, K., & Wang, T. F. (2010). The efficiency analysis of container port production using DEA panel data approaches. *OR Spectrum, 32*(3), 717–738.

Cullinane, K., Song, D. W., & Gray, R. (2002). A stochastic frontier model of the efficiency of major container terminals in Asia: Assessing the influence of administrative and ownership structures. *Transportation Research Part A, 36,* 743–762.

Cullinane, K., Wang, T. F., & Cullinane, S. (2004). Container terminal development in Mainland China and its impact on the competitiveness of the port of Hong Kong. *Transport Reviews, 24*(1), 33–56.

Cullinane, K., Ji, P., & Wang, T. F. (2005). The relationship between privatisation and DEA estimates of efficiency in the container port industry. *Journal of Economics and Business, 27*(5), 433–462.

Cullinane, K., Wang, T. F., Song, D., & Ji, P. (2006). The technical efficiency of container ports: Comparing data envelopment analysis and stochastic frontier analysis. *Transportation Research Part A, 40*(4), 354–374.

De Langen, P. W. (2002). Clustering and performance: The case of maritime clustering in the Netherlands. *Maritime Policy and Management, 29*(3), 209–221.

De Martino, M., & Morvillo, A. (2008). Activities, resources and inter-organisational relationships: Key factors in port competitiveness. *Maritime Policy and Management, 35*(6), 571–589.

De Monie, G. (1987). *Measuring and Evaluating Port Performance and Productivity* (UNCTAD Monographs on Port Management No. 6). Geneva: UNCTAD.

Estache, A., & Trujillo, L. (2009). Global economic changes and the future of pot authorities. In H. Meersman, E. Van de Voorde, & T. Vanelslander (Eds.), *Future Challenges for the Port and Shipping Sector* (pp. 69–87). London: Informa.

Figueiredo, D., Oliverira, G., & Cariou, P. (2015). The impact of competition on container port (in)efficiency. *Transportation Research Part A, 78,* 124–133.

Fleming, D. K., & Baird, A. J. (1999). Some reflections on port competition in the United States and Western Europe. *Maritime Policy and Management, 26*(4), 383–394.

Foster, T. (1978). Ports: What shippers should look for. *Chilton's Distribution Worldwide, 77*(1), 41–48.

Foster, T. (1979). What's important in a port. *Chilton's Distribution Worldwide, 78*(1), 32–36.

Fung, K. F. (2001). Competition between the ports of Hong Kong and Singapore: A structural vector error correction model to forecast the demand for container handling services. *Maritime Policy and Management, 27*(1), 3–22.

Garcia-Alonso, L., & Martin-Bofarull, M. (2007). Impact of port investment on efficiency and capacity to attract traffic in Spain: Bilbao versus Valencia. *Maritime Economics and Logistics, 9*(3), 254–267.

Gonzalez, M. M., & Trujillo, L. (2009). Efficiency measurement in the port industry: A survey of the empirical evidence. *Journal of Transport Economics and Policy, 43*(2), 157–192.

Guy, E., & Urli, B. (2006). Port selection and multicriteria analysis: An application to the Montreal-New York alternative. *Maritime Economics and Logistics, 8*(2), 169–186.

Ha, M. S. (2003). A comparison of service quality at major container ports: Implications for Korean ports. *Journal of Transport Geography, 11,* 131–137.

Haezendonck, E., & Notteboom, T. (2002). The competitive advantage of seaports. In M. Huybrechts, et al. (Eds.), *Port Competitiveness: An Economic and Legal Analysis of the Factors Determining the Competitiveness of Seaports* (pp. 67–87). Antwerp: De Boeck.

Haralambides, H. E. (2002). Competition, excess capacity, and the pricing of port infrastructure. *Maritime Economics and Logistics, 4*(4), 323–347.

Heaver, T. (1995). The implications of increased competition for port policy and management. *Maritime Policy and Management, 22,* 125–133.

Heaver, T., Meersman, H., & Van de Voorde, E. (2001). Co-operation and competition in international container transport: Strategies for ports. *Maritime Policy and Management, 28*(3), 293–305.

Heaver, T., Meersman, H., Moglia, F., & Van de Voorde, E. (2000). Do mergers and alliances influence european shipping and port competition? *Maritime Policy and Management, 27*(4), 363–373.

Homosombat, W., Ng, A., & Fu, X. (2016). Regional transformation and port cluster competition: The case of the Pearl River Delta in South China. *Growth and Change, 47*(3), 349–362.

Hoshino, H. (2010). Competition and collaboration among container ports. *The Asian Journal of Shipping and Logistics, 26*(1), 31–47.

Huybrechts, M., Meersman, H., Van de Voorde, E., Van Hooydonk, E., Verbeke, A., & Winkelmans, W. (Eds.). (2002). *Port Competitiveness: An*

Economic and Legal Analysis of the Factors Determining the Competitiveness of Seaports. Antwerp: De Boeck Ltd.

Ishii, M., Lee, P. T. W., Tezukac, K., & Chang, Y. T. (2013). A game theoretical analysis of port competition. *Transportation Research Part E: Logistics and Transportation Review, 49*(1), 92–106.

Jara-Diaz, S. R., Cortes, C., & Ponce, F. (2001). Number of points served and economies of spatial scope in transport cost functions. *Journal of Transport Economics and Policy, 35*(2), 327–342.

Jeon, I.-S., Kim, H.-S., & Kim, B.-J. (1993). *Strategy for Improvement of Competitive Power in Korea Container Port*. Seoul: Korea Maritime Institute.

Kim, H.-S. (1993). *Decision Components of Shippers' Port Choice in Korea*. Seoul: Korea Maritime Institute.

Lirn, T. C., Thanopoulou, H. A., & Beresford, A. K. C. (2003). Transhipment port selection and decision-making behaviour: Analysing the Taiwanese case. *International Journal of Logistics: Research and Applications, 6*(4), 229–244.

Lirn, T. C., Thanopoulou, H. A., Beynon, M. J., & Beresford, A. K. C. (2004). An application of AHP on transhipment port selection: A global perspective. *Maritime Economics and Logistics, 6*(1), 70–91.

Liu, Z. (1995, September). The comparative performance of public and private enterprises. *Journal of Transportation Economics and Policy, 29*(3), 263–274.

Lloyd's List. (2016). *Top 100 Container Ports 2016*. Available at https://maritimeintelligence.informa.com/~/media/Informa-Shop.../LL_Top_Ports. pdf. Accessed 25 January 2017.

Luo, M., & Grigalunas, T. A. (2003). A spatial economic multimodal transportation simulation model for US coastal container ports. *Maritime Economics and Logistics, 5*(2), 158–178.

Malchow, M., & Kanafani, A. (2001). A disaggregate analysis of factors influencing port selection. *Maritime Policy and Management, 28*(3), 265–277.

Malchow, M. B., & Kanafani, A. (2004). A disaggregate analysis of port selection. *Transportation Research Part E, 40,* 317–337.

Marcadon, J. (1999). Containerisation in the ports of Northern and Western Europe. *GeoJournal, 48*(1), 15–20.

Martinez-Budría, E., Diaz-Armas, R., Navarro-Ibanez, M., & Ravelo-Mesa, T. (1999). A study of the efficiency of Spanish port authorities using data envelopment analysis. *International Journal of Transport Economics, 26*(2), 237–253.

McCalla, R. (1999). Global change, local pain: Intermodal seaport terminals and their service areas. *Journal of Transport Geography, 7,* 247–254.

Meersman, H., Van de Voorde, E., & Vanelslander, T. (2010). Port competition revisited. *Review of Business Economic Literature, 55*(2), 210–232.

Merkel, A. (2017). Spatial competition and complementarity in European port regions. *Journal of Transport Geography, 61,* 40–47.

Ng, A. K. Y. (2006). Assessing the attractiveness of ports in the North European container transhipment market: An agenda for future research in port competition. *Maritime Economics and Logistics, 8*(3), 234–241.

Ng, A. K. Y. (2013). The evolution and research trends of port geography. *Professional Geographer, 65*(1), 65–86.

Nguyen, H. O., Nguyen, H. V., Chang, Y., Chin, A., & Tongzon, J. (2016). Measuring port efficiency using bootstrapped DEA: The case of Vietnamese ports. *Maritime Policy and Management, 43*(5), 644–659.

Nir, A., Lin, K., & Liang, G. (2003). Port choice behaviour-from the perspective of the shipper. *Maritime Policy and Management, 30*(2), 165–173.

Notteboom, T. E. (2002, November 13–15). The interdependence between liner shipping networks and intermodal networks. *Proceedings of the Annual Conference of the International Association of Maritime Economists (IAME),* Panama City.

Notteboom, T. (2008, March). *The Relationship Between Seaports and the Inter-Modal Hinterland in Light of Global Supply Chains* (OECD Discussion Paper No. 2008–2010). OECD/ITF Joint Transportation Research Centre.

Notteboom, T. (2012, April 18). Dynamics in Port Competition in Europe: Implications for North Italian Ports. *Workshop 'I porti del Nord'-Milan.*

Notteboom, T. E., & Rodrigue, J.-P. (2005). Port regionalisation: Towards a new phase in port development. *Maritime Policy and Management, 32*(3), 297–313.

Notteboom, T. E., & Winkelmans, W. (2001). Structural changes in logistics: How will port authorities face the challenge? *Maritime Policy and Management, 28*(1), 71–89.

Notteboom, T., & Yap, W. Y. (2012). Port competition and competitiveness. In W. Talley (Ed.), *The Blackwell Companion to Maritime Economics,* pp. 549–570. Malden: Blackwell.

Notteboom, T., Coeck, C., & Van Den Broeck, J. (2000). Measuring and explaining the relative efficiency of container terminals by means of Bayesian stochastic frontier models. *International Journal of Maritime Economics, 2,* 83–106.

OECD. (2011). *Competition in Ports and Port Services* (OECD Working Paper). Paris: OECD.

Ohashia, H., Kim, T., Oum, T., & Yuc, C. (2005). Choice of air cargo transshipment airport: An application to air cargo traffic to/from Northeast Asia. *Journal of Air Transport Management, 11,* 149–159.

Pallis, A., & Vaggelas, G. (2005). Port competitiveness and the EU Port Services Directive: The case of Greek ports. *Maritime Economics and Logistics, 7,* 116–140.

Parola, F., Risitano, M., Ferretti, M., & Panetti, E. (2017). The drivers of port competitiveness: A critical review. *Transport Reviews, 37*(1), 116–138.

Perez-Labajos, C., & Blanco, B. (2004). Competitive policies for commercial sea ports in the EU. *Marine Policy, 28,* 553–556.

Porter, M. E. (1990). *The Competitive Advantage of Nations.* New York: Free Press.

Rimmer, P. (1998). Ocean liner shipping services: Corporate restructuring and port selection/competition. *Asia Pacific Viewpoint, 39*(2), 193–208.

Robinson, R. (1998). Asian hub/feeder nets: The dynamics of restructuring. *Maritime Policy and Management, 25*(1), 21–40.

Robinson, R. (2002). Ports as elements in value driven chain systems: The new paradigm. *Maritime Policy and Management, 29*(3), 241–255.

Roe, M. (2009). Maritime governance and policy-making failure in the European Union. *International Journal of Shipping and Transport Logistics, 1*(1), 161–174.

Seabrooke, W., Hui, E. C. M., Lam, W. H. K., & Wong, G. K. C. (2003). Forecasting cargo growth and regional role of the port of Hong Kong. *Cities, 20*(1), 51–64.

Slack, B., & Fremont, A. (2005). Transformation of port terminal operators: From the local to the global. *Transport Reviews, 25*(1), 117–130.

Slack, B., Comtois, C., & McCalla, R. (2002). Strategic alliances in the container shipping industry: A global perspective. *Maritime Policy and Management, 29*(1), 65–76.

Song, D. W. (2003). Port co-opetition in concept and practice. *Maritime Policy and Management, 30*(1), 29–44.

Song, D. W., & Yeo, K.-T. (2004). A competitive analysis of Chinese container ports using the analytic hierarchy process. *Maritime Economics and Logistics, 6,* 34–52.

Thai, V. V. (2008). Service quality in maritime transport: Conceptual model and empirical evidence. *Asia Pacific Journal of Marketing and Logistics, 20*(4), 493–518.

Thai, V. V. (2015). The impact of port service quality on customer satisfaction: The case of Singapore. *Maritime Economics and Logistics, 18*(4), 458–475.

Tiwari, P., Itoh, H., & Doi, M. (2003). Shippers' port and carrier selection behaviour in China: A discrete choice analysis. *Maritime Economics and Logistics, 5*(1), 23–39.

Tongzon, J. (1989). The impact of wharfage costs on Victoria's export-oriented industries. *Economic Paper, 8,* 58–64.

Tongzon, J. (2001). Efficiency measurement of selected Australian and other international ports using data envelopment analysis. *Transportation Research Part A, 35*(2), 113–128.

Tongzon, J., & Heng, W. (2005). Port privatisation, efficiency and competitiveness: Some empirical evidence from container ports (terminals). *Transportation Research Part A, 39*(5), 405–424.

Tongzon, J. L., & Sawant, L. (2007). Port choice in a competitive environment: From the shipping lines' perspective. *Applied Economics, 39,* 477–492.

Trujillo, L., & Tovar, B. (2007). The European port industry: An analysis of its economic efficiency. *Maritime Economics and Logistics, 9*(2), 148–171.

Tsai, M. C., & Su, C. H. (2005). Political risk assessment of five East Asian ports: The viewpoints of global carriers. *Marine Policy, 29*(4), 291–298.

Valentine, V. F. (2002). *Measuring Efficiency of Container Ports: An Analysis By Organisational and Ownership Structure* (PhD thesis). University of Plymouth, UK.

Van de Voorde, E., & Winkelmans, W. (2002). A general introduction to port competition and management. In M. Huybrechts, H. Meersman, E. Van de Voorde, E. Van Hooydonk, A. Verbeke, & W. Winkelmans (Eds.), *Port Competitiveness* (pp. 1–15). Antwerp: De Boeck.

Veldman, S., & Buckmann, E. H. (2003). A model on container port competition: An application for the West European container hub-ports. *Maritime Economics and Logistics, 5,* 3–22.

Veldman, S. J., Buckmann, E. H., & Saitua, R. N. (2005). River depth and container port market shares: The impact of deepening the Scheldt River on the West European container hubport market shares. *Maritime Economics and Logistics, 7*(4), 336–355.

Wan, Y., & Zhang, A. (2013). Urban road congestion and seaport competition. *Journal of Transport Economics and Policy, 47*(1), 55–70.

Wang, J., & Slack, B. (2000). The evolution of a regional container port system: Pearl River Delta. *Journal of Transport Geography, 8*(4), 263–275.

Wang, J., Ng, A. K. Y., & Olivier, D. (2004). Port governance in China: A review of policies in an era of internationalising port management practices. *Transport Policy, 11*(3), 237–250.

Yap, W. Y., & Lam, J. S. L. (2004). An interpretation of inter-container port relationships from the demand perspective. *Maritime Policy and Management, 31*(4), 337–355.

Yap, W. Y., & Lam, J. S. L. (2006a). Competition dynamics between container ports in East Asia. *Transportation Research Part A, 40*(1), 35–51.

Yap, W. Y., & Lam, J. S. L. (2006b). A measurement and comparison of cost competitiveness of container ports in South East Asia. *Transportation, 33,* 641–654.

Yap, W. Y., Lam, J. S. L., & Notteboom, T. (2006). Developments in container port competition in East Asia. *Transport Reviews, 26*(2), 167–188.

Yeo, G. T. (2007). *Port Competitiveness in North East Asia: An Integrated Fuzzy Approach to Expert Evaluations* (PhD thesis). University of Plymouth, UK.

Yeo, G. T., Roe, M., & Dinwoodie, J. (2008). Evaluating the competitiveness of container ports in Korea and China. *Transportation Research Part A, 42*(6), 910–921.

Zeng, Z., & Yang, Z. (2002). Dynamic programming of port position and scale in the hierarchized container ports network. *Maritime Policy and Management, 29*(2), 163–177.

4

Models of Container Port Security

In Chapters 2 and 3, the related maritime security issues and framework, the Container Security Initiative (CSI) and its controversial implications and port competition theories have been reviewed. A study on the long-term analysis on the effects of security initiatives on EU seaports is needed to fill the research gap identified in Chapter 2. Therefore, we now focus on the CSI and its implications for EU container seaport competition. A conceptual model and five conceptual assumptions are developed to assist in achieving the aim and objectives.

Conceptual Model

The conceptual model is presented in Fig. 4.1. This model aims to explore the effects of the CSI on EU container seaport competition, rather than testing or explaining relationships.

The model is based on research Objective O1 that contains two major themes: maritime security measures and EU container seaport competition. Maritime security in this research refers to maritime terrorism. The model illustrates the synthesis of the literature review and

© The Author(s) 2019   **87**
X. Zhang and M. Roe, *Maritime Container Port Security*,
https://doi.org/10.1007/978-3-030-03825-0_4

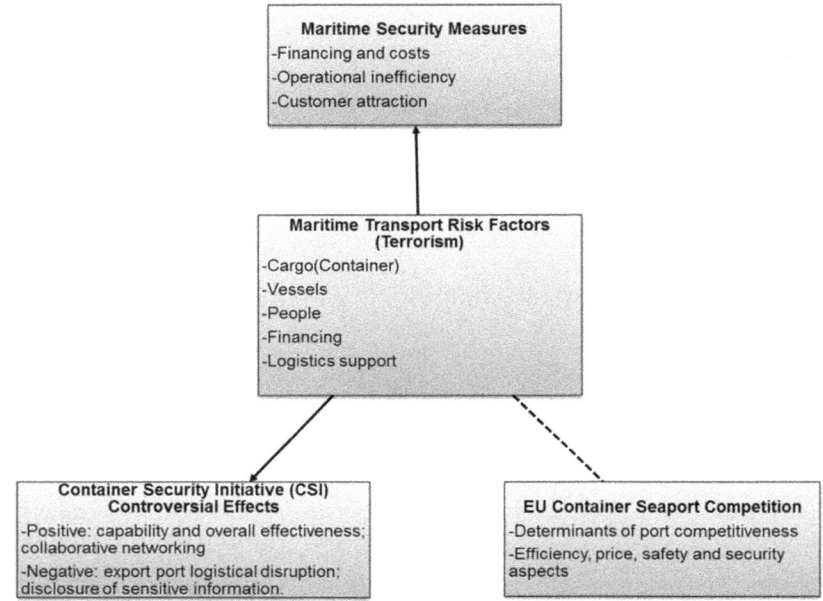

Fig. 4.1 Conceptual model for container port security (*Source* The authors)

consists of four pillars that are: (1) maritime transport risk factors; (2) maritime security measures; (3) the CSI and its controversial effects; and (4) EU container seaport competition. The maritime transport risk factors in maritime terrorism, as the first pillar, are the starting point of this model since various maritime security regulations and measures have been developed in response to these potential threats. The maritime security measures, as the second pillar, include existing theories and arguments of the positive and negative effects of maritime security measures compliance. There is a lack of data and empirical analysis to support these arguments. This pillar directs this research to collect relevant data to fill the research gap. The third pillar, the CSI and its controversial effects, is built upon the research aim. The CSI, as one of the most influential maritime security measures, has remained controversial since it was established in 2002. This research aims at analysing the impacts of the CSI on EU container seaport competition; hence, this pillar is essential for this model. As discussed, port competition varies between regions. The influential factors discussed in Chapter 3 have different impacts on port competition to a varying degree. Thus, the fourth pillar is designed to find out the determinants of container seaport competitiveness in the EU. In turn, the impacts of the CSI on the identified factors will be analysed accordingly to deduce how EU container seaport competition could be altered.

Five conceptual assumptions (C.A.1, C.A.2, C.A.3, C.A.4, and C.A.5) are developed to connect each pillar to indicate how one affects the others. These conceptual assumptions are derived from the review in Chapters 2 and 3. C.A.1 aims to find out the importance of implementing maritime security measures, despite the negative implications mentioned by various scholars (Allen 2006; Bichou and Evans 2007; Miller 2007; Bichou 2008; Dekker and Stevens 2007; Bichou 2011). C.A.2 serves two purposes. The connection between the first pillar and third pillar is to find out whether the CSI improves maritime security since it was introduced. The CSI has shared similar arguments with other maritime security measures in terms of its benefits and negativities. However, there has been little evidence to support these arguments. Therefore, the connection between the second and third pillar aims at finding out whether the CSI has negative impacts on ports and directing data collection to settle the conjuncture. C.A.3 is designed based on the fourth pillar to identify the key determinants of EU container seaport competitiveness. C.A.4 and C.A.5 are designed to achieve the research aim. In addition to directly analysing the collected primary and secondary data, the analyses of these two assumptions will also take two aspects into consideration. The first aspect is how the CSI affects the identified port competitiveness determinants (illustrated by the arrow from the third to the fourth pillar). The second aspect is to conclude how maritime security measures affect port operations and port competition (illustrated by the arrow from the second to the fourth pillar).

Maritime Transport Risk Factors

The term 'security' refers to terrorism and port/maritime security issues are clearly often terrorism related. Terrorism has been a global concern because various transportation modes have been utilised to transport weapons or become a target due to the vulnerabilities which lead to economic loss and human casualties. Seaborne transport poses several additional security challenges by its complex and international transportation network nature. Sea-going vessels can be the target of attacks or used for illegal cargo movement. The OECD (2003) identified five major risk factors in maritime transport: cargo, vessels, people, financing and logistics support (see Fig. 2.1).

Cargo ships, especially containerised ships, transport most of the global non-bulk cargoes. Containerised shipping's increasing trade volume, its high velocity in the world trade and its uniformity have caused formidable security challenges. Weapons of mass destruction, drugs and illegal goods can be concealed within containers by terrorists and criminals. Vessels can be used as a weapon in a terrorist attack against a population area next to a port or intermodal transportation node to damage port facilities or block access to a port facility (UNCTAD 2004). Additionally, seafarers and port workers are often directly targeted or indirectly suffer from terrorism attacks. The OECD (2003) mentioned that some seafarers could actually be the terrorist group's accomplices or members. In the latter scenario, it would be more difficult to detect terrorism activities. Last but not least, financing and logistic support cannot be overlooked. Terrorist groups can operate vessels to finance and support their logistics operations. An example as we noted earlier is that of the LTTE in Sri Lanka.

Maritime Security Measures

In response to the potential maritime security threats, various supply chain and maritime security measures have been developed and imposed by regulatory bodies. The categories and significance have been discussed in Chapter 2. The benefits such as increasing the level of security awareness and lowering the possibility of a terrorist attack have been stressed by many studies (e.g. Stasinopoulos 2003; Bichou et al. 2007; Park 2013). Thibault et al. (2006) found that the security initiatives have formed a cooperative security relationship between industry and government. Security improvements resulting from maritime security requirements have enhanced service quality in terms of service reliability, social responsibility awareness and operation and management efficiency (Thai 2007).

Financing and Costs

Arguments arise out of the potential problems caused by maritime security requirements. Additional costs and operational inefficiency are the two major issues raised by many studies (e.g. OECD 2003; Dekker and Stevens 2007; Miller 2007; Bichou and Evans 2007; UNCTAD 2007; Kruk and Donner 2008; Bichou 2011). A major cause of cost burden comes from container scanning required by the security regime. In order to comply with the regime, initialisation costs occur for purchasing, installation, initial training and civil engineering works. Moreover, operational costs arise as ongoing expenses incurred operating the container scanning equipment. Cost estimates from a variety of sources imply that the additional cost could cause issues for both low-volume export container ports and high-volume export container ports (OECD 2003; Miller 2007; Bichou and Evans 2007; UNCTAD 2007; Dekker and Stevens 2007). However, there are some studies focusing mostly on the cost efficiency of regime compliance. Thai (2007) pointed out that ports and terminals could increase revenue by creating a new income stream. The total cost of cargo inspection can be lower than conventional random physical inspections (Gutiérrez et al. 2007). Compliance can also provide fast-lane treatment and access certificates as well as reduced insurance costs (Bichou 2011). According to much research, the unresolved debate is over whether port security should be paid for by jurisdictional stakeholders, export stakeholders or import stakeholders. Although costs would ultimately cascade down to importers and final customers, the stakeholders may absorb some of the costs themselves due to political or strategic factors.

Efficiency

While security regimes enhance maritime security, they slow down cargo movement due to additional inspections. According to the

WSC (2007), Asian port operations were predicted to suffer the most from a range of US supply chain security initiatives since China heavily relies on exports to the USA. Bichou (2011) argued that the procedural requirements of a security regime harm operational and logistical efficiency. Direct functional redundancies and indirect supply chain disruptions stemming from longer lead times could both lead to less reliable demand and supply scenarios. Nevertheless, the productivity of the entire supply chain can be improved due to better procedural arrangements. Security regime compliance is also commercially rewarding. Many papers focus on positive impacts regarding logistical efficiency (e.g. Crutch 2006; Gutiérrez et al. 2007; Thai 2007). Positive impacts include reduced transit time and improvement of lead-time predictability (Thai 2007; Bichou 2011), reductions in stowaways (Timlen 2007), improved manpower utilisation (Thai 2007), better document processing and cargo handling (Thai 2007), and improved customers' satisfaction and enhanced branding (Gutiérrez et al. 2007; Thai 2007; Bichou 2011).

However, to date, there is little data or empirical analysis to support the positive and negative operational and financial impacts of maritime security regime compliance (Bichou 2008). There are a few studies that have examined the existence of these impacts, based on conceptual work, the economic situation or anecdotal evidence (Babione et al. 2003; Lee and Whang 2005; Thai 2007; Rabadi et al. 2007; Gutiérrez et al. 2007; Bennett and Chin 2008; Yang 2010; Urciuoli et al. 2010; Voss et al. 2009; Talas and Menachof 2009). Therefore, to fill the research gap, this conceptual model includes the operational and cost factors caused by maritime security regime compliance.

The CSI and Its Controversial Effects

As one of the voluntary maritime security programmes, the CSI has received increasing attention in recent years. It aims at protecting container trading systems between CSI and US ports by forming a bilateral agreement between the USA and foreign-trade country partners.

The US Customs and Border Protection (CBP) claimed a number of benefits that the CSI brings, including increasing the level of security awareness, and improvement of overall effectiveness through international collaboration between customs. However, some benefits still remain controversial. In similar vein to the maritime security initiative, the additional security checks transferred from a container unloading point in the USA to loading point overseas may bring costs and logistical interference to the affiliated ports. Additionally, CSI's development of a collaborative network among connected ports inevitably involves sensitive business information disclosure that port operators and users are not always willing to share. From this viewpoint, CSI compliance could be a 'hidden' burden for participant ports. The overlaps between the IMO and WCO measures and the CSI (see Fig. 2.2) may potentially lead to administrative confusion and an overly bureaucratic system which is contrary to the initial purposes of these initiatives (Parliament of Australia 2003). Another feature of the CSI programme is that it is voluntary. It is possible that smaller and less economically independent countries would be intimidated by US threats of isolation in the event of a terrorist attack and would join the programme simply to ensure US constant support. Not joining the programme may cause ports to lose their competitiveness and the market share of US-inbound container trade. On the other hand, the smaller participating ports could suffer from the high initialisation and operational costs of CSI compliance. The CSI programme may put these ports in a dilemma.

Nevertheless, there is little research to investigate and analyse the implications of the CSI programme for participating and non-participating ports. Therefore, this conceptual model sets up two major concerns regarding the positive and negative effects of the CSI and facilitates analysis of the impacts of the CSI on ports.

EU Container Seaport Competition

It has been widely discussed that the increasingly severe situation of terrorism and the corresponding security initiatives have significantly affected maritime transportation and port operations (Bichou 2004; Park 2013). According to Dekker and Stevens (2007), three topics regarding maritime security and transportation were required for further study. One was to conduct a long-term analysis on how security initiatives influence seaports' competitive positions. It is important therefore to analyse the CSI's long-term effects on EU seaports' competition.

Much seaport competitiveness analysis has concentrated on port selection criteria. The paper by Yeo et al. (2008) summarised port selection criteria from research undertaken since the 1980s. Malchow and Kanafani (2004) studied another significant characteristic of a port, which was its location. In 2005, Tongzon and Heng suggested eight factors that affect port competitiveness. Bichou and Gray (2005, p. 89) proposed that port competition has shifted to cross-border, cross-industry levels. They also proposed that port competition would shift from *'the institutional, functional and/or spatial levels to channel management level'*.

The port environment has become increasingly competitive. Port competition varies between regions depending on the extent to which the influential factors have affected the nature of the port environment (Tongzon and Heng 2005). A variety of regional research projects on the competition among ports has been undertaken, particularly in Asia (Kim 1993; Jeon et al. 1993; Fung 2001; Tiwari et al. 2003; Cullinane et al. 2004; Song and Yeo 2004; Yap et al. 2006; Anderson et al. 2008). Therefore, in order to analyse the implications of the CSI for EU container seaport competition, factors that impact upon port competition in the EU should be identified first.

Fleming and Baird (1999) targeted the UK, the USA and north-western Europe and suggested six sets of factors that affect port competitiveness. They are port tradition and organisation, port accessibility by land and sea, state aid and its influence on port costs, port productivity, port selection preferences of carriers and comparative locational advantage (Valentine 2002). Huybrechts et al. (2002) evaluated the attractiveness of the port of Antwerp and concluded that it needed to address the issue of port accessibility in order to become a market leader within North Europe. The components of port competitiveness that Yeo (2007) and Parola et al. (2017) summarised and selected are presented in Table 3.3. They are in three categories and include: port location, port facilities including superstructure (berth, depth, channel length), terminal efficiency, hinterland networks, value-added logistics; and port services, safe handling of cargoes, confidence in port schedules, operational efficiency, electronic data interchange, IT, integration, simplification of procedures, incentives, operational transparency and port labour and skills. On the other hand, according to studies focusing on the impacts of maritime security measures on sea transportation, costs/ financing and logistical disruption caused by port inefficiency are two major issues affecting port competitiveness. Therefore, it is important to include the endogenous factors (cost factor, efficiency factor and service factor), together with safety and security (component of software drivers) to investigate major EU container seaport competitiveness determinants and how they are influenced by the CSI.

Conceptual Assumptions

The assumptions of the conceptual model are classified under four conceptual categories, which denote the main issues of maritime safety and security in container shipping that have been identified (Fig. 4.1). They are: (1) the necessity of pursuing maritime security initiatives; (2) introduction of the CSI and its controversial influences; (3) determinants of EU container seaport competitiveness; (4) the implications of the CSI for EU container seaport competition. A set of conceptual assumptions are developed based on each of these conceptual categories. The conceptual assumptions attempt to direct analysis towards the implications of the CSI for EU container seaport transportation. A set of statements, is derived which forms the basis for the Delphi survey introduced in the following chapters. These statements were developed from the results of a research synthesis from Chapters 2 and 3. Each statement contains controversial and debatable viewpoints taken from the extant literature. The sources will be presented in Table 5.5.

Conceptual Category 1: The Necessity of Pursuing Maritime Security Initiatives

Conceptual Assumption 1: It is necessary to carry out a maritime security initiative despite the fact that additional inspections may cause supply chain disruption and financial burden.

Statements:

S1.1—Maritime security has become a great concern worldwide. The increasing volume of container movements, their relatively high velocity in international trade and their uniformity have posed formidable security challenges. As the loading and unloading points of a sea transport process, container ports are the most important nodes for maritime safety. However, only around 2–10% of containers are actually inspected. US ports normally inspect roughly 5% of the 17 million containers arriving at the border every year. Great concern about container security emerged from this low inspection rate. Container security is far more important than efficiency and profit for the port. Therefore, security should be seen as the first priority.

S1.2—As the world's largest national economy, USA plays a vital role in global trade. After 9/11, the USA has reacted to the needs for strengthening security measures to enhance maritime transport safety. Some of the maritime security initiatives have influence on some export ports in terms of logistics efficiency and financing. Nevertheless, those export ports should be prepared to comply with the US container port security initiatives for maritime safety.

Conceptual Category 2: Introduction of the CSI and Its Controversial Influences

Conceptual Assumption 2: The Container Security Initiative (CSI) can facilitate global container seaborne trade safety and security, adding competitiveness to CSI-affiliated ports.

S2.1—The CSI programme managed by the US CBP is an influential voluntary initiative. The CSI was proposed to ensure that all containers that pose a potential risk for terrorism are identified and inspected at foreign ports before they are loaded on to vessels and imported to the USA. Without a doubt, the CSI has dramatically increased the level of awareness for the need to secure global trade.

S2.2—Unlike the 24-Hour Rule, the CSI is a voluntary initiative. However, in order to keep the market share for US-inbound trade, the major exporters have to join the programme. Not joining the programme could make the export ports lose competitiveness over their rivals.

Conceptual Category 3: Determinants of EU Container Seaport Competitiveness

Conceptual Assumption 3: The EU container port industry is highly competitive. Port efficiency, service and cost related elements are still the most important competitiveness components.

S3—The port environment generally has become increasingly competitive, it varies between regions and places depending upon the extent to which these forces have impacted upon the nature of the port environment. According to prior studies, the components of port competitiveness are port location, port facilities, overall efficiency, hinterland networks, value-added logistics; and port services, safe handling of cargoes, confidence in port schedules, simplification of procedures, operational transparency and port labour and skills. Among these factors, for EU ports, since port location is static, port efficiency, service and cost-related elements are still the most important competitiveness components. Port safety and security is not an incentive for port selection.

Conceptual Category 4: The Implications of the CSI for EU Container Seaport Competition

Conceptual Assumption 4: CSI compliance does not cause global supply chain disruption or financial problems for the EU container ports.

S4.1—To obtain the minimum required level of compliance, ports need to implement technical and organisational measures that will bring additional costs to maritime industries. Enhancing the technical measures due to security regulations, such as the ISPS Code, has brought additional costs to European maritime industries. Smaller ports in the EU may stop their US-inbound business since they cannot bear the financial costs. Larger ports may 'steal' new business from smaller ports which are financially strained to meet the scanning requirements. A distortion of EU container port market share will arise.

S4.2—While port security measures enhance port security, procedural requirements of the new security regime act against operational and logistical efficiency. The proponents of this view list a number of operational inefficiencies ranging from direct functional redundancies such as additional inspections and lengthy procedures, to indirect supply chain disruptions stemming from longer lead times and less reliable demand and supply scenarios.

S4.3—Productivity could improve due to better procedural arrangements. With the reinforcement of security, there is reduced likelihood of security incidents, a probability of fewer incidents being recorded and higher port reliability. Increased reliability which leads to higher trust between a port and its upstream and downstream partners in a container supply chain, contributes to the reduction of cargo processing time and results in reduction of cargo processing cost. Decreased cargo processing cost has a positive effect on port selection, thus attracting more container volume. Consequently, from the viewpoint of the above analysis, improving security level and increasing port reliability can attract more containers. Compliant participants would benefit from access certification and fast-lane treatment as well as reduced insurance costs and risk exposure.

S4.4—Although the US CBP stated that the CSI can bring benefits to member ports, those benefits are still controversial. The CSI has negative effects on port profit. In addition to the significant initial investment in new equipment, the CSI makes the cargo inspection process more complicated, creating an increase in cargo processing time and processing cost. That can change important performance characteristics of the port such as the port efficiency and price. With the perspective of a long-term economic model, these consequences produce negative impacts on relative attractiveness of ports for various stakeholders, namely exporters, and cargo carriers. The reduced attractiveness will decrease the competitiveness of a port. Moreover, the deepening cost and time may initiate a vicious circle of decreasing port competitiveness. The CSI is actually a heavy burden for those ports that have joined.

S4.5—The CSI could improve the capabilities and the overall effectiveness of the targeting process. However, this programme transfers the container examinations from unloading ports in the USA to the loading ports overseas. On the other hand, all the checks are carried out in the host countries which bear the equipment cost. In case of unloading and emptying of any potential threat posed by a dangerous container, the costs are borne by the importer to a US port. The US Customs sacrifices the export ports to save the USA unloading port's time and cost. The CSI is a unilateral and unfair programme without considering the host ports.

S4.6—CSI bilateral system of information exchange requires a host country to offer to conduct a security check on containers shipping to a US port. In return, the host country can send its officers to any US port to target ocean-going containerised cargo being exported to their country. Under this system, there can be sensitive information exchange, according to the US government, which may be deemed necessary to ensure the safety of any ports involved. However, the host countries are not willing to offer any confidential information.

Conceptual Assumption 5: The introduction of the CSI does not cause small ports to lose market share. EU container port market competition is not disrupted by CSI introduction.

S5—There are many ports in Europe. However, there are 'only' about 130 seaports handling containers of which around 40 accommodate intercontinental container services. About 70% of the total container throughput in the EU port system passes through the top 17 load centres; 14 of those have joined the CSI programme. In the short term, small container ports have to stop their US-inbound business and large EU container ports will gain new market share. In the long run, with further CSI implementation, the EU host countries will absorb the extra cost through transferring them to customers. However, the distortion in the competitiveness of large EU container ports will be minor.

With the agreement of the statements, we can now proceed to the process of analysing the significance of the CSI for US/EU port security and competitiveness.

References

Allen, N. H. (2006). The container security initiative costs, implications and relevance to developing countries. *Public Administration and Development, 26*(5), 439–447.

Anderson, C. M., Park, Y. A., Chang, Y. T., Yang, C. H., Lee, T. W., & Luo, M. (2008). A game-theoretic analysis of competition among container port hubs: The case of Busan and Shanghai. *Maritime Policy and Management, 35*(1), 5–26.

Babione, R., Kim, C. K., Phone, E., & Sanjaya, E. (2003). *Post 9/11 Security Cost Impact on Port of Seattle Import/Export Container Traffic* (Working Paper GTTL 502). The University of Washington.

Bennett, A. C., & Chin, Y. Z. (2008). *100% Container Scanning: Security Policy Implications for Global Supply Chains* (Master of Science Dissertation). Massachusetts Institute of Technology.

Bichou, K. (2004). The ISPS Code and the cost of port compliance: An initial logistics and supply chain framework for port security assessment and management. *Maritime Economics and Logistics, 6,* 322–348.

Bichou, K. (2008). *Security and risk-based models in shipping and ports: Review and critical analysis, in ITF, terrorism and international transport: Towards risk-based security policy.* Paris: OECD Publishing.

Bichou, K. (2011). Assessing the impact of procedural security on container port efficiency. *Maritime Economics and Logistics, 13*(1), 1–28.

Bichou, K., & Evans, A. (2007). Maritime security and regulatory risk-based models: Review and critical analysis. In K. Bichou, M. G. H. Bell, & A. Evans (Eds.), *Risk Management in Port Operations, Logistics and Supply Chain Security* (pp. 265–280). London: Informa.

Bichou, K., & Gray, R. (2005). A critical review of conventional terminology for classifying seaports. *Transportation Research A, 39,* 75–92.

Bichou, K., Lai, K. H., Lun, Y. H. V., & Cheng, T. C. E. (2007). A quality management framework for liner shipping companies to implement the 24-hour advance vessel manifest rule. *Transportation Journal, 46*(1), 5–21.

Crutch, M. (2006). *The Benefits of Investing in Global Supply Chain Security: Executive Summary from the DVDR 2006 Roundtable Meeting*. Lehigh University Centre for Value Chain Research.

Cullinane, K., Fei, W. T., & Cullinane, S. (2004). Container terminal development in Mainland China and its impact on the competitiveness of the port of Hong Kong. *Transport Reviews, 24*(1), 33–56.

Dekker, S., & Stevens, H. (2007). Maritime security in the European Union-empirical findings on financial implications for port facilities. *Maritime Policy and Management, 34*(5), 458–499.

Fleming, D. K., & Baird, A. J. (1999). Some reflections on port competition in the United States and Western Europe. *Maritime Policy and Management, 26*(4), 383–394.

Fung, K. F. (2001). Competition between the ports of Hong Kong and Singapore: A structural vector error correction model to forecast the demand for container handling services. *Maritime Policy and Management, 27*(1), 3–22.

Gutiérrez, X., Hintsa, J., Wieser, P., & Hameri, A. P. (2007). Voluntary supply chain security program impacts: An empirical study with BASC member companies. *World Customs Journal, 1*(2), 31–48.

Huybrechts, M., Meersman, H., Van de Voorde, E., Van Hooydonk, E., Verbeke, A., & Winkelmans, W. (Eds.). (2002). *Port Competitiveness: An Economic and Legal Analysis of the Factors Determining the Competitiveness of Seaports*. Antwerp: De Boeck Ltd.

Jeon, I.-S., Kim, H.-S., & Kim, B.-J. (1993). *Strategy for Improvement of Competitive Power in Korea Container Port*. Seoul: Korea Maritime Institute.

Kim, H.-S. (1993). *Decision Components of Shippers' Port Choice in Korea*. Seoul: Korea Maritime Institute.

Kruk, C., & Donner, M. (2008). *Review of Cost of Compliance with The New International Freight Transport Security Requirements*. Washington, DC: The World Bank.

Lee, H. L., & Whang, S. (2005). Higher supply chain security with lower cost: Lessons from total quality management. *International Journal of Production Economies, 96*(3), 289–300.

Malchow, M. B., & Kanafani, A. (2004). A disaggregate analysis of port selection. *Transportation Research Part E, 40*, 317–337.

Miller, J. (2007, October 25). New Shipping Law Makes Big Waves in Foreign Ports. *Wall Street Journal*.

OECD. (2003). *Maritime Transport Committee Security in Maritime Transport: Risk Factors and Economic Impact*. Available at https://www.oecd.org/newsroom/4375896.pdf.

Park, H. G. (2013). *Impact of Supply Chain Security Orientation on Port Performance* (PhD dissertation). Cardiff University, UK.

Parliament of Australia. (2003). *The US Container Security Initiative and Its Implications for Australia*. Available at http://www.aph.gov.au/About_Parliament/Parliamentary_Departments/Parliamentary_Library/Publications_Archive/CIB/cib0203/03cib27.

Parola, F., Risitano, M., Ferretti, M., & Panetti, E. (2017). The drivers of port competitiveness: A critical review. *Transport Reviews, 37*(1), 116–138.

Rabadi, G., PintoI, C. A., Talley, W., & Arnaout, J. P. (2007). Port recovery from security incidents: A simulation approach. In K. Bichou, M. Bell, & A. Evans (Eds.), *Risk Management in Port Operations, Logistics and Supply Chain Security* (pp. 83–94). London: Informa.

Song, D. W., & Yeo, K.-T. (2004). A competitive analysis of Chinese container ports using the analytic hierarchy process. *Maritime Economics and Logistics, 6*, 34–52.

Stasinopoulos, D. (2003). Maritime security: The need for a global agreement. *Maritime Economics and Logistics, 5*(3), 311–320.

Talas, R., & Menachof, D. (2009). The efficient tradeoff between security and cost for seaports: A conceptual model. *International Journal of Risk Assessment and Management, 13*(1), 46–59.

Thai, V. V. (2007). Impacts of security improvements on service quality in maritime transport: An empirical study of Vietnam. *Maritime Economics and Logistics, 9*(4), 335–356.

Thibault, M., Brooks, M., & Button, K. (2006). The response of the US maritime industry to the new container security initiatives. *Transportation Journal, 45*(1), 5–15.

Timlen, T. (2007, April/May). The ISPS Code: Where are we now? *Cargo Security International, 5*(3), 14–15.

Tiwari, P., Itoh, H., & Doi, M. (2003). Shippers' port and carrier selection behaviour in China: A discrete choice analysis. *Maritime Economics and Logistics, 5*(1), 23–39.

Tongzon, J., & Heng, W. (2005). Port privatisation, efficiency and competitiveness: Some empirical evidence from container ports (terminals). *Transportation Research Part A: Policy and Practice, 39*(5), 405–424.

UNCTAD. (2004, February 26). *Container Security: Major Initiatives and Related International Developments*. Report by the UCTAD Secretariat, Geneva.

UNCTAD. (2007). *Maritime Security: ISPS Code Implementation, Costs and Related Financing UNCTAD/SDTE/TLB/2007.* Available at http://unctad. org/en/Docs/sdtetlb20071_en.pdf.

Urciuoli, L., Sternberg, H., & Ekwall, D. (2010, July 11–15). *The Effects of Security on Transport Performances.* Paper Presented at the 12th World Conference on Transport Research, Lisbon, Portugal.

Valentine, V. F. (2002). *Measuring Efficiency of Container Ports: An Analysis By Organisational and Ownership Structure* (PhD thesis). Plymouth University, UK.

Voss, M., Whipple, J., & Closs, D. (2009). The role of strategic security: Internal and external security measures with security performance implications. *Transportation Journal, 48*(2), 5–23.

WSC. (2007). *Statement Regarding Legislation to Require 100% Container Scanning.* Available at http://www.worldshipping.org/pdf/wsc_legislation_ statement.pdf.

Yang, Y. C. (2010). Impact of the container security initiative on Taiwan's shipping industry. *Maritime Policy and Management, 37*(7), 699–722.

Yap, W. Y., Lam, J. S. J., & Notteboom, T. (2006). Developments in container port competition in East Asia. *Transport Reviews, 26*(2), 167–188.

Yeo, G. T. (2007). *Port Competitiveness in North East Asia: An Integrated Fuzzy Approach to Expert Evaluations* (PhD thesis). Plymouth University, UK.

Yeo, G. T., Roe, M., & Dinwoodie, J. (2008). Evaluating the competitiveness of container ports in Korea and China. *Transportation Research Part A, 42*(6), 910–921.

5

Research Methodology for Container Port Security

Research Strategy and Method

The choice of research strategy is determined by the research objectives as well as the relevant literature. It is important to use a suitable methodology by which the impacts on EU port competition will be determined. In choosing the methodology for data collection, the available and applicable methods need to be considered first. Whether these techniques suit the research aim and objectives is another substantial consideration. The methodology for data collection and analysis will be discussed and presented in this chapter.

Outlining a framework of research aim and objectives is essential to guide methodological development. The purpose of this study is to explore and explain the implications of the CSI for EU container port competition. The limited amount of research related to this subject means that this research is exploratory, aiming at identification and description. Moreover, due to the abductive research approach, a model was developed to interpret the facts discovered in the Delphi survey.

© The Author(s) 2019
X. Zhang and M. Roe, *Maritime Container Port Security*,
https://doi.org/10.1007/978-3-030-03825-0_5

Research Methods and Port Competitiveness Studies

In Chapter 3, research on port competitiveness was reviewed. The methods scholars adopted together with major influential factors were identified (Tables 3.1 and 3.2).

Kent and Ashar (2001) suggested a conceptual model that consists of four elements for monitoring port competitiveness. The four elements were: transportation, operational performance, tariff comparison and financial performance. Cullinane et al. (2002) used the economic inputs of capital and labour for analysing port efficiency. Tiwari et al. (2003) used a discrete choice model to analyse how shippers select liner companies and ports. They examined the characteristics of ports, shipping line and shipper by analysing proxies. Veldman and Buckmann (2003) originally intended to analyse port competition and choice using two factors which are cost and service quality. However, owing to limitations in obtaining sufficient data, only service factors were analysed.

The Choice of Qualitative Approach for This Research

In Chapter 2, studies regarding the implications of maritime security measures on ports were reviewed. Much of the available analysis is based on conceptual work, modelling techniques, the economic situation and efficiency measurement which are in the field of quantitative research. However, there is little evidence of qualitative analysis to explore how the maritime security measures affect port competitive positions. On the other hand, in earlier work which adopted a quantitative approach to investigate port competitiveness, very limited and abstracted input factors have been used. To obtain these quantitative data, major obstacles such as business confidentiality, evaluation complexities, difficulties in measurement and unavailability still remain.

For example, Cullinane et al. (2002) had problems in data collection regarding port cost since there were no secondary sources available for the targeted areas. As a result, an alternative approach using the physical characteristics of ports was adopted. Kent and Ashar (2001) also stated that difficulties existed in data collection since the assumptions they made for the model were based on industry standards which may vary from country to country. Sanchez et al. (2003) did not include transport cost charged to the shippers in their analysis of international transport costs owing to the problems with obtaining key information. Malchow and Kanafani (2004) were restrained by data availability and the complexities of port tariffs, and finding data on port charges, the transport cost and the intermodal transfer process was very difficult. Tiwari et al. (2003) had to exclude shipping line service factors and variables from their input factors due to lack of information. Tongzon and Heng (2005) omitted factors such as cargo handling charges, average delay time and product differentiation because of confidentiality issues and technological difficulties.

Bearing in mind the opinions of port industrial and administrative experts on ideological issues as well as obtaining attitudes concerning the application of this ideology to EU container ports, a qualitative approach will stimulate a more in-depth response than a quantitative survey because of the obstacles in obtaining data.

Primary and Secondary Data Collection

Primary and secondary data were gathered to fulfil the research objectives. Secondary data collected from the literature review will be used to achieve Objectives 1, 2 and partially Objective 3. To fully achieve Objectives 3 and 4, primary data will be collected through a Delphi survey. Developing the Delphi survey will be based on key areas in the literature review on the implications of maritime security measures and influential factors of port competition. Discussion of the findings will be made based on a synthesis of the literature and the Delphi results. As this research is shaped by an abductive approach, a model will be developed to interpret the findings. In order to build such a model, secondary data including existing theories and port-related data will be collected. Figure 5.1 illustrates the research phases and data sources for this abductive research.

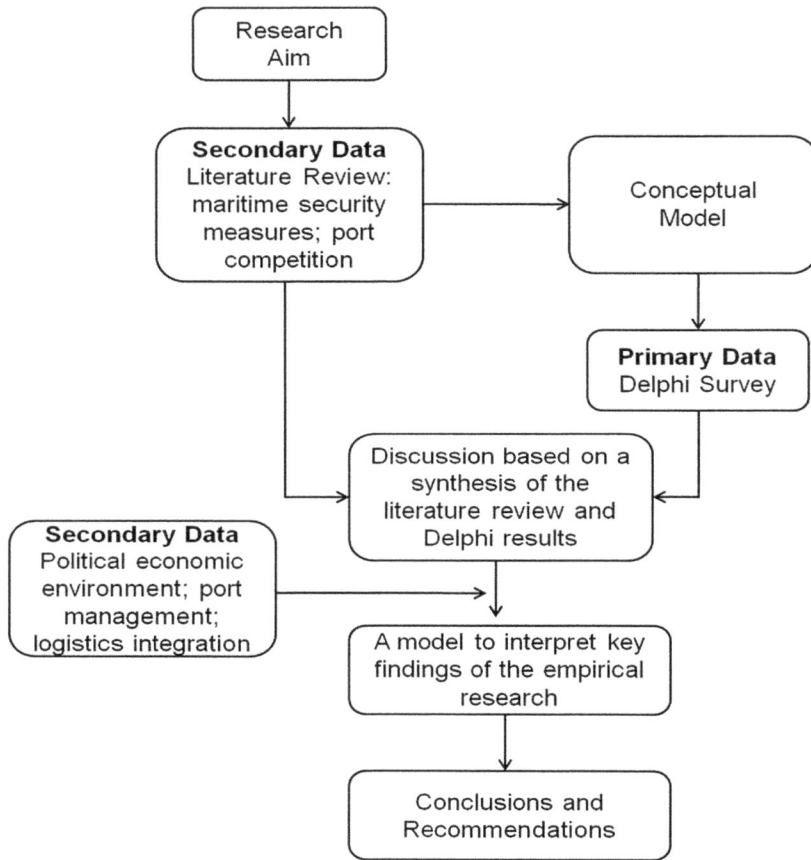

Fig. 5.1 Abductive research phases (*Source* The authors)

Rationale for Adopting a Delphi Technique as the Qualitative Approach

According to Berg (1995) and Wengraf (2004), there are three main approaches for qualitative data gathering: group discussions or focus groups, in-depth interviews and questionnaires or surveys.

The process of group discussion or focus groups involves the researcher and a specific group of people, which could be structured, semi-structured or unstructured (Barbour 2007). The researcher acts as a moderator or facilitator (Rubie-Davies 2007). Group discussion or focus groups are used when the researcher is guided by research objectives and aims to initiate a dialogue between group members (Denzin and Lincoln 2011). However, this method was criticised by Flick (2009) as the discussion could be dominated by a strong personality and other group members may just agree which could lead to a failure to collect varying views from experts with different backgrounds.

Hannes and Lockwood (2012) described questionnaires or surveys as the sending out of a list of questions to specific individuals, and the individuals sending back their responses. The questions can be structured, semi-structured or unstructured. The logical sequencing of questions and the context setting should be taken into consideration (Barbour 2007). The researcher needs to identify and select a large enough sample to detect statistically significant effects because the goal is to generalise the findings to a larger population (Okoli and Pawlowski 2004). However, regarding a research topic that involves political and security issues and port operations, there are a limited number of potential participants who are willing to contribute their professional opinions. Moreover, limitations of questionnaires emerge when visual aids, open-ended questions and complex questions are needed (Neuman 2011). In addition, according to Silverman (2011), Myers (2008), and Gibbs (2008), a poor respondent return rate, lack of control over who responds to the questionnaire and potential person-specific and situation-specific bias constitute other limitations.

Considering the limitations discussed above, primary data were collected through a Delphi study. According to Keeney et al. (2001), a Delphi survey involves sending out a number of rounds until consensus is reached, where in each round the panellists are asked to comment on a specific subject. Unlike a traditional questionnaire or survey, Delphi does not require visual aids and open-ended questions. Brooks (1985), Linstone and Turoff (2002), and Geist (2010) highlighted that Delphi could prevent a few dominant individuals from imposing their ideologies on other members. In addition, the limitation over who responds to the questionnaire does not exist in this case since the questionnaires will be sent directly to the identified participants who have agreed in advance to answer (Cottam 2012). Consequently, the rate of return will increase. Based on this, the Delphi technique is the most appropriate method because it offers a systematic qualitative approach for data collection and analysis, and reporting the findings facilitates greater depth of understanding regarding the targeted issue.

Wechsler (1978, p. 23) gave a fully comprehensive definition for Delphi: '*it is a survey which is steered by a monitoring group, comprises several rounds of a group of experts, who are anonymous among each other and for whose subjective-intuitive prognoses a consensus is aimed*'. The Delphi technique has been identified by many as a means for consensus building through using a set of questionnaires to collect data from a panel of specific experts. The experts are encouraged to reassess their initial opinions on the information from the previous iteration during the Delphi feedback process. Thereby, '*in a Delphi study, the results of previous iterations regarding specific statements and/or items can change or be modified by individual panel members in later iterations based on their ability to review and assess the comments and feedback provided by the other Delphi panellists*' (Hsu and Sandford 2007, p. 2).

The Origins and Use of Delphi

The Delphi technique was mainly developed by Dalkey and Helmer at the RAND Corporation in the 1950s. It has been widely adopted and accepted for achieving convergence of opinions from experts on real-world knowledge within certain topic areas, such as programme planning, needs assessment and resource utilisation, exploring assumptions and correlating judgements on a topic across a wide range of disciplines (Hsu and Sandford 2007; Turoff and Hiltz 1996). Over the years, both the number and diversity of research topics using Delphi have grown, thereby confirming the flexibility of this method (Bryman 2012). Cottam (2012, p. 213) reviewed varying Delphi research projects and noted that research fields implementing Delphi include: nursing (Keeney et al. 2001); administration and planning (Watkins 2011);

leadership; business (Bleicher 2011); marketing; education (Zeedick 2011); and management. Delphi has been used for research on supply chain management (SCM) and transport fields. Professor J. B. Schneider at the University of Washington used the Delphi technique for the exploration of transportation planning (Linstone and Turoff 2002). In 1987, Kapoor adopted Delphi to examine the international trade system and to develop a model to identify areas of system failure regarding maritime fraud (Kapoor 1987). Cooper (1994) used a Delphi technique to analyse future logistics in Europe. Akkermans et al. (2003) concluded a Delphi study on how Enterprise Resource Planning (ERP) affected SCM. Brett and Roe (2010) adopted Delphi to study if Ireland has the potential ability to develop as a maritime service centre of excellence. Islam et al. (2006) applied Delphi to collect local experts' opinion on how to develop effective multimodal freight transport in Bangladesh. Mason and Alamdari (2007) used a Delphi panel of 26 experts in air transport to predict the structure of the industry in the EU in 2015 regarding network carriers, low-cost airlines and passenger behaviour. Seuring and Müller (2008) used Delphi for sustainable SCM and stated that it allowed a structured gathering of opinions. Piecyk and McKinnon (2009) conducted a Delphi survey with 100 logistics specialists to analyse future freight transport and environmental trends in the UK up to 2020. Parsons et al. (2011) included the Delphi technique to collect opinions from stakeholders and experts towards Arctic icebreaking services. Schuckmann et al. (2012) ran a Delphi-based scenario in terms of the factors that would affect transport infrastructure development up to 2030. Dinwoodie et al. (2013) used classic Delphi to analyse perceptions of changing patterns of maritime oil freight flows to 2050. The Delphi technique was chosen since it could facilitate remote group communications and ensure anonymity. In the research of Dinwoodie et al. (2014), a classic quantitative Delphi was chosen as the most appropriate method to explore dry bulk shipping flows to 2050. Liimatainen et al. (2014) used Delphi to investigate the future of carbon dioxide (CO_2) emissions of road transport in Finland.

Characteristics of the Delphi Technique

According to Powell (2003), the Delphi technique has six common characteristics. Firstly, it focuses on topics which are unresearched, in future or areas about which little is known. Delphi can be used for developing estimations of future events and conceptualising (Aligica and Herritt 2009).

Secondly, Delphi relies on the use of experts in a certain subject brought together in groups via these panels (Clayton 1997). An expert is a person who has profound knowledge about a specific subject (Davidson et al. 1997). Their informed opinions are the source of information for the Delphi study (Powell 2003). Panel members can be national or international, from industry, government or academia, or from different social/professional stratifications (Okoli and Pawlowski 2004).

Another primary characteristic and advantage of adopting the Delphi technique for this research is that anonymity can reduce the effects of dominant individuals during group-based processes in which information is collected and synthesised (Dalkey et al. 1972). Delphi can also be used to avoid direct confrontation of the experts with one other (Dalkey and Helmer 1963, p. 4). They observed that the disadvantages of direct confrontation with experts were that it '*induces the hasty formulation of preconceived notions, an inclination to close one's mind to novel ideas, a tendency to defend a stand once taken, or alternatively and sometimes alternately, a predisposition to be swayed by persuasively stated opinions of others*'. Anonymity is vital since it allows experts with different backgrounds such as port users, government officials and academics from different countries to express their true opinion. Only the Delphi facilitator knows all panellists. It helps to improve judgemental accuracy as the Delphi study is conducted anonymously, which ensures that the participants focus on the study rather than being affected by the other participants' opinion (Rowe et al. 2005). Additionally, '*the issue of confidentiality is facilitated by geographic dispersion of the subjects as well as the use of electronic communication such as e-mail to solicit and exchange information*' (Hsu and Sandford 2007, p. 2).

Fourthly, Delphi adopts an iterative research process (Hasson et al. 2000). The process is viewed as a series of rounds (questionnaires) that are required to be responses from the panel members. Each round includes synthesised information derived from an earlier round to allow panel members to refine and reassess their opinions from round to round (Zeedick 2011). The iteration provides flexibility and adaptability to suit the complex competition environment of EU ports.

In addition, the possibility to control feedback in the process to reduce the effect of 'noise' also calls for the use of a Delphi study. Dalkey et al. (1972) defined 'noise' as communication which distorts the data and concerns group and/or individual interests rather than focusing on problem-solving in a group process. According to Hsu and Sandford (2007), the information extracted from 'noise' is generally constituted by bias irrelevant to the purpose of the study. The feedback procedures assure that only directly relevant information is offered to the panellists and they are asked to make judgements (Greatorex and Dexter 2000). Controlled feedback allows the panel members stimulated thinking to achieve a valid and reliable set of conclusions. Through this, Delphi can create a consensus of opinion.

Types of Delphi

There are many different types of Delphi that vary in their difficulty to plan and conduct (Table 5.1). Four main Delphi techniques were discussed by van Zolingen and Klaassen (2003), namely the classical Delphi, the policy Delphi, the decision Delphi and the group Delphi/expert workshop. Additionally, some other types of Delphi, such as modified Delphi, real-time Delphi, e-Delphi, technological Delphi, disaggregative Delphi and fuzzy Delphi, have been adopted. Generally speaking, they share similar difficulties in planning and conducting. They are all time-consuming and labour intensive and require expert preparation in advance; hence, they are relatively expensive (Sindi 2016).

Table 5.1 Different types of Delphi technique

Types of Delphi	Description and features
Classical Delphi	Individual basis, data gathering from anonymous experts in a number of rounds, stability reached through iteration, consensus achieved for forecast.
Policy Delphi	Policy issue and social situation, various number of rounds, anonymity, not decision making, clarifying an understanding of different plurality standpoints. (Linstone and Turoff 2002)
Decision Delphi	Prepare, help and make decisions, actual decision-makers form panellists for analysis of decisions, deals with reality rather than predicted or described
Group Delphi/expert workshop	Efficient for lessening doubt around knowledge of predictions and interpretations, more convenient than classical Delphi, provides a rationale behind disagreement and tests them in a 'peer review', provides only a brief summary of expert opinions
Real time Delphi	Sometimes referred to as a consensus conference, aims to ensure expert availability to reduce drop-out rates and increase process efficiency, participants are provided with a hyperlink to a welcome page where they read the details of the study and what is required and access the initial questionnaire. The process uses a refined interface, and the authors argue the outcomes. (Gnatzy et al. 2011)
e-Delphi (adopted for this research)	Similar to real time Delphi, replicates the classical Delphi process, the questionnaire, feedback, and participation of the expert panel is all done via email or online surveys. It can be argued that this approach is categorised under modified Delphi. (Gnatzy et al. 2011)
Technological Delphi	Similar to real time Delphi, difference is that the technological Delphi uses handheld devices to respond immediately to the questions.
Disaggregative Delphi	Critical of classical Delphi, consensus is formed when panellists are asked to give estimates of probable and preferable futures, uses cluster analysis to disaggregative responses of key variables, first round contains quantitative questions, second round is qualitative
Fuzzy Delphi	Traditional forecasting, mostly utilised to generate a professional consensus for complex topics, reduces time of investigation and consumption of cost and time, round vary and anonymity

Source The authors adapted from Sindi (2016) and Elgarhy (2016)

Delphi Method Adopted

The literature review in Chapter 2 indicated that there is a lack of empirical data in the case of how maritime security measures generally affect port competition. In order to find out how the CSI impacts upon EU port competition, Delphi can help to obtain comprehensive opinions and judgements in terms of the past, present and future. Additionally, Delphi can be applied to a wide range of subjects, such as policy-making and industry predictions (Cottam 2012). It can expose all the different opinions (agreement and disagreement) and arguments on these opinions (Iqbal and Pipon-Young 2009). A broader spectrum of responses can be gathered since the panel consists of stakeholders with a variety of backgrounds. Moreover, anonymity between panellists is important because the participants are freer to state their position in a less pressed environment without being influenced by others (De Meyrick 2003). With regard to port security, which involves politics, terrorism and conflicts among different interest groups, the anonymity of Delphi could encourage varying individuals to contribute both their knowledge and problem-solving skills. In addition, participants can explore the original conceptual assumptions and subsequent developments to offer a range of inclusive indicators for the research. Furthermore, Delphi questionnaires can be facilitated through email which is cost-effective and time saving for the participants since Delphi does not require physical contact to collect the required data (Iqbal and Pipon-Young 2009). Since this research focuses on industrial and political issues, people who contribute data to this research are most likely to have busy schedules and prefer to remain anonymous. As a result, taking into account various factors such as cost, timing and anonymity, the e-Delphi which utilises email and an online survey is the most suitable method.

The Criticisms of Delphi

Despite the advantages of the Delphi technique, some criticisms have been expressed. According to Tzeng et al. (2002), person-specific and situation-specific biases can be possible and impact upon the reliability of Delphi as a judgement method. Person-specific bias can be difficult to avoid since there are 58 CSI container seaports globally and the number of experts who have interests in maritime security and port operations is quite limited. As a result, the study relies on experts' professionalism to gather unbiased opinions.

Another criticism is that whether participants commit to complete the Delphi process often depends upon their interest and involvement in the research topic (Rowe and Wright 2011). Some participants drop out from the survey during the process, especially after the first round. Therefore, to increase the commitment level, great care will be taken when choosing participants. The Delphi questionnaire must be carefully prepared and tested to avoid ambiguity. The Delphi process must be managed and scheduled rigidly. In addition, the high level of anonymity helps to maintain the participation rate (Landeta et al. 2011). However, Sackman (1975) argued that anonymity may lead to unaccountability since the response is untraceable. However, it is normally considered a good quality which allows participants to express their opinions freely and reduce the dropout rate. Hasson et al. (2000) also suggested that consensus cannot be well explained in studies that employ Delphi. It has also been argued that a consensus approach may lead to *'a diluted version of the best opinion and the result representing the lowest common denominator'* (Cottam 2012, p. 236). However, all approaches to gain consensus have the same risk. Furthermore, it is often claimed in that time and labour-intensity are negative attributes, therefore leading to high costs. However, the adoption of e-Delphi reduced costs whereby email communication was used as the major communication approach and an online survey could be set up to acquire experts' opinions.

The Delphi Study Process

Scholars have presented a variety of means of carrying out Delphi studies. Based on Linstone and Turoff (2002, pp. 5–6), usually Delphi undergoes four distinct phases as follows:

- *'Characterised by exploration of the subject under discussion, wherein each individual contributes additional information he feels is pertinent to the issue'.*
- *'The process of reaching an understanding of how the group views the issue'.*
- *'If there is significant disagreement, then that disagreement is explored in the third phase to bring out the underlying reasons for the differences and possibly to evaluate them'.*
- *'A final evaluation occurs when all previously gathered information has been initially analysed and the evaluations have been fed back for consideration'.*

According to Beech (1997), two or three rounds are ideal and have proven sufficient to reach consensus; more rounds would not increase this (Powell 2003). Consequently, it was anticipated that two to three rounds of Delphi would be utilised to analyse how EU container port competition changes with the implementation of the CSI. Figure 5.2 illustrates the adopted Delphi process, consisting of ten stages from the design of the research conceptual statements to the validity of the third round.

Formulating research conceptual assumptions is the very first step towards implementing the Delphi technique. The conceptual assumptions would direct the research to find out the implications of the CSI for EU container seaport competition. In Chapter 4, the assumptions were classified under four conceptual categories. They are: (1) the necessity of pursuing a maritime security initiative; (2) introduction of the CSI and its controversial influences; (3) determinants of EU container seaport competitiveness; and (4) the implications of the CSI for EU container seaport competition. Each conceptual category led to a set of conceptual assumptions. Each of these conceptual assumptions derived a set of statements, which were sent out to panel experts for data collection. The objectives of the Delphi study were to gain consensus about the necessity of maritime security initiatives; the positive effects of the CSI on maritime industry; the EU container port competitiveness components; and the implications of the CSI implementation for

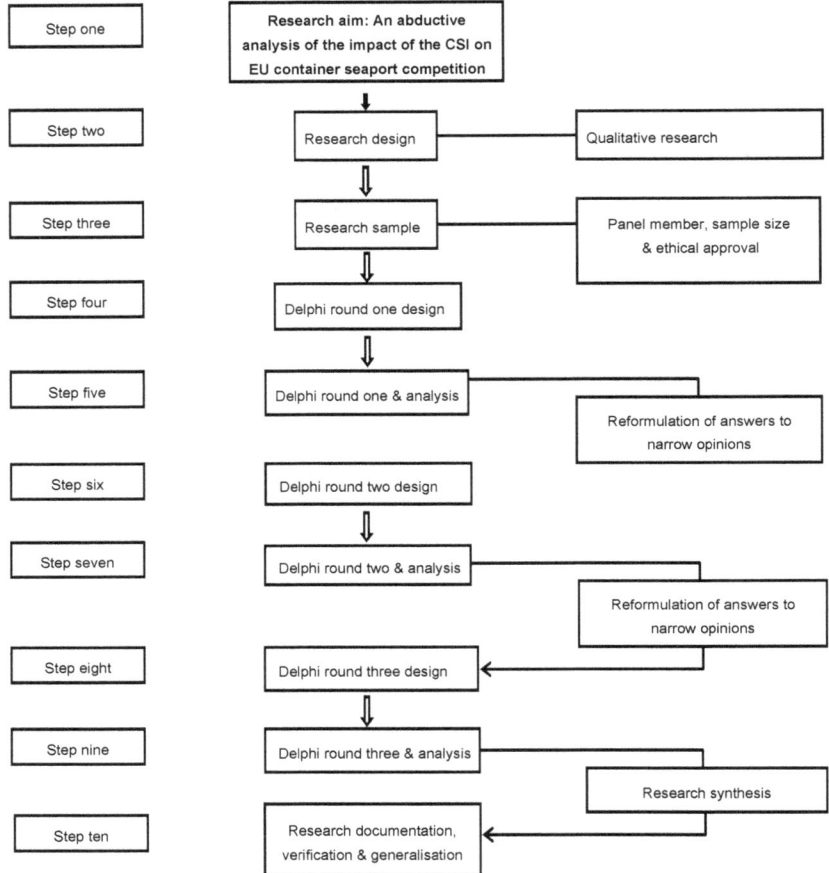

Fig. 5.2 The Delphi process (*Source* The authors adapted from Fowles [1978] and Linstone and Turoff [2002])

EU container seaports through affecting the identified competitiveness components.

After developing a series of feasible assumptions, the next step was to design the Delphi survey at the micro-level. Selecting Delphi panel members is the first critical step since the outcomes of the Delphi are based on the experts' opinions.

Panellist Formation

The selection of appropriate participants as the first stage in the Delphi process has been described as the 'linchpin of the method' (Green et al. 1999, p. 200). The knowledge and cooperation of experts are the key factors that determine the success of a Delphi study, and therefore, it is essential to include people who are likely to contribute valuable ideas. The selection of the panellist is not a random process. Unlike a statistically based study in which participants are assumed to be representative of a larger population, the Delphi needs non-representative and knowledgeable people (Linstone and Turoff 2002). This means that each respondent is an expert who also has an incentive and is motivated to participate in the area of the research (Day and Bobeva 2005). Experts can be a group of 'informed individuals' and specialists in their domain or a knowledgeable person in a specific subject (McKenna 1994; Goodman 1987). This research adopted four main criteria for experts summarised by Cottam (2012, p. 219): '*(i) knowledge and experience with the issues under investigation; (ii) capacity and willingness to participate; (iii) sufficient time to participate in the survey; and (iv) effective communication skills*'. Delphi participants must be highly trained in their specialised field and richly knowledgeable with regard to the targeted academic field (Powell 2003). Therefore, the panel selection for this study is extremely rigorous.

Panellists with Different Backgrounds

Bichou (2008a, p. 26) argued that '*a problem with survey inquiries occurs when the findings of a case-specific survey are generalised to all stakeholders and security programmes*' and '*even when survey inquiries investigate a single security programme, their results may show inconsistent cost figures, either over time or between participants*'. In order to study whether the CSI is beneficial to the whole community or not, it is very important to consider the differences between stakeholders' values and perspectives. Therefore, for this specific Delphi research, participants with various backgrounds and interests are needed for analysing the fragmented maritime industry.

The Delphi research comprised three groups: (i) academics who encompass the opinions and expertise of scholars researching maritime security and container port competition; (ii) industrial experts, specifically holding opinions and industry experience of EU container port management and CSI implementation; and (iii) administrators, occupying positions and experience in major organisations involved in maritime security regulation and maritime governance at international, supranational and national levels. All participants remained anonymous, with rigorous attention to protect their identity and the integrity of the companies and organisations involved.

Panel Size

There is no agreement on the Delphi panel size or precise approach for identifying it, and it is impossible to recognise a positive relationship between Delphi group size and Delphi group performance (Rowe and Wright 2011). Keeney et al. (2001) suggested that the panel size should depend on the research aim, design selected and time frame for data collection. In addition, the nature of the different viewpoints included and the resources available can help to determine the panel size (Landeta et al. 2011; Sharkey and Sharples 2003). Previous Delphi research used different techniques for panel formation. Van Zolingen and Klassen (2003) formed one panel with four different stakeholder groups. Wang et al. (2003) included two panels with two different nationalities: Chinese and international. Therefore, the panel size varies and ultimately depends upon the nature of the research (Nowack et al. 2011). Delbecq et al. (1975) recommended a panel with 10–15 similar panellists as the ideal number. Warner (2014) suggested that at least 13 experts should be included to achieve a reliable sample. Kapoor (1987) included 39 experts in his Delphi. Delbecq et al. (1975) argued that using too many panellists would lead to extreme difficulty in data analysis. However, Whitman (1990) used 75 experts, and Campbell et al. (2000) sent the first questionnaire to 305 experts across the UK.

Therefore, there is no agreed optimum number for panels or participants (Lai et al. 2002). Nowack et al. (2011) commented that the panel size can be much larger in a real-time Delphi, whereas for a Delphi which relies on interviews, the panel size would be much smaller for practical reasons.

In the context of this study, a single panel of experts with different backgrounds, namely academics, industrial experts and administrators, was chosen for the research. The single panel was chosen because the study would be less complex than that of multiple panels (Hanafin 2004) and it allowed the opportunity to share their ideas across all panel members through feedback between rounds (Nowack et al. 2011; Goluchowicz and Blind 2011). However, experts are required to state their background in the questionnaire in order to interpret their different viewpoints. In addition, experts may have overlaps between the three backgrounds. An expert who is categorised as academic may also have working experience as an industrial consultant. Therefore, it is essential for them to identify themselves and express opinions based on how they position themselves in this specific research. Many experts are needed so that rich data on maritime security and port competition can be collected for deep analysis.

Process of Panel Selection

Academic Panellist Selection

Identification of individuals forming the academic group was difficult and complex. In order to guarantee the quantity and quality of the potential participants, two steps were taken to identify the desired academic experts. Firstly, two groups of academic experts were identified separately: (i) experts in maritime security policies and (ii) experts in port competition. A laborious task was taken to identify the first group because there is an absence of a central database for maritime security academics or researchers. Therefore, refereed publications and books were used to obtain the names of authors writing in the area of maritime security especially container port security and its influence on port performance. The names were populated using the function of 'related articles' in academic and industrial journals. It was relatively easier to identify the experts in port competition since a considerable number of studies have been conducted since the 1970s. The names were mostly obtained at the stage of the literature review, and a few experts were recommended by the contacted academicians. The second step was to identify overlaps between the two groups. The overlapping experts were chosen as potential participants who have expertise in both maritime security and port competition. After identification of experts' names, various search tools such as Google and LinkedIn were used to gain their contacts. Most of the candidates' contacts were available on the Internet, especially the academics. Therefore, emails were quite easy to acquire on Google. Some participants' emails were provided by their co-workers/colleagues or the institutions for which they worked. LinkedIn, as an auxiliary tool, helped to identify desired individuals since various interest groups and their contact methods are available on it. A total of 30 academic experts were identified and received the invitation email for participation. Table 5.2 shows the number of the academic participants contacted and their current occupations.

Table 5.2 Delphi participants contacted

Panellist category	No. of participants	% of the total panellists	Current positions of employment/qualification
Academic	30	36.14	PhD, post-doctoral, senior research fellow, professor, associate professor
Industrial	28	33.73	Operation manager, harbour master, CEO, COO, CFO, infrastructure director, port safety and security supervisor, liner manager, port agency, broker, port operation consultant
Administrative	25	30.12	Maritime security policy maker, consultant, secretary, committee member
Total	83	100	N/A

Source The authors

Industrial Panellist Selection

It was necessary to identify individual participants with industrial backgrounds. In order to validate their response, stakeholders who were relevant to EU container seaports would constitute the industrial panel experts. Therefore, identifying and selecting relevant EU container ports was essential. Table 5.3 provides an overview of the top 20 container ports in Europe. According to Notteboom (2012, p. 2), many of them '*act as almost pure transhipment hubs with a transshipment incidence of 75% or more (i.e. Gioia Tauro, Marsaxlokk, Algeciras) while other load centres can be considered as almost pure gateways or a combination of a dominant gateway function with sea-sea transhipment activities (e.g. Hamburg, Rotterdam, Le Havre, Antwerp)*'.

Table 5.3 shows that about 80% of the total container throughput in the European port system passes through the top 20 load centres. However, Russia and Turkey are not EU members. Since this research focuses on EU container ports, the ports of Ambarli, St Petersburg and Mersin were not included. As a result, only 17 ports were chosen as sample ports. The relevant stakeholders of those ports, such as the port management team, port users and port authorities, were selected as the experts with industrial background to form the Delphi panel. In addition, trans-Atlantic line managers from major container shipping companies, consultants of liner shipping agents and consultants of port management and operations were also included as industrial experts. Names were obtained from online sources such as company official websites, industrial seminars or conference records. Nevertheless, most of their contacts were not shown on the websites. Therefore, in order to acquire the experts' emails, the companies' headquarters and management teams were contacted as intermediaries. Twenty-eight practitioners were identified and invited as the industrial experts, of which 20 were from the 17 CSI ports in the EU. Eight experts were from trans-Atlantic shipping lines and port consulting companies. Their current positions are presented in Table 5.2.

Table 5.3   The Top 20 European Container Ports in 2013

Rank	Name	Country	Handling volume in million TEU
1	Rotterdam	Netherlands	11.87
2	Hamburg	Germany	8.86
3	Antwerp	Belgium	8.64
4	Bremen	Germany	6.12
5	Valencia	Spain	4.47
6	Algeciras	Spain	4.11
7	Felixstowe	UK	3.70
8	Ambarli	Turkey	3.10 Not EU
9	Piraeus	Greece	2.75
10	GionaTauro	Italy	2.72
11	Duisburg	Germany	2.60
12	Maarsaxlokk	Malta	2.54
13	St Petersburg	Russia	2.52 Not EU
14	Le Havre	France	2.31
15	Genoa	Italy	2.06
16	Zeebrugge	Belgium	1.95
17	Barcelona	Spain	1.76
18	Southampton	UK	1.48
19	Mersin	Turkey	1.26 Not EU
20	Las Palmas	Spain	1.25
Share of Top 20 of Europe total container throughput: 80%			

Source The authors adapted from Lloyd's List (2014)

Administrative Panellist Selection

Identification of policy-makers was the most difficult procedure, due to security and confidentiality issues. Distinguishing maritime security-regulating bodies, selecting the candidates to contact and obtaining contact details were time-consuming and laborious operations. A three-tiered approach based on current maritime governance jurisdiction was taken: national, supranational and international. Since the CSI was established as part of the CBP layered cargo security strategy, the CBP was contacted as the most suitable organisation in terms of national level, however, as the largest US federal law enforcement agent, was unlikely to respond. A general invitation email was sent to its team through its online contact page, and no response was received from them. At the other end of the spectrum, the United Nations Conference on Trade and Development (UNCTAD); the Organisation for Economic Co-operation and Development (OECD); and the International Maritime Organisation (IMO) were all liaised with as part of panel formation. Relevant experts were identified from the organisations' official website. Phone calls were made to the headquarters, asking for emails. Invitation emails were sent out to those experts. Although no expert from the CBP was contacted, some experts from the aforementioned organisations have experience either working with the CBP or working for the US relevant entities. The number of invited administrative participants was 25, and their external roles are presented in Table 5.2.

Table 5.2 also shows that the total experts invited to participate were 83. Every effort was made to make each category proportional. Nevertheless, academic experts were the largest proportion, accounting for 33.73% of the total number. This is because identifying academicians and acquiring their contacts is the easiest among three categories. The second largest group was the industrial experts. Most of them were from EU container port/terminal operators, ranking from top management team to operation supervisors. Other industrial participants also included trans-Atlantic liner operators, consultants and brokers. The administrative expert group had the smallest number but still accounted for more than 30% of the total. This is not surprising, considering the difficulty of acquiring their contacts.

Other Issues in Delphi Design

This Delphi survey consists of three rounds in which experts were invited to comment on the main conceptual statements of the study. Participants were asked to state if they 'agree', 'disagree' or are 'either agree or disagree' on 12 statements and answer one additional open-ended question. Statements were developed from the literature review and the conceptual model (see Chapter 4) derived from the research objectives.

When adopting a Delphi method, it is important to achieve a desirable response rate in the first round and also to maintain response rates in the following rounds (Ludwig 1997). Regarding the potential scarcity of qualified participants for panel formation, based on Parente and Anderson-Parente (2011), the ability to achieve and maintain a desirable response rate is vital to the validity of a Delphi study. Cottam (2012, p. 222) reviewed a number of key approaches used to decrease attrition between rounds and summarised them as '*making contact with the participant prior to the launch of the survey* (Zeedick 2011)*; ensuring participants are fully informed about the study* (Hasson et al. 2000)*; having short follow up periods between rounds, issuing reminders by email, telephone and personal contact* (Gupta and Clarke 1996)*; and offering incentives such as stamped addressed envelopes and thank you notes* (Campbell et al. 2004)'.

In this study, each selected panel member was sent an invitation email. The content of the invitation email stated: (1) the participant would be personally written to, to invite them to participate in the Delphi study; (2) the reasons why they have been chosen; (3) a concise description and justification of the research project; (4) a time frame for the Delphi; (5) confidentiality and anonymity assurances; (6) importance and contribution of their views; (7) contact details for further information about this research; and (8) the survey link and participation instructions.

The next stage after the identification of panel experts was to formulate the Delphi round one questionnaire. The initial conceptual category defined and guided the context in which the statements were placed. The role of round one is to generate ideas (Keeney et al. 2001) and identify issues to be addressed in later iterations (Crisp et al. 1997). Nowack et al. (2011) suggested using open-ended questions when Delphi serves the purpose of idea generation. A judgement was to be made on whether the CSI has negatively influenced port operations and EU port competition based on the Delphi results. According to Nowack et al. (2011), if the Delphi is used for judgement purpose, its success depends upon the extent of creativity needed. Cottam (2012) noted that open-ended questions can increase the richness of the data collected. Therefore, in the light of the nature of the research topic and the disciplines involved, a combination of open-ended and structured questions was used in the study (Cottam and Roe 2004).

Survey Method for Identification of EU Port Competitiveness

The port competition environment varies between regions. Consequently, factors that influence EU port competition needed to be identified first.

Aronietis et al. (2010) reviewed numerous studies on port competitiveness and adopted approaches. Methods that have been used for studying port competitiveness are summarised in Table 5.4.

As Table 5.4 shows, the most popular methodology for approaching the problem of port competitiveness is the survey instrument. It was widely used in the papers which study port choice and port competitiveness determinants. In 1985, Slack conducted a survey which focused on shippers and forwarders of trans-Atlantic container trades to identify criteria of port selection. After that, as Table 5.4 shows, Bird and Bland (1988), Murphy et al. (1992), Murphy and Daley (1994), Mangan et al. (2002), Nir et al. (2003), Tongzon (1995, 2009), Ha (2003), Tongzon and Sawant (2007), Acosta et al. (2007), De Langen (2007), and Grosso and Monteiro (2008) all adopted survey instruments to study port competitiveness and selection criteria. This provided a good basis for selecting the survey instrument to establish the determinants of EU container seaport competitiveness.

The components of port competitiveness have been presented in Table 3.3. These determinants include: port location, port facilities, overall efficiency, hinterland networks, value-added logistics and port services, safe handling of cargoes, confidence in port schedules, simplification of procedures, operational transparency, and port labour and skills (Yeo 2007). Since the choice of survey for EU container seaport competitiveness component identification is consistent with the choice of Delphi as a survey method, these competitiveness components,

Table 5.4 Summary of adopted methods for port competitiveness Components Identification

Source	Participants	Methods
Slack (1985)	Shippers; forwarders	Survey
Bird and Bland (1988)	Forwarders	Survey
Frankel (1992)	Governmental bodies; shipping companies; shippers; freight forwarders	Analytic hierarchy process
Murphy et al. (1992)	Large/small shippers; international water carriers; international water ports; international freights forwarders	Survey; Univariate analysis; Multivariate factor analysis
Murphy and Daley (1994)	Purchasing manager (shipper)	Survey
Kumar and Rajan (2002)	Shipper	Analytic hierarchy process
Mangan et al. (2002)	Decision makers (on ferry choice) in transport companies	Modelling; Survey
Nir et al. (2003)	Shipper	Survey; Revealed preference multinomial logical model
Lirn et al. (2004)	Shipping lines	Analytic hierarchy process
Tongzon (1995, 2009) and Tongzon and Sawant (2007)	Forwarders	Survey
Tiwari et al. (2003)	Shippers	Literature review; Discrete choice analysis
Ha (2003)	Shipping companies	Literature review; Discrete choice analysis
Malchow and Kanafani (2001, 2004)	Shippers (commodity types)	Discrete choice model
Song and Yeo (2004)	Ship owners; shipping companies shippers; terminal operators; academics	Analytic hierarchy process; Experts surveys
Cullinane et al. (2005)	Shippers (demand trends) Port authorities (supply)	Relative competitiveness analysis
Guy and Urli (2006)	Shipping companies	Multi-criteria analysis
Ugboma et al. (2006)	Shippers	Analytic hierarchy process

(continued)

Table 5.4   (continued)

Source	Participants	Methods
Acosta et al. (2007)	Terminal operators	Survey
De Langen (2007)	Shippers; forwarders	Survey
Shintani et al. (2007)	Shipping companies	Algorithm-based
De Martino and Morvillo (2008)	Port authorities; shippers; forwarders; shipping companies	Literature review
Grosso and Monteiro (2008)	Forwarding companies	Literature review Survey
Leachman (2008)	Importers	Economic optimisation model
Meersman et al. (2008)	Shipping companies Terminal operating companies Port authorities	Analysis of expected trends
Wiegmans et al. (2008)	Container terminal operators	Interviews Literature review
Donner and Kruk (2009)	Shipping company	Modeling

Source The authors adapted from Aronietis et al. (2010, pp. 4–7)

together with port safety and security, are hypothesised as influential in affecting EU container seaport competitive position and can be tested in this Delphi survey. Therefore, through analysing how maritime security initiatives influence these components, the effects on port competition can be then concluded.

Delphi Conceptual Statements and Rationale

The conceptualised assumptions identified in Chapter 4 led to the formation of the 13 questions for Delphi round one, comprising 12 statements and one open-ended question. The statements were developed from the results of a numerical research synthesis. Each statement contains controversial and debatable viewpoints taken from the literature. Table 5.5 indicates the sources for each statement. The 13 questions are categorised into four topics and one open-ended question for experts to express their comments that help to answer the original research question.

Table 5.5 Delphi statements literature synthesis sources

Statement	Sources
1.1	OECD (2003) and Koch (2002)
1.2	Martonosi et al. (2005), Allen (2006), Dekker and Stevens (2007), Bichou (2008a), and Metaparti (2010)
2.1	Thai (2007) and CBP (2006, 2014)
2.2	Parliament of Australia (2003), Banomyong (2005), Dallimore (2008), and Donner and Kruk (2009)
3	Haezendonck and Notteboom (2002), Ha (2003), Veldman and Buckmann (2003), Cullinane et al. (2005), Tongzon and Heng (2005), Yap and Lam (2006a, b), Yeo (2007), and Notteboom and Yap (2012)
4.1	Parliament of Australia (2003), UNCTAD (2003), Banomyong (2005), Dallimore (2008), Dekker and Stevens (2007), Bichou (2008a), and Donner and Kruk (2009).
4.2	Martonosi et al. (2005), Bennett and Chin (2008), and Bichou (2008b, 2011)
4.3	Allen (2006), CBP (2006), Thai (2007), and Bichou (2011)
4.4	Allen (2006), Dekker and Stevens (2007), Bichou (2005, 2011), CBP (2006, 2011, 2014), and Yeo et al. (2013)
4.5	Machalaba (2001), Limao and Venables, (2001), and Bichou (2011)
4.6	Parliament of Australia (2003), Metaparti (2010), and CBP (2011)
5	Allen (2006) and Dallimore (2008)

Source The authors

The statements were outlined in Chapter 4 but are repeated here for ease of discussion.

Delphi Conceptual Category, Assumption and Statements

Conceptual Category 1: The necessity of carrying out a maritime security initiative

Conceptual Assumption 1: It is necessary to carry out a maritime security initiative despite the fact that additional inspections may cause supply chain disruption and financial burden.

S1.1—Maritime security has become a great concern worldwide. The increasing volume of container movements, their relatively high velocity in the international trade and their uniformity have posed formidable security challenges. As the loading and unloading points of a sea transport process, container ports are the most important nodes for maritime safety. However, only around 2–10% of containers are actually inspected. US ports normally inspect roughly 5% of the 17 million containers arriving at the border every year. A great concern about container security emerged from this low inspection rate. Container security is far more important than efficiency and profit for the port. Therefore, security should be seen as the first priority.

The design of this statement is to test the experts' opinion on the importance of maritime security. Containerised shipping has been playing an increasingly important role in global transportation, largely due to the numerous technical and economic advantages. According to the OECD (2003), the increasing volume of container movements, their relatively high velocity in international trade and their uniformity have posed formidable security challenges. However, by contrast, the inspection rate of containers is considerably low. Therefore, experts' opinion is essential to testify the need for improving the inspection rate. What is more, it can also help to compare the different perceptions of experts who have different backgrounds, i.e. academic, policy-maker and industry, and what they value the most as the first priority.

S1.2—As the world's largest national economy, the USA plays a vital role in global trade. After 9/11, the USA has reacted to the needs for strengthening security measures to enhance maritime transport safety. Some of the maritime security initiatives have influence on some export ports in terms of logistics efficiency and financing. Nevertheless, those export ports should be prepared to comply with the US container port security initiatives for maritime safety.

This statement serves two purposes. The first one is to give a brief description of the background of the topic. As the biggest import and export country, the USA has become a major target of terrorism. Many security programmes and much legislation were proposed and developed by the USA. The second purpose is to collect expert opinions on the fact that most exports ports need to react to US unilateral security initiatives.

Conceptual Category 2: Introduction of the CSI and its controversial influences

Conceptual Assumption 2: The Container Security Initiative (CSI) can facilitate global container seaborne trade safety and security, adding competitiveness to CSI-affiliated ports.

S2.1—The Container Security Initiative (CSI) programme managed by US Customs and Border Protection (CBP) is an influential voluntary initiative. The CSI was proposed to ensure that all containers that pose a potential risk for terrorism are identified and inspected at foreign ports before they are loaded onto vessels and imported to the USA. Without a doubt, the CSI has dramatically increased the level of awareness for the need to secure global trade.

The CBP is one of the DHS's largest and most complex components. Its priority mission is keeping terrorists and their weapons out of the USA. The CSI, as one of the CBP multi-layer approach measurements, has affected maritime security to some extent. The design of this statement is to test to what extent the experts appreciate the CSI can affect maritime security.

S2.2—Unlike the 24-hour rule, the CSI is a voluntary initiative. However, in order to keep market share for US-inbound trade, the major exporters have to join the programme. Not joining the programme could make export ports lose competitiveness over their rivals.

Based on the literature review, there is an argument about the need to join the CSI programme. With the premise of 24-hour rule and 100% scanning, the voluntary CSI could improve the overall process efficiency. The possibility of gaining competitive advantage in terms of overall efficiency could be one of the reasons why the export ports join the CSI. This statement is designed to test experts' opinions over that conjecture.

Conceptual Category 3: Determinants of the EU container seaport competitiveness

Conceptual Assumption 3: The EU container port industry is highly competitive. Port efficiency, service and cost-related elements are still the most important competitiveness components.

S3—The port environment generally has become increasingly competitive; it varies between regions and places depending on the extent to which these forces have impacted upon the nature of the port environment. According to prior studies, the components of port competitiveness are: port location, port facilities, overall efficiency, hinterland networks, value-added logistics, port services, safe handling of cargoes, confidence in port schedules, simplification of procedures, operational transparency, and port labour and skills. Among these factors, for the EU ports, since port location is static, port efficiency, service and cost-related elements are still the most important competitiveness components. Port safety and security is not an incentive for port selection.

This research aims to find out the implications of the CSI for EU port competition. Based on the discussion in Chapter 3, identifying port competitive determinants is essential. Therefore, this statement is designed to test expert opinions on the determinants which are to be applied. Although there have been a number of studies on port competitiveness, this research looks at EU ports specifically. Port competition and competitiveness vary in different regions and places. As a result, the identification of key factors that determine EU port competitiveness is necessary. According to the discussion and Table 3.3, costs, service factors and efficiency factors are included in this statement, assuming they are the major competitiveness drivers for EU ports. Based on the synthesis of the literature review and the research aim, 'port safety and security' constitutes the last part of the statement and will be commented on by the panellists.

Conceptual Category 4: The implications of introduction of the CSI on EU port competition

Conceptual Assumption 4: CSI compliance does not cause global supply chain disruption or financial problems for the EU container ports.

S4.1—To obtain the minimum required level of compliance, ports need to implement technical and organisational measures that will bring additional costs to maritime industries. Enhancing the technical measures due to security regulations, such as the ISPS Code, has brought additional costs to European maritime industries. Smaller ports in the

EU may stop their US-inbound business since they cannot bear the financial costs. Larger ports may 'steal' new business from smaller ports which are financially strained to meet the scanning requirements. A distortion of EU container port market share will arise.

This statement is designed to test an expert's opinion on how the CSI could affect EU port competition from the aspect of financial burden. Based on the literature, it is strongly believed that the implementation of the CSI could bring a considerable amount of extra cost to ports, which would be a particular burden for smaller ports. Since cost is closely related to port competitiveness, it can be deduced that joining the CSI programme could influence the EU port competitive position.

S4.2—While port security measures enhance port security, procedural requirements of the new security regime act against operational and logistical efficiency. The proponents of this view list a number of operational inefficiencies ranging from direct functional redundancies such as additional inspections and lengthy procedures to indirect supply chain disruptions stemming from longer lead times and less reliable demand and supply scenarios.

This statement is designed to test expert opinion on the negative effects in terms of operational and logistics efficiency that the CSI may bring. There has been some debate about the inefficiencies mentioned by Bichou (2008a, 2011) which have not been tested.

S4.3—Productivity could improve due to better procedural arrangements. With the reinforcement of security, there is reduced likelihood of security incidents, a probability of fewer incidents being recorded and higher port reliability. Increased reliability which leads to higher trust between a port and its upstream and downstream partners in a container supply chain contributes to the reduction of cargo processing time and results in reduction of cargo processing cost. Decreased cargo processing cost has a positive effect on port selection, thus attracting more container volume. Consequently, from the viewpoint of the above analysis, improving security level and increasing port reliability can attract more containers. Compliant participants would benefit from access certification and fast-lane treatment as well as reduced insurance costs and risk exposure.

This statement is designed to test expert opinions on the positive effect brought by the CSI. The benefits brought by the CSI are controversial. Measures such as the CSI fundamentally emphasise prevention and source inspection, which theoretically could be more cost-effective and less time-consuming than conventional random physical checks (Bichou 2011). The CBP claimed that due to a better procedural arrangement, the overall efficiency of the process can be improved, which could decrease the overall handling time and cost. In addition to lower incidents records and higher port reliability, both increased port reliability and decreased cost could increase customer attraction. However, according to the literature review, there might be a possibility that the CBP neglects the operational inefficiencies that include direct functional redundancies and indirect supply chain disruptions. These factors may have negative effects on the EU export ports. Therefore, experts with different backgrounds may have different points of view on this statement that will contribute to the analysis.

S4.4—Although US Customs and Border Protection stated that the CSI can bring benefits to member ports, those benefits are still controversial. The CSI has negative effects on port profit. In addition to the significant initial investment in new equipment, the CSI makes the cargo inspection process more complicated, creating an increase in cargo processing time and cost. That can change important performance characteristics of the port such as port efficiency and price. From the perspective of a long-term economic model, these consequences produce negative impacts for relative attractiveness of ports for various stakeholders, namely exporters, and cargo carriers. The reduced attractiveness will decrease the competitiveness of a port. Moreover, the deepening cost and time may initiate a vicious circle of decreasing port competitiveness. The CSI is actually a heavy burden for those ports that have joined.

This statement aims at testing expert opinion on the negative effects CSI has on port competitiveness. According to the literature review, the positive effects the CSI brings to joining ports are disputable. There is more than one result that could be deduced from CBP's claim about how the CSI can benefit those ports. For example, a better procedural arrangement for container scanning could lead to higher efficiency of the whole process. However, it will have negative effect on export terminal operators. Moreover, in order to absorb extra costs, a port could increase port charges for its customers. Port price may still be the first priority for port selection, rather than port reliability. Nevertheless, based on the current literature, there is commonly evidence to support both arguments. Therefore, this statement can help to collect expert opinion on this controversial topic.

S4.5—The CSI could improve the capabilities and the overall effectiveness of the targeting process. However, this programme transfers container examinations from unloading ports in the USA to the loading ports overseas. On the other hand, all the checks are carried out in the host countries which bear the equipment cost. In case of unloading and emptying of any potential threat posed by a dangerous container, the costs are borne by the importer to a US port. The US Customs sacrifices the export ports to save the US unloading port's time and cost. The CSI is a unilateral and unfair programme without considering the implications for host ports.

This statement is designed to test expert opinion on the negative effects CSI could bring to the emerging EU export ports. Based on the literature review, there are two major debates over port efficiency due to the CSI programme. Some literature indicates that joining the CSI will bring negative effects to export ports such as lower efficiency. However, there is little evidence to support this argument.

S4.6—CSI bilateral system of information exchange requires a host country to offer to conduct a security check on containers shipping to a US port. In return, the host country can send its officers to any US port to target ocean-going containerised cargo being exported to their country. Under this system, there can be sensitive information exchange, according to the US government, which may be deemed necessary to ensure safety of any ports involved. However, the host countries are not willing to offer any confidential information.

This statement aims at testing expert opinions on sensitive information exchange involved within CSI. It is specifically designed for experts with industrial background such as the port management team or terminal operators since they are more concerned about their business confidentiality. The CSI programme aims at fostering a collaborative working relationship with the participating foreign authorities. Donner and Kruk (2009) commented that this collaborative work is vital which deals with increased risk, heightened threat levels and re-establishment of commerce flow in the event of a terrorist attack. However, this network involves confidential business information that port operators and users are not willing to offer.

Conceptual Assumption 5: The introduction of the CSI does not cause small ports to lose market share. EU container port market competition is not disrupted by the CSI introduction.

S5—There are many ports in Europe. However, there are 'only' about 130 seaports handling containers of which around 40 accommodate intercontinental container services. About 70% of the total container throughput in the EU port system passes through the top 17 load centres. Fourteen of those have joined the CSI programme. In the short term, small container ports have to stop their US-inbound business and large EU container ports will gain new market share. In the long run, with further CSI implementation, the EU host countries will absorb the extra cost through transferring them to customers. However, the distortion in the competitiveness of large EU container ports will be minor.

This statement aims at testing expert opinion on how CSI implementation would affect EU port competition in the long term. An increasing maritime security level is inevitable, and CSI has increased the level of awareness of stakeholders to enhancing global trade security. The programme is participating in developing a world standard. It adds protection for the primary system of international trade on which the worldwide economy depends. At the early stage of its introduction and implementation, CSI would have certain effects on joining port competitiveness. However, in the long term, it is possible that the situation can be stabilised and minimised.

Q13—Are there any further comments you would like to make on these statements and how do you think the CSI will change EU container port competition? In addition to cost, efficiency and port charges, what other aspect do you think the CSI will/have affected in short/long term?

This question is to encourage experts to express different points of view. It will not be analysed as a single statement. Information obtained from this question will be treated as supplementary opinions to relevant statements.

Outlining Delphi Design and Process

Good practices in the development of the first Delphi round were followed, based on Cottam (2012). This included: the questionnaire length; the ambiguity of the statements, the response format; and having a heterogeneous group of participants. Nevertheless, it is the correlation between the statements and the original research conceptual assumptions that is most important. The correlation is addressed by the following questions: (1) Are the statements applicable and relevant to the implications of maritime security initiatives on EU container port competition? (2) Are the statements completed without requiring additional support to address the issues? (3) Are the statements understandable?

In order to ensure the success of the Delphi study, a pilot test was conducted before the formal survey was sent out. Polit et al. (2001) explained that a pilot study is a small-scale version or trial run when preparing for a major study. Pilot testing was argued by Powell (2003) as optional; nevertheless, its benefits such as testing instructions, clearness of the statements and formatting were stated by Creswell (2014). Further, a pilot survey could also save financial resources. Therefore, a pilot survey that contained an invitation email and round one questionnaire was sent to six current active senior academic experts in related fields who did not take part in the main study. In terms of this specific pilot survey, the following measures were conducted:

- The participants were asked for feedback to identify ambiguities and difficult questions.
- The time taken to complete round one questionnaire was recorded.
- Whether each question was answered adequately was assessed.
- It was established that replies could be interpreted regarding the information that was required.

Based on the results of the pilot survey and the recommendations of participants, the survey was changed. The implementation of the pilot survey is discussed in Chapter 6.

After the Delphi statement formation and pilot testing, the next step was to distribute round one of the questionnaire to participants by emails, to be completed on the Delphi 'Qualtrics' site. On return of the questionnaire, the results were then analysed based on the research paradigm. Statements failing to reach consensus (measured by Average Percentage of Majority Opinion) entered into the second round.

Based on the Delphi process illustrated in Fig. 5.2, and after Delphi round one analysis, the next step was to form questions for Delphi round two. The round two questionnaire was developed on the basis of round one responses. Rowe and Wright (2011) mentioned that the researcher may direct the focus of the research, or be directed by the participants' opinions. Regarding this Delphi, expert opinions on maritime security and the CSI were analysed and where appropriate used in Delphi round two.

The round two questionnaire was then sent out and returned for analysis. Statements not reaching consensus were included in Delphi round three.

In a similar way to the second round Delphi statement formation, developing the round three questionnaire required the researcher to have an understanding of the research boundaries and where the results could be extended (Neuman 2011; Okoli and Pawlowski 2004). The questions became more focused and specific as the iterations continued (Aligica and Herritt 2009). As the rounds progressed, controversial viewpoints were collected and analysed, namely in the fields of: maritime security measure implementation and impacts, the effects of the CSI on EU container seaport competition and distortion on EU container port competition in the short run and long run.

The next step was to analyse final round results, following a similar process used to analyse the data in first and second round. The participants were also given the opportunity to verify and share their answers with other panel experts. The Delphi iteration ceased when the research question was satisfactorily answered, which meant that consensus was achieved and theoretical stability was reached.

Feedback on questionnaire analysis was provided to participants after the first round. Feedback in a Delphi study is defined by Rowe and Wright (2011, p. 370) as *'the means by which information is passed between panellists so that individual judgement may be improved and debiasing may occur'*. Experts can revise their own judgement in the light of the judgement of the others (van Zolingen and Klaassen 2003). According to von der Gracht (2008), three types of feedback situations can be distinguished. They are: *'feedback in case of numerical estimations; feedback in case of evaluation of developments, succeeding problems, scenarios; and feedback in case of open questions'* (von der Gracht 2008, p. 50). Numerical data are the simplest way to provide feedback. In this case, feedback was provided between the first and second round, providing participants with the percentage of 'agree', 'disagree' and 'unable to comment' under each statement. According to Cottam (2012), the timing of feedback is important too since the quality of the Delphi increases as the time between responding a questionnaire and the next round being sent out shortens. Although it is difficult to control the duration that participants needed to complete the questionnaire, the next round was sent out with feedback within three weeks once all responses were received.

Consensus Level

Consensus is defined as an agreement in opinion of all concerned, or as a major view, and it is one of the most controversial components of the Delphi technique. According to Williams and Webb (1994), Delphi originates from an ancient Greek method for future forecasting. As a long-term forecasting method, the early Delphi surveys used consensus as a stopping criterion. However, consensus is not a straightforward concept. Keeney et al. (2001) suggested that consensus does not indicate the correct answer. Bolger et al. (2011) described consensus as more like the explanation for decreased variance since panel experts could simply alter their estimates to comply with the group without actual opinions changing. Goluchowicz and Blind (2011) found that most changes in response occur in the first two rounds. Cottam (2012) stated that some authors judge consensus from a qualitative angle such as Millar (2001), but an empirical approach is taken in most studies. According to Hanafin (2004, p. 36), consensus can be determined by '*statistically measuring the variance in responses across rounds*'. Rowe and Wright (1999) argued that less variance can be seen as greater consensus, although this interpretation has been controversial. Rowe and Wright (2011) stated that participants with more extreme views were more likely to leave the research than those with relatively moderate views. The decrease in variance can be a result of attrition rather than consensus (Hanafin 2004).

Hussler et al. (2011) noted that stability of results between rounds can be a more appropriate stopping criterion since few changes will be made to the responses after two rounds. Before the second round, it has to be decided which statements from the first round proceed to the second round, and then the same for the second to third round. In terms of this study, consensus was adopted to determine which statements entered into the next round. A further interpretation was applied to statements that still did not reach consensus after three rounds.

Average Percentage of Majority Opinions (APMO)

Aligica and Herritt (2009) argued that in most Delphi studies when a certain percentage of the votes which can be either agreement or disagreement is in a predetermined range, consensus is assumed to have been achieved (Saldanha and Gray 2002). There is no universally agreed guideline to determine when a consensus level is achieved, similar to the panel size and the Delphi rounds. McKenna (1994) recommended 51% agreement among the experts as a consensus. Sumsion (1998) suggested 70% as a consensus level, while 80% agreement is suggested by Green et al. (1999). Von der Gracht (2008) summarised a number of consensus measures, including stipulated number of rounds, subjective analysis, certain level of agreement, APMO cut-off rate, standard deviation and mean, coefficient of variation, Spearman's rank-order correlation coefficient, interquartile range (IQR) and post-group consensus. Among the measures, the APMO equation defined by Kapoor (1987) as a specific consensus measure has been sporadically used in UK Delphi research (von der Gracht 2008). The Delphi studies of Abdel-Fattah

(1997), Kapoor (1987), Saldanha and Gray (2002), Makukha and Gray (2004), Cottam and Roe (2004), and Cottam (2012) are further examples for the employment of APMO rate. APMO produces a cut-off rate to determine if consensus has been achieved. Therefore, to reach consensus level, a statement must achieve a percentage which can be either 'agree' or 'disagree' that is higher than the APMO cut-off rate, otherwise statements have to proceed to the next round until agreement (Kapoor 1987).

$$\text{APMO} = \frac{\text{Majority Agreements} + \text{Majority Disagreements}}{\sum \text{Opinions Expressed}} \tag{5.1}$$

Equation 5.1: APMO cut-off rate for consensus
Source Kapoor (1987)

Cottam (2012) described the APMO equation in detail. Firstly, the number of majority agreements and disagreements needs to be calculated by counting the comments 'agree', 'disagree' and 'unable to comment' in percentages per statement. A comment's majority is reached when its percentage is above 50% (Kapoor 1987). Secondly, the majority agreements and disagreements need to be summed up. These sums are then divided by the total number of opinions expressed (Eq. 5.1). However, different scholars have different ways to interpret this equation. For example, although a majority has been defined as a percentage above 50%, Cottam (2012) took it as above 48%. In the Delphi studies of Makukha and Gray (2004), 50% was accepted as the majority agreement rate. What is more, it is difficult to define the 'total opinions expressed'. In the Delphi studies of Cottam et al. (2004), Cottam (2012), Makukha and Gray (2004), and Saldanha and Gray (2002), 'unable to comment' was excluded from 'total opinions expressed'. Nevertheless, in Briouig (2013), 'total opinions expressed' included the 'unable to comment'. Therefore, it is difficult to be firm in defining each variable in the APMO cut-off rate equation. Here, the majority agreement, majority disagreement and the total opinions expressed for the APMO equation were justified for each round and slightly differed for each round.

Research Ethics

The researcher's topic and methodology should be carefully chosen with ethical considerations. According to Grix (2004), a researcher must be guided by a set of moral principles to conduct the study when the topics involve issues of confidentiality, anonymity, legality, professionalism and privacy. Therefore, the researcher needs to check with any person involved in the research if they agree to participate in the first place and instruct them in the data collection and analysis approach.

The choice of a Delphi technique is believed to be an ethical approach. First of all, compared to other group methods, Delphi stipulates and facilitates the engagement of more expertise in relevant fields. It provides each participant with an equal opportunity to have their opinions taken into account to give a fairer representation of the viewpoints than focus groups. Secondly, careful attention was given to ethical issues including consent, privacy and confidentiality of data at the beginning of each Delphi round and ensure the participants gave informed consent throughout the process. The four main criteria for 'expert' were the only basis when choosing the participants. Hence, the potential for harm in this research is relatively low.

Participants were informed about the research purpose, the procedures, the anticipated time commitment and contact details of the researcher. Their privacy was protected in every possible way. The participants' information was confidential, and they remained anonymous throughout the research. The core of anonymity is that '*information provided by participants should in no way reveal their identity*' (Hanafin 2004, p. 43), and such anonymity is ensured by the Delphi technique. The survey feedback showed no link between the names or positions of participants and their responses. This Delphi study also paid careful attention to ensure confidentiality since anonymity is one key feature of Delphi. Any primary data collected including its sources were and will remain confidential unless participants agreed to their disclosure.

We can now move on to the application of the Delphi process to maritime safety initiatives in the US/EU container market.

References

Abdel-Fattah, N. (1997). *Privatisation of the Road Freight Industry in Egypt and Hungary* (PhD thesis). University of Plymouth, UK.

Acosta, M., Coronado, D., & Cerban, M. M. (2007). Port competitiveness in container traffic from an internal point of view: The experience of the Port of Algeciras Bay. *Maritime Policy and Management, 34*(5), 501–520.

Akkermans, H. A., Bogerd, P., Yucesan, E., & van Wassenhove, L. N. (2003). The impact of ERP on supply chain management: Exploratory findings from a European Delphi study. *European Journal of Operational Research, 146*(2), 284–301.

Aligica, P. D., & Herritt, R. (2009). Epistemology, social technology, and expert judgement: Olaf Helmer's contribution to future research. *Futures, 41*(5), 253–259.

Allen, N. H. (2006). The container security initiative costs, implications and relevance to developing countries. *Public Administration and Development, 26*(5), 439–447.

Aronietis, R., Van de Voorde, E., & Vanelslander, T. (2010). *Port Competitiveness Determinants of Selected European Ports in The Containerised Cargo Market.* International Association of Maritime Economists Conference IAME (Vol. 10). Lisbon, Portugal.

Banomyong, R. (2005). The impact of port and trade security initiatives on maritime supply chain management. *Maritime Policy and Management, 32*(1), 3–13.

Barbour, R. (2007). *Doing Focus Groups.* London: Sage.

Beech, B. F. (1997). Studying the future: A Delphi survey of how multi-disciplinary clinical staff view the likely development of two community mental health centres over the course of the next two years. *Journal of Advanced Nursing, 25,* 331–338.

Bennett, A. C., & Chin, Y. Z. (2008). *100% Container Scanning: Security Policy Implications for Global Supply Chains* (Master of Science Dissertation). Massachusetts Institute of Technology.

Berg, B. (1995). *Qualitative Research Methods for the Social Sciences.* London: Allyn and Bacon.

Bichou, K. (2005). *Maritime Security: Framework, Methods and Applications* (Report to UNCTAD). Geneva: UNCTAD.

Bichou, K. (2008a). *Security and Risk-Based Models in Shipping and Ports: Review and Critical Analysis*, in ITF. Terrorism and International Transport: Towards Risk-based Security Policy. Paris: OECD Publishing.

Bichou, K. (2008b). Security of ships and shipping operations. In Talley, W. (Ed.), *Ship Piracy and Security* (pp. 73–88). London: Informa.

Bichou, K. (2011). Assessing the impact of procedural security on container port efficiency. *Maritime Economics and Logistics, 13*(1), 1–28.

Bird, J., & Bland, G. (1988). Freight forwarders speak: The perception of route competition via seaports in the European Communities Research Project. Part 1. *Maritime Policy and Management, 15*(1), 35–55.

Bleicher, J. (2011). *Scenario Methods as a Means for Enhancing Organisational Learning: A Delphi Study* (Proquest, Umi Dissertation Publishing).

Bolger, F., Stranieri, A., Wright, G., & Yearwood, J. (2011). Does the Delphi process lead to increased accuracy in group-based judgmental forecasts or does it simply induce consensus amongst judgmental forecasters? *Technological Forecasting and Social Change, 78*(9), 1671–1680.

Brett, V., & Roe, M. (2010). The potential for the clustering of the maritime transport sector in the Greater Dublin Region. *Maritime Policy and Management, 37*(1), 1–16.

Briouig, M. (2013). *Risk Management in Liquefied Natural Gas Ports and Marine Terminals Supply Chains* (PhD thesis). Plymouth University, UK.

Brooks, M. (1985). An alternative theoretical approach to the evaluation of liner shipping—Part 2: Choice criteria. *Maritime Policy and Management, 12*(2), 145–155.

Bryman, A. (2012). *Social Research Methods*. Buckingham: Open University Press.

Campbell, S., Cantrill, J., & Roberts, D. (2000). Prescribing indicators for UK general practice: Delphi consultation study. *British Medical Journal, 321,* 425–428.

Campbell, S. M., Shield, T., Rogers, A., & Gask, L. (2004). How do stakeholder groups vary in a Delphi technique about primary mental health care and what factors influence their ratings? *QualSaf Health Care, 13*(6), 428–434.

CBP. (2006). *Container Security Initiative: Strategic Plan 2006–2011*. Available at http://www.cbp.gov/linkhandler/cgov/trade/cargo_security/csi/csi_strategic_plan.ctt/csi_strategic_plan.pdf. Accessed 30 July 2013.

CBP. (2011). *Container Security Initiatives in Summary*. Available at https://www.cbp.gov/sites/default/files/documents/csi_brochure_2011_3.pdf. Accessed 7 August 2016.

CBP. (2014). *CSI: Container Security Initiatives*. Available at https://www.cbp.gov/border-security/ports-entry/cargo-security/csi/csi-brief. Accessed 27 August 2016.

Clayton, M. J. (1997). Delphi: A technique to harness expert opinion for critical decision-making tasks in education. *Educational Psychology: An International Journal of Experimental Educational Psychology, 17*(4), 373–386.

Cooper, J. C. (1994). *Logistics Futures in Europe—A Delphi Study*. Centre for Logistics and Transportation, Cranfield University, UK.

Cottam, H. (2012). *An Analysis of Eastern European Liner Shipping During the Period of Transition* (PhD thesis). Plymouth University, UK.

Cottam, H., & Roe, M. (2004). The impact of transitional changes on maritime transport in Central and Eastern Europe. *Maritime Policy and Management, 31*(4), 287–308.

Cottam, H., Roe, M., & Challacombe, J. (2004, January). Outsourcing of trucking activities by relief organisations. *Journal of Humanitarian Assistance*, 1–26.

Creswell, J. W. (2014). *Research Design Qualitative, Quantitative, and Mixed Methods Approaches*. London: Sage.

Crisp, J., Pelletier, D., Duffield, C., Adams, A., & Nagy, S. (1997). The Delphi method? *Nursing Research, 46*(2), 116–118.

Cullinane, K., Song, D. W., & Gray, R. (2002). A stochastic frontier model of the efficiency of major container terminals in Asia: Assessing the influence of administrative and ownership structures. *Transportation Research Part A, 36,* 743–762.

Cullinane, K., Wang, T., Song, D., & Ji, P. (2005). The technical efficiency of container ports: Comparing data envelopment analysis and stochastic frontier analysis. *Transportation Research Part A, 40*(4), 354–374.

Dalkey, N., & Helmer, O. (1963). An experimental application of the Delphi method to the use of experts. *Management Science, 9*(3), 458–467.

Dalkey, N. C., Rourke, D. L., Lewis, R., & Snyder, D. (1972). *Studies in the Quality of Life*. Lexington, MA: Lexington Books.

Dallimore, C. (2008). *Securing the Supply Chain: Does the Container Security Initiative Comply with WTO Law?* (Dissertation). University of Muenster.

Available at https://www.wwu-customs.de/fileadmin/downloads/pdfs/diss_dallimore.PDF. Accessed 30 January 2016.

Davidson, P., Merritt-Gray, M., Buchanan, J., & Noel, J. (1997). Voices from practice: Mental health nurses identify research priorities. *Archives of Psychiatric Nursing, XI*(6), 340–345.

Day, J., & Bobeva, M. (2005). A generic toolkit for the successful management of Delphi studies. *The Electronic Journal of Business Research Methodology, 3*(2), 103–116.

De Langen, P. W. (2007). Port competition and selection in contestable hinterlands: The case of Austria. *European Journal of Transport and Infrastructure Research, 7*(1), 1–14.

De Martino, M., & Morvillo, A. (2008). Activities, resources and inter-organisational relationships: Key factors in port competitiveness. *Maritime Policy and Management, 35*(6), 571–589.

De Meyrick, J. (2003). The Delphi method and health research. *Health Education, 103,* 7–16.

Dekker, S., & Stevens, H. (2007). Maritime security in the European Union-empirical findings on financial implications for port facilities. *Maritime Policy and Management, 34*(5), 458–499.

Delbecq, A. L., Van de Ven, A. H., & Gustafson, D. H. (1975). *Group Techniques for Program Planning: A Guide to Nominal Group and Delphi Processes.* Glenview, IL: Scott, Foresman.

Denzin, N. K., & Lincoln, Y. S. (2011). *The Sage Handbook of Qualitative Research.* London: Sage.

Dinwoodie, J., Tuck, S., & Rigot-Müller, P. (2013). Maritime oil freight flows to 2050: Delphi perceptions of maritime specialists. *Energy Policy, 63*(3), 553–561.

Dinwoodie, J., Landamore, M., & Rigot-Muller, P. (2014). Dry bulk shipping flows to 2050: Delphi perceptions of early career specialists. *Technological Forecasting and Social Change, 88,* 64–75.

Donner, M., & Kruk, C. (2009). *Supply Chain Security Guide.* The World Bank/DFID, 1, pp. 1–107. Available at http://siteresources.worldbank.org/INTPRAL/Resources/SCS_Guide_Final.pdf. Accessed 20 April 2016.

Elgarhy, A. M. (2016). *An Analysis of Policy Making for Dry Port Location Capacity: A Case Study on Alexandria* (PhD thesis). University of Plymouth, UK.

Flick, U. (2009). *Managing Quality in Qualitative Research.* London: Sage.

Fowles, J. (1978). *Handbook of Futures Research*. Westport, CO: Greenwood Press.

Frankel, E. G. (1992). Hierarchical logic in shipping policy and decision-making. *Maritime Policy and Management, 19*(3), 211–221.

Geist, M. R. (2010). Using the Delphi method to engage stakeholders: A comparison of two studies. *Evaluation and Programme Planning, 33*(2), 147–154.

Gibbs, G. (2008). *Analysing Qualitative Data (Qualitative Research Kit)*. London: Sage.

Gnatzy, T., Warth, J., der Gracht, Von, & Darkow, I.-L. (2011). Validating an innovative real-time Delphi approach—A methodological comparison between real-time and conventional Delphi studies. *Technological Forecasting and Social Change, 78*(9), 1681–1694.

Goluchowicz, K., & Blind, K. (2011). Identification of future fields of standardisation: An explorative application of the Delphi methodology. *Technological Forecasting and Social Change, 78*(9), 1526–1541.

Goodman, C. M. (1987). The Delphi technique: A critique. *Journal of Advanced Nursing, 12,* 729–734.

Greatorex, J., & Dexter, T. (2000). An accessible analytical approach for investigating what happens between the rounds of a Delphi study. *Journal of Advanced Nursing, 32*(4), 1016–1024.

Green, B., Jones, M., & Hughes, D. (1999). Applying the Delphi technique in a study of GPs information requirement. *Health and Social Care in the Community, 7*(3), 198–205.

Grix, J. (2004). *The Foundations of Research*. London: Palgrave Macmillan.

Grosso, M., & Monteiro, F. (2008). *Relevant Strategic Criteria When Choosing a Container Port—The Case of the Port of Genoa*. European Transport Conference 2008.

Gupta, U. G., & Clarke, R. E. (1996). Theory and applications of the Delphi technique: A bibliography (1975–1994). *Technological Forecasting and Social Change, 53*(2), 185–211.

Guy, E., & Urli, B. (2006). Port selection and multi criteria analysis: An application to Montreal-New York alternative. *Maritime Economic and Logistics, 8*(2), 169–186.

Ha, M. S. (2003). A comparison of service quality at major container ports: Implications for Korean ports. *Journal of Transport Geography, 11,* 131–137.

Haezendonck, E., & Notteboom, T. (2002). The competitive advantage of seaports. In M. Huybrechts, et al. (Eds.), *Port Competitiveness: An Economic and Legal Analysis of the Factors Determining the Competitiveness of Seaports* (pp. 67–87). De Boeck: Antwerp.

Hanafin, S. (2004). *Review of Literature on the Delphi Technique.* Available at https://www.dcya.gov.ie/documents/publications/Delphi_Technique_A_Literature_Review.pdf. Accessed 26 April 2018.

Hannes, K., & Lockwood, C. (2012). *Synthesizing Qualitative Research: Choosing the Right Approach* (Vol. 1). London: Wiley-Blackwell.

Hasson, F., Keeney, S., & Mckenna, H. (2000). Research guidelines for the Delphi survey technique. *Journal of Advanced Nursing, 32*(4), 1008–1015.

Hsu, C. C., & Sandford, B. A. (2007). The Delphi technique: Making sense of consensus. *Practical Assessment Research and Evaluation, 12*(10), 2.

Hussler, C., Muller, P., & Ronde, P. (2011). Is diversity in Delphi panellist groups useful? Evidence from a French forecasting exercise on the future of nuclear energy. *Technological Forecasting and Social Change, 78*(9), 1642–1653.

Iqbal, S., & Pipon-Young, L. (2009). The Delphi method. *Psychologist, 22*(7), 598–601.

Islam, D. M. Z., Dinwoodie, J., & Roe, M. (2006). Promoting development through multimodal freight transport in Bangladesh. *Transport Reviews, 26*(5), 571–591.

Kapoor, P. (1987). *A Systems Approach to Documentary Maritime Fraud* (PhD thesis). University of Plymouth, UK.

Keeney, S., Hasson, F., & Mckenna, H. P. (2001). A critical review of the Delphi technique as a research methodology for nursing. *International Journal of Nursing Studies, 38,* 195–200.

Kent, P., & Ashar, A. (2001). Port competition regulation: A tool for monitoring for anticompetitive behaviour. *International Journal of Maritime Economics, 3,* 27–51.

Koch, C. (2002). *Testimony Before the House Transportation and Infrastructure Committee.* Available at http://www.house.gov/transportation/cgmt/03-13-02/koch.html. Accessed 13 March 2016.

Kumar, S., & Rajan, V. (2002). An analysis of intermodal transport carrier selection criteria for Pacific-Rim imports to New England. *Journal of Transportation Management, 13*(1), 19–27.

Lai, V. S., Wong, B. K., & Cheung, W. (2002). Group decision-making in a multiple criteria environment: A case using the AHP in software selection. *European Journal of Operational Research, 137,* 134–144.

Landeta, J., Barrutia, J., & Lertxundi, A. (2011). Hybrid Delphi: Methodology to facilitate contribution from experts in professional contexts. *Technological Forecasting and Social Change, 78*(9), 1629–1641.

Leachman, R. C. (2008). Port and modal allocation of waterborne containerized imports from Asia to the United States. *Transportation Research Part E, 44*(2), 313–331.

Liimatainen, H., Kallionpää, E., Pöllänen, M., Stenholm, P., Tapio, P., & McKinnon, A. (2014). Decarbonizing road freight in the future—Detailed scenarios of the carbon emissions of Finnish road freight transport in 2030 using a Delphi method approach. *Technological Forecasting and Social Change, 81*(1), 177–191.

Limao, N., & Venables, A. J. (2001). Infrastructure, geographical disadvantage, transport costs and trade. *The World Bank Economic Review, 15*(3), 451–479.

Linstone, H. A., & Turoff, M. (2002). *The Delphi Method: Techniques and Applications.* Available at http://is.njit.edu/pubs/delphibook/delphibook. pdf. Accessed 7 July 2013.

Lirn, T. C., Thanopoulou, H. A., Beynon, M. J., & Beresford, A. K. C. (2004). An application of AHP on transhipment port selection: A global perspective. *Maritime Economics and Logistics, 6*(1), 70–91.

Lloyd's List. (2014). *Top 20 European Ports.* Available at https://www.lloydslist. com/ll/incoming/article431990.ece. Accessed 25 May 2015.

Ludwig, B. (1997). Predicting the future: Have you considered using the Delphi methodology? *Journal of Extension, 35*(5), 1–4.

Machalaba, D. (2001, July 9). US Ports Are Losing the Battle to Keep Up with Overseas Trade. *The Wall Street Journal. 2001.* Available at http:// www.nc.gsu.edu/_ecojxm/7030/notes/articles/w070901.htm. Accessed 2 December 2016.

Makukha, K., & Gray, R. (2004). Logistics partnerships between shippers and logistics service providers: The relevance of strategy. *International Journal of Logistics: Research and Applications, 7*(4), 361–377.

Malchow, M., & Kanafani, A. (2001). A disaggregate analysis of factors influencing port selection. *Maritime Policy and Management, 28*(3), 265–277.

Malchow, M. B., & Kanafani, A. (2004). A disaggregate analysis of port selection. *Transportation Research Part E, 40*, 317–337.

Mangan, J., Lalwani, C., & Gardner, B. (2002). Modelling port/ferry choice in RoRo freight transportation. *International Journal of Transport Management, 1*(1), 15–28.

Martonosi, S. E., Ortiz, D. S., & Willis, H. H. (2005). Evaluating the viability of 100 percent container inspections at America's ports, in Richardson, H. W., Gordon, P., & Moore, J. E. II (Eds.), *The Economic Impacts of Terrorist Attacks*. Cheltenham: Edward Elgar Publishing Ltd.

Mason, K. J., & Alamdari, F. (2007). EU network carriers, low cost carriers and consumer behaviour: A Delphi study of future trends. *Journal of Air Transport Management, 13*(5), 299–310.

McKenna, H. (1994). The Delphi technique: A worthwhile research approach for nursing? *Journal of Advanced Nursing, 19,* 1221–1225.

Meersman, H., Pauwels, T., Van de Voorde, E., & Vanelslander, T. (2008). *The Relation Between Port Competition and Hinterland Connections: The Case of the 'Iron Rhine' and the 'Betuweroute'*, International Forum on Shipping, Ports and Airports (IFSPA 2008)—Trade-Based Global Supply Chain and Transport Logistics Hubs: Trends and Future Development, Hong Kong.

Metaparti, P. (2010). Rhetoric, rationality and reality in post-9/11 maritime security. *Maritime Policy and Management, 37*(7), 723–736.

Millar, G. (2001). The development of indicators for sustainable tourism: Results of a Delphi survey of tourism researchers. *Tourism Management, 22,* 351–362.

Murphy, P. R., & Daley, J. M. (1994). A framework for applying logistical segmentation. *International Journal of Physical Distribution and Logistics Management, 24*(10), 13–19.

Murphy, P. R., Daley, J. M., & Dalenberg, D. R. (1992). Port selection criteria: An application of a transportation research framework. *Logistics and Transportation Review, 28,* 237–255.

Myers, M. D. (2008). *Qualitative Research in Business and Management*. London: Sage.

Neuman, W. L. (2011). *Social Research Methods: Qualitative and Quantitative Approaches*. Boston, MA: Allyn & Baker.

Nir, A., Lin, K., & Liang, G. (2003). Port choice behaviour-from the perspective of the shipper. *Maritime Policy and Management, 30*(2), 165–173.

Notteboom, T. (2012). Dynamics in Port Competition in Europe: Implications for North Italian Ports. *Workshop 'I porti del Nord'-Milan*, 18 April.

Notteboom, T., & Yap, W. Y. (2012). Port competition and competitiveness, in Talley, W. (Ed.), *The Blackwell Companion to Maritime Economics* (pp. 549–570). West Sussex: Wiley-Blackwell.

Nowack, M., Endrikat, J., & Guenther, E. (2011). Review of Delphi-based scenario studies: Quality and design considerations. *Technological Forecasting and Social Change, 78*(9), 1603–1615.

OECD. (2003). *Maritime Transport Committee Security in Maritime Transport: Risk Factors and Economic Impact.* Available at https://www.oecd.org/newsroom/4375896.pdf.

Okoli, C., & Pawlowski, S. D. (2004). The Delphi method as a research tool: An example, design considerations and applications. *Information & Management, 42,* 15–29.

Parente, R., & Anderson-Parente, J. (2011). A case study of long-term Delphi accuracy. *Technological Forecasting and Social Change, 78*(9), 1705–1711.

Parliament of Australia. (2003). *The US Container Security Initiative and Its Implications for Australia.* Available at http://www.aph.gov.au/About_Parliament/Parliamentary_Departments/Parliamentary_Library/Publications_Archive/CIB/cib0203/03cib27.

Parsons, J., Dinwoodie, J., & Roe, M. (2011). Northern opportunities: A strategic review of Canada's Arctic icebreaking services. *Marine Policy, 35*(4), 549–556.

Piecyk, M. I., & McKinnon, A. (2009). *Environmental Impact of Road Freight Transport in 2020: Full Report of a Delphi Survey.* Edinburgh: Heriot-Watt University.

Polit, D. F., Beck, C. T., & Hungler, B. P. (2001). *Essentials of Nursing Research: Methods, Appraisal, and Utilization* (5th ed.). Philadelphia, PA: Lippincott.

Powell, C. (2003). The Delphi technique: Myths and realities. *Journal of Advanced Nursing, 41*(4), 376–382.

Rowe, G., & Wright, G. (2011). The Delphi technique: Past, present and future prospects. *Technological Forecasting and Social Change, 78*(9), 1487–1490.

Rowe, G., Wright, G., & McColl, A. (2005). Judgment change during Delphi-like procedures: The role of majority influence, expertise and confidence. *Technological Forecasting and Social Change, 72,* 377–399.

Rubie-Davies, C. M. (2007). Classroom interactions: Exploring the practices of high and low expectation teachers. *British Journal of Educational Psychology, 77,* 289–306.

Sackman, H. (1975). *Delphi Critique.* Lexington, MA: Lexington Books.

Saldanha, J., & Gray, R. (2002). The potential for British coastal shipping in a multimodal chain. *Maritime Policy and Management, 29*(1), 77–92.

Sanchez, R., Hoffmann, J., Micco, A., Pizzolitto, G., Sguti, M., & Wilmsmeier, G. (2003). Port efficiency and international trade: Port efficiency as a determinant of maritime transport costs. *Maritime Economics and Logistics, 5*, 199–218.

Schuckmann, S. W., Gnatzy, T., Darkow, I., & von der Gracht, H. A. (2012). Analysis of factors influencing the development of transport infrastructure until the year 2030—A Delphi based scenario study. *Technological Forecasting and Social Change, 79*(8), 1373–1387.

Seuring, S., & Müller, M. (2008). From a literature review to a conceptual framework for sustainable supply chain management. *Journal of Cleaner Production, 16*(15), 1699–1710.

Sharkey, S. B., & Sharples, A. (2003). The impact on work-related stress of mental health teams following team-based learning on clinical risk management. *Journal of Psychiatric and Mental Health Nursing, 10*(1), 73–81.

Shintani, K., Imai, A., Nishimura, E., & Papadimitriou, S. (2007). The container shipping network design problem with empty container repositioning. *Transportation Research Part E, 43*(1), 39–59.

Silverman, D. (2011). *Interpreting Qualitative Research*. London: Sage.

Sindi, S. H. O. (2016). *Development of a Multi-Dimensional Matrix for Supply Chain Management* (PhD thesis). Plymouth Uiversity, UK.

Slack, B. (1985). Containerisation inter-port competition and port selection. *Maritime Policy and Management, 12*(4), 293–303.

Song, D. W., & Yeo, K.-T. (2004). A competitive analysis of Chinese container ports using the analytic hierarchy process. *Maritime Economics and Logistics, 6*, 34–52.

Sumsion, T. (1998). The Delphi technique: An adaptive research tool. *British Journal of Occupational Therapy, 61*(4), 153–156.

Thai, V. V. (2007). Impacts of security improvements on service quality in maritime transport: An empirical study of Vietnam. *Maritime Economics and Logistics, 9*(4), 335–356.

Tiwari, P., Itoh, H., & Doi, M. (2003). Shippers' port and carrier selection behaviour in China: A discrete choice analysis. *Maritime Economics and Logistics, 5*(1), 23–39.

Tongzon, J. (1995). Determinants of port performance and efficiency. *Transportation Research Part A, 29*(3), 245–252.

Tongzon, J. L. (2009). Port choice and freight forwarders. *Transportation Research Part E: Logistics and Transportation Review, 45*(1), 186–195.

Tongzon, J., & Heng, W. (2005). Port privatisation, efficiency and competitiveness: Some empirical evidence from container ports (terminals). *Transportation Research Part A, 39*(5), 405–424.

Tongzon, J. L., & Sawant, L. (2007). Port choice in a competitive environment: From the shipping lines' perspective. *Applied Economics, 39,* 477–492.

Turoff, M., & Hiltz, S. R. (1996). Computer based Delphi processes. In M. Adler & E. Ziglio (Eds.), *Gazing into the Oracle: The Delphi and Its Application to Social Policy and Public Health.* London: Jessica Kingsley.

Tzeng, G., Teng, M., Chen, J., & Opricovic, S. (2002). Multicriteria selection for a restaurant location in Taipei. *International Journal of Hospitality Management, 21,* 171–187.

Ugboma, C., Ugboma, O., & Ogwude, I. C. (2006). An Analytic Hierarchy Process (AHP) approach to port selection decisions—Empirical evidence from Nigerian ports. *Maritime Economics and Logistics, 8*(3), 251–266.

UNCTAD. (2003, February 24–28). *Report on the Expert Meeting on Efficient Transport and Trade Facilitation to Improve Participation by Developing Countries in International Trade: Problems and Potential for the Application of Current Trade Facilitation Measures by Developing Countries.* Trade and Development Board. Commission on Enterprise, Business Facilitation and Development Seventh session, Geneva, pp. 2–9.

van Zolingen, S. J., & Klaassen, C. A. (2003). Selection processes in a Delphi study about key qualifications in senior secondary vocational education. *Technological Forecasting and Social Change, 70*(4), 317–340.

Veldman, S., & Buckmann, E. H. (2003). A model on container port competition: An application for the West European container hub-ports. *Maritime Economics and Logistics, 5,* 3–22.

von der Gracht, H. A. (2008). *The Future of Logistics: Scenarios for 2025.* Berlin: Springer Science & Business Media.

Wang, C. C., Wang, Y., Zhang, K., Fang, J., Liu, W., Luo, S., et al. (2003). Reproductive health indicators for China's rural areas. *Social Science and Medicine, 57*(2), 217–225.

Warner, L. (2014). *Using the Delphi Technique to Achieve Consensus: A Tool for Guiding Extension Programmes.* Department of Agricultural Education and Communication, UF/IFAS Extension, AEC521.

Watkins, J. (2011). *Shaping the Future of Northeast Michigan: Utilising the Delphi Method to Inform Planning Scenario Construction.* Milton Keynes, UK: Lightning Source UK Ltd.

Wechsler, W. (1978). *Delphi-Methode, Gestaltung und Potential für betriebliche Prognoseprozesse.* Schriftenreihe Wirtschaftswissenschaftliche Forschung und Entwicklung, München. p. 23.

Wengraf, T. (2004). *Qualitative Research Interviewing: Biographic Narrative and Semi-Structured Methods.* London: Sage.

Whitman, N. (1990). The committee meeting alternative: Using The Delphi technique. *Journal of Nursing Administration, 20*(7), 30–36.

Wiegmans, B. W., Van Der Hoest, A., & Notteboom, T. E. (2008). Port and terminal selection by deep-sea container operators. *Maritime Policy and Management, 35*(6), 517–534.

Williams, P., & Webb, C. (1994). The Delphi technique: A methodological discussion. *Journal of Advanced Nursing, 19,* 180–186.

Yap, W., & Lam, J. (2006a). Competition dynamics between container ports in East Asia. *Transportation Research Part A, 40*(1), 35–51.

Yap, W., & Lam, J. (2006b). A measurement and comparison of cost competitiveness of container ports in South East Asia. *Transportation, 33,* 641–654.

Yeo, G. T. (2007). *Port Competitiveness in North East Asia: An Integrated Fuzzy Approach to Expert Evaluations* (PhD thesis). Plymouth University, UK.

Yeo, G., Pak, J., & Yang, Z. (2013). Analysis of dynamic effects on seaports adopting port security policy. *Transportation Research Part A, 49,* 285–301.

Zeedick, D. (2011). *The Modified Delphi Method to Analyse the Application of Instructional Design Theory to Online Graduate Education* (Proquest, Umi Dissertation Publishing).

6

The Delphi Research Process

The previous chapter confirmed the Delphi technique is a suitable methodology for primary data collection in the analysis of the impacts of the CSI on EU container seaport competition. Various sources have claimed that the US maritime security initiatives have either positive or negative effects on EU container port competitiveness. Based on that, the conceptual model and related assumptions were developed to achieve the research aim and objectives. The conceptual model structured five assumptions that derived a list of statements, which in turn were used to formulate Delphi round one.

This chapter presents the process used to analyse the results from the Delphi survey. It starts with the presentation of the pilot study and then outlines the process of each round of Delphi. The results of the three rounds are presented, including the response rate, the consensus level and formulation of next round statement if one did not reach consensus. For statements that reach consensus level, comments and discussions will be presented in Chapter 7.

© The Author(s) 2019
X. Zhang and M. Roe, *Maritime Container Port Security*,
https://doi.org/10.1007/978-3-030-03825-0_6

Pilot Delphi Study

The necessity and benefits of conducting a pilot study have been discussed in Chapter 5. In order to test the validity, reliability and credibility of the Delphi research, a preliminary pilot Delphi study was undertaken. Baker (1994) suggested that 10–20% of sample size for the actual study is a reasonable number for pilot study participants. The total number of potential participants for the main Delphi study was 83. Therefore, the pilot survey—containing an invitation email and round one questionnaire, was sent to six current active senior academic experts in related fields who were not included in the 83 potential participants for the main study. The participants were identified using the same panel selection procedure as the main survey. The invitation email included a brief introduction of this specific Delphi research and instruction for using the Qualtrics online survey tool. Three weeks were given to participants to finish the pilot study and provide recommendations. The pilot Delphi study was conducted over a four-week period, from June to July 2015 since it contained only one instead of three rounds. Two out of the six pilot study participants sent back their feedback within one week. One more participant finished the survey before the required deadline. Hence, there were three participants in the pilot survey, accounting for 50% of those invited. Based on the procedures suggested by Peat et al. (2002), the following measures were conducted:

- The participants were asked for feedback to identify ambiguities and difficult questions.
- The time taken to complete the round one questionnaire was recorded.
- Assess whether each question was answered adequately.
- Establish that replies could be interpreted regarding the information that is required.

Based on the result of the pilot survey and the recommendations of participants, the layout and the invitation letter of the survey were changed to provide clearer instructions and better user-friendliness. Further, the time limit of each round was increased from three weeks to five in order to achieve a higher response rate.

The Delphi Survey

The Delphi study began in September 2015 and did not complete until mid-May 2016. The study included three rounds of questionnaires, consisting of 12 statements and one open-ended question. An average of five weeks was given to participants to complete each round. The length of time between rounds was designed to be ample to encourage experts to participate. A three-week turnaround time was employed, to maintain momentum, increase accuracy and reduce the occurrence of any changes in the context of the actual research (Goodman 1987).

After the appropriate amendments and corrections based on the pilot study, invitation emails were sent out to the potential 83 participants on 1 September 2015. The email contained an explanatory covering letter which presented the aim and context of the research and explained how panel members were chosen. It provided a survey link, utilising the Qualtrics online survey tool. A clear instruction of how to use Qualtrics was included as well. A Word document that briefly described the research background, methodology and research justification was also attached. The author's contacts were given if further information was needed.

On 15 September 2015, a reminder email was sent to participants who had not completed the survey, addressing the significance of their contribution to the research. The reminder email also included the original copy of the invitation email.

Delphi round one closed October 2015. It took around three weeks to analyse responses and formulate round two statements. The Delphi round two survey was sent out on 1 December 2015. Eight weeks were given to the participants to complete the second round, considering the Christmas break. The Delphi round three survey was sent out on 1 April 2016 and closed in mid-May 2016. All experts who were included in round two finished round three within three weeks as required.

Panel Participation

Of the initial 83 potential participants that were invited to participate in the survey, 17 agreed to participate and completed the first-round survey, 65 did not respond to the invitation email and 1 agreed to participate but did not complete the survey. Table 6.1 presents panel participation rate for Delphi round one.

People fail to respond to a survey due to a variety of reasons. For example, time factors, poor survey design, a lack of interest in the subject, uncomprehensive instructions and inappropriate language use could influence non-participation (Grix 2004; Denzin and Lincoln 2011; Goluchowicz and Blind 2011). However, since a pilot study was conducted before the Delphi was launched, poor design, uncomprehensive instructions and ambiguous language were not the overriding factors for non-participation. The time factor could have an effect on the experts and their response rate (Grix 2004). Many of them are quite busy or the time span of the survey does not fit their schedule. Another major reason is a lack of interest in the subject of study. This research looks at one specific initiative and port operations. Therefore, the participant needs to have expertise in both container port security and EU container port operations. This inevitably leads to a limited number of potential participants.

Table 6.1 Delphi round one panel participation rate

Delphi round one participation rate		
Responses	Participation	Percentage (%)
Participation	17	21
No response	65	78
Participate but did not complete	1	1
Total contacted	83	100

Source The authors

Size and Structure of Panel

There were 17 participants in the first round. The panel was categorised into three categories that were academic, industrial and administrative. Table 6.2 presents the initial size and structure of the panel.

According to Table 6.2, besides academic, industrial and administrative categories, three panel members identified themselves as 'other background'. However, they stated their background as 'government', 'transportation advisor' and 'academic', respectively. Therefore, after the authors modified 'government' as 'administrative' and 'transportation advisor' as 'industrial', Table 6.2 was amended as shown in Table 6.3.

According to Cottam (2012), stakeholders are mutually interdependent among interest groups holding different rights, objectives, expectations and responsibilities. Therefore, they can contribute different perceptions with their experience and knowledge. Academics are people who have rich knowledge in maritime security and port competition. The identification of 'academics' implies that their viewpoints are from their experience in academia and have no personal interests in the port industry or maritime administration. Therefore, their opinions

Table 6.2 Size and structure of panel based on Delphi round one responses

Category	Response	Percentage (%)
Academic	9	53
Industrial	3	18
Administrative	2	12
Other	3	17
Total	17	100

Source The authors

Table 6.3 Adjusted size and structure of panel: Delphi round one

Category	Response	Percentage (%)
Academic	10	56
Industrial	4	25
Administrative	3	19
Total	17	100

Source The authors

will be the most neutral among the three expert groups. The industrial group experts are the stakeholders who have commercial interests in the port industry. Maritime security measures compliance could bring negative impacts on port operations, and the shipping and port industry expressed concern about the negativities. Therefore, the viewpoints from the industrial group are anticipated to be opposed to additional security checks and to speak for their commercial interests. Practical and historical information on maritime security initiative implementation is expected and rich qualitative data can be obtained from their comments. Administrative experts were expected to provide opposite perceptions to the industrial experts. They are the policy-makers and regulatory bodies, and their viewpoints are expected to stress the necessity of implementing security measures. A comprehensive consideration of all three groups' viewpoints and perceptions was necessary to maintain the trustworthiness of this Delphi study.

The first category contributing to the Delphi study was academics and consisted of the largest number of participants, representing 56% of the panel. Among the 83 initial participants, 30 were academics, counting as the largest portion of the total contacts (see Table 5.2). The actual number of participants is 10, which means 20 academic experts did not respond to the survey. This proportion is predictable since academics are commonly associated with and contribute most to the relevant field. As this research is designed to study maritime security measures and port competition, academics who have a personal interest in the subject or know of another who does were contacted first.

The second largest category was industrial, given that the aim of this research was to study the EU container seaport competition, representing 25% of the panel. As Table 5.2 presents, the number of initial industrial experts was 28 and counts as the second largest category of the initial panel. The number of actual participants was 4, which means 24 initial participants failed to complete the survey. According to the literature review and conceptual model, there was only a limited discussion of negative impacts of maritime security management. The lack of empirical research on the negative impacts of maritime security management on port operations emphasised the need for industrial stakeholders such as port/terminal operators, shippers and carriers to contribute their opinions. Stakeholders such as managers and directors from the Top 17 EU container seaports based on the TEU throughput were contacted to join the Delphi panel. What is more, consultants on EU port operations and liner brokers who worked for trans-Atlantic lines were invited to take part as well.

The last category was professionals with administrative background, making up 19% of the panel. Judging from the number of initial and actual participants (see Tables 5.2 and 6.3), 22 administrative experts did not complete the survey. This proportion is not surprising since administrative stakeholders are commonly more conservative in their opinions than academic and industrial stakeholders and is also constrained by their employers. Nevertheless, their knowledge and contribution to this research is undeniable. Administrative professionals influence, determine and supervise the implementation of maritime security regimes. Therefore, they are a good source of knowledge on seaborne trade security and safety, providing a different insight from academics and industrial.

Analysis of Delphi Round One

Analysing the Delphi study serves important purposes. Analysis between each round could provide feedback and allow the identification of when consensus has been reached (Rowe and Wright 1999). Statements which did not reach consensus would enter into re-evaluation. This study employed Average Percentage of Majority Opinions (APMO) as the statistical measure to identify consensus for each Delphi round. According to Cottam et al. (2004) and Von der Gracht (2008), the numbers of majority agreements and disagreements are calculated based on participants comment 'agree', 'disagree' and 'unable to comment' in percentages per statements. A majority was here defined as over 50%. The majority agreements and disagreements need to be summed and then divided by the total number of opinions expressed. Table 6.4 presents the full results from round one and Eq. 6.1 shows the equation and calculation of the APMO.

Table 6.4 APMO cut-off rate for consensus in Delphi round one

Delphi round one, Average Percentage of Majority Opinions (APMO)	
Majority agreements	73
Majority disagreements	8
Total opinions expressed (excl. U.C)	146
APMO	56%
Number of statements reached consensus	5
Number of statements to be formulated into Delphi round two	7

Source The authors

$$\text{APMO} = \frac{\text{Majority Agreements} + \text{Majority Disagreements}}{\sum \text{Opinions Expressed}}$$
$$= \frac{73 + 8}{146} = 56\% \tag{6.1}$$

Equation 6.1: APMO cut-off rate equation and calculation
Source The authors

Table 6.4 and Eq. 6.1 illustrate the process of calculation of APMO cut-off rates. As they show, 56% is the APMO rate that will be used in the first-round Delphi analysis. In other words, if the percentage of either 'agreement' or 'disagreement' for each statement is greater than 56%, consensus is reached. Table 6.5 illustrates the rate of 'agreement', 'disagreement' and 'unable to comment' for Delphi round one analysis.

Abdel-Fattah (1997) provided a conceptualisation of the various phases used to identify consensus in individual statements from each Delphi round. The process is repeated until an optimal consensus level is achieved and utilised to support all three rounds.

Consensus Reached After Round One

With the result of the AMPO calculation, it can be determined which statements from round one have achieved consensus level. As Table 6.5 demonstrates, five statements—S1.1, S1.2, S2.1, S2.2 and S4.3—achieved a percentage of agreement over 56%, and therefore reached consensus. The panellists' comments will be discussed in Section

Table 6.5 Delphi round one analysis

Conceptual category	Statement no.	Agreed No.	Agreed %	Disagreed No.	Disagreed %	U.C No.	U.C %	Total opinion expressed (excl. U.C)	Consensus	
The necessity of pursuing maritime security initiative	1.1	10	58.8	3	17.6	4	23.5	13	Yes	Agreed with 58.8%
	1.2	11	64.7	2	11.8	4	23.5	13	Yes	Agreed with 64.7%
Introduction of the CSI and its controversial influences	2.1	15	88.2	0	0	2	11.8	15	Yes	Agreed with 88.2%
	2.2	10	58.8	1	5.9	6	35.3	11	Yes	Agreed with 58.8%
Determinants of EU container seaport competitiveness	3	9	52.9	7	41.2	1	5.9	16	No	
The implication of the CSI for EU container seaport competition	4.1	5	29.4	4	23.5	8	47.1	9	No	
	4.2	7	41.2	6	35.3	4	23.5	13	No	
	4.3	10	58.8	3	17.6	4	23.5	13	Yes	Agreed with 58.8%
	4.4	4	23.5	7	41.2	6	35.3	11	No	
	4.5	4	23.5	8	47.1	5	29.4	12	No	
	4.6	5	29.4	4	23.5	8	47.1	9	No	
	5	8	47.1	3	17.6	6	35.3	11	No	
Majority agreed/disagreed		73		8				146		

U.C = Unable to comment
Source The authors

'Delphi Round One: Statements Reaching Consensus Level and Comments' in Chapter 7.

Reformulation of Statements for Delphi Round Two

The statements that did not reach consensus from Delphi round one were reformulated based on panel comments and included in round two. Based on the first-round result, there were seven statements which were agreed at less than 56%. Therefore, those statements were brought into the second round. The Delphi statements inevitably become more focused and specific to the research aim and objectives as each round comes to pass. The original Delphi round one statements and the reformulated statements entered into round two are specified in the following sections.

S3 Original Statement

The port environment generally has become increasingly competitive; it varies between regions and places depending on the extent to which these forces have impacted upon the nature of the port environment. According to prior studies, the components of port competitiveness are: port location, port facilities, overall efficiency, hinterland networks, value-added logistics; and port services, safety handling of cargoes, confidence in port schedules, simplification of procedures, operational transparency, and port labour and skills. Among these factors, for the EU ports, since port location is static, port efficiency, service and cost related elements are still the most important competitiveness components. Port safety and security are not an incentive for port selection.

Reformulated Statement

The port environment generally has become increasingly competitive; it varies between regions and places. Ports and terminals no longer enjoy de facto monopolies. Ports need to compete for individual hinterlands and terminals need to compete with other operators within a port. According to prior studies, the components of port competitiveness are: port location, port facilities, overall efficiency, hinterland networks, value-added logistics; and port services, safe handling of cargoes, confidence in port schedules, simplification of procedures, operational transparency, and port labour and skills. Among these factors, for EU ports, carriers will use a multitude of tangible criteria such as port efficiency, and cost related elements which are still the most important competitiveness components. Port safety and security are considered as intangible criteria. These criteria are also important and ports/terminals as an absolute minimum need to match industry standards and best practices.

Arguments

This statement achieved 53% agreement which is lower than the APMO rate. Historically, ports and terminals enjoyed de facto monopolies, and there was little competition among them. However, at present and in the future, the reality is that several ports compete for individual hinterlands and within one port several terminals exist. As a result, ports and terminals need to adapt to this environment and those which fail to do so will suffer profit losses and ultimately exit the industry. Most panel members, if not all, agreed that efficiency and price are still the most important components of port competitiveness. They stated that carriers use a multitude of tangible criteria which are related to the total cost of ownership to select the best ports and terminals for their networks. All costs including direct and indirect cost will be considered. Moreover, numerous intangible criteria such as port security and safety are becoming more evident, along with '*ease of doing business*'. Therefore, port security and safety are also important factors in port selection.

S4.1 Original Statement

To obtain the minimum required level of compliance, ports need to implement technical and organisational measures that will bring additional costs to maritime industries. Enhancing the technical measures due to security regulations, such as the ISPS Code, has brought additional costs to European maritime industries. Smaller ports in the EU may stop their US-inbound business since they cannot bear the financial costs. Larger ports may 'steal' new business from smaller ports which are financially strained to meet the scanning requirements. A distortion of EU container port market share will arise.

Reformulated Statement

To obtain the minimum required level of the ISPS compliance, ports need to implement technical and organisational measures. Theoretically, the additional cost brought by security regulations would affect EU container ports, making some small EU ports lose business. Nevertheless, the constraint of handling ever larger container ships efficiently is the major reason. The influence of additional cost is minor and it depends on what level of security the smaller ports are willing to agree to. Moreover, European consumers are contributing to the costs since ports/terminals pass them onto shippers/forwarders/3PLs and ultimately to retailers and then end consumers. Larger ports may gain new business from smaller ports. A distortion of EU container port market share will arise. Nevertheless, the positive effect of increasing worldwide maritime security overcomes the negative distortion.

Arguments

Smaller ports are far more likely to lose business due to not being able to handle mega container ships efficiently rather than ISPS compliance. Additionally, the USA is not the main business for the smaller container ports. Therefore, based on the panellists, the market share changes are not serious. The compliance costs from ports and terminals are levied to line/carriers who in turn pass them onto shippers, forwarders and 3PLs and ultimately to retailers and then end consumers. Moreover, this has created a new revenue stream for ports and terminal operators. A few more cents/pence per consumer pays can create a better and safer maritime environment. Therefore, the positive effects of spending extra compliance costs outweigh the negative market share changes.

S4.2 Original Statement

While port security measures enhance port security, procedural requirements of the new security regime act against operational and logistical efficiency. The proponents of this view list a number of operational inefficiencies ranging from direct functional redundancies such as additional inspections and lengthy procedures to indirect supply chain disruptions stemming from longer lead times and less reliable demand and supply scenarios.

Reformulated Statement

While port security measures enhance port security, procedural requirements of the new security regime act against operational and logistical efficiency. The proponents of this view list a number of operational inefficiencies ranging from direct functional redundancies such as additional inspections and lengthy procedures to indirect supply chain disruptions stemming from longer lead times and less reliable demand and supply scenarios. However, security inspections cannot be repealed. Better administrative processes and better IT tools can help to mitigate inefficiency. Port operations consist of many factors, and efficiency and security are two of them. If a port is efficient, good security will not cause it not to be.

Arguments

Experts who agreed with this statement believed that security procedures bring additional inspections and lengthy procedures. However, opinions against argued that inefficiency always exists in an inefficient port regardless of what kind of operations there are. Port operations consist of many factors and security is one of them. A better use of

IT tools and administrative processes could facilitate the security procedure. The supply chain and logistics process can be managed and disruptions can be mitigated through process enhancement.

S4.4 Original Statement

Although the US Customs and Border Protection stated that the CSI can bring benefits to member ports, those benefits are still controversial. The CSI has negative effects on port profit. In addition to the significant initial investment in new equipment, the CSI makes cargo inspection process more complicated, creating an increase in cargo processing time and cargo processing cost. That can change important performance characteristics of the port such as the port efficiency and price. From the perspective of a long-term economic model, these consequences produce the negative impacts on relative attractiveness of ports for various stakeholders, namely exporters and cargo carriers. The reduced attractiveness will decrease the competitiveness of a port. Moreover, the deepening cost and time may initiate a vicious circle of decreasing port competitiveness. The CSI is actually a heavy burden for those ports that have joined.

Reformulated Statements

Although the US Customs and Border Protection stated that the CSI can bring benefits to member ports, those benefits are still controversial. This programme transfers the container examinations from unloading ports in the USA to the loading ports overseas. On the other hand, all the checks are carried out in the host countries which bear the equipment cost. Some research claims that CSI creates competitive disadvantages due to additional investment and running cost. However, in reality, all terminal/port investment is surcharged to direct customers, with the costs ultimately being born by the Beneficial Cargo Owners (BCOs). The real burden falls to the BCOs, and ultimately to US importers/retailers and the end consumers. In fact, security regulations compliance such as ISPS has created new revenue streams.

Argument

It was pointed out by panellists that a policy will have its good and bad impacts and its implementation is key to its success. As current security inspection has been improved, there is no evidence to show that the CSI has created a heavy burden for ports which have chosen to join. The levels of compliance to the CSI are very similar among competing ports and terminals that share the same hinterland and foreland. ISPS compliance has created a new revenue stream and therefore ports and terminals levy very similar security surcharges/fees. The extra costs are passed down to the BCOs. Notwithstanding all ports and terminals being vocal about additional costs during the launch of the CSI, no port or terminal claimed that the CSI negatively affected the volume or profitability since they joined.

S4.5 Original Statement

The CSI could improve the capabilities and the overall effectiveness of the targeting process. However, this programme transfers the container examinations from unloading ports in the USA to the loading ports overseas; on the other hand, all the checks are carried out in the host countries which bear the equipment cost. In case of unloading and emptying of any potential threat posed by a dangerous container, the costs are borne by the importer to a US port. The US Customs sacrificed the export ports to save the USA unloading port's time and cost. The CSI is a unilateral and unfair programme without considering the host ports.

Reformulated Statement

The CSI could improve the capabilities and the overall effectiveness of the targeting process. However, this programme transfers the container examinations from unloading ports in the USA to the loading ports overseas. Opponents argue that it would slow down loading port efficiency. However, from a security perspective, the optimum is to intercept suspect containers as early as possible in the logistics chain. Moreover, the CSI is merely a documentation process in which terminals and ports are not directly involved. Very few containers experience a physical inspection. The process is driven by pre-shipment submission of cargo manifests, from which a few containers require non-obtrusive inspections, and very few of these actual physical inspections.

Arguments

Theoretically, CSI can improve the overall effectiveness of port operations. Nevertheless, arguments suggested that the CSI is not considered comprehensive and does not display better performance and thus improve port efficiency. Proponents of the CSI considered it a process that ought to be implemented worldwide. For any perceived security threat, scanning and physical inspection will be required. Carrying out the essential inspection at destination has been described as '*closing the gate of the pen after all the sheep have run away*'. From a security perspective, intercepting suspect containers as early as possible is the best solution in the supply chain. Moreover, with the USA having relatively inefficient ports and the highest labour costs, performing inspections at loading ports achieves cost reductions and efficiency improvements for the entire supply chain.

S4.6 Original Statement

CSI bilateral system of information exchange requires a host country to offer to conduct a security check on containers shipping to a US port. In return, the host country can send its officers to any US port to target ocean-going containerised cargo being exported to their country. Under this system, there can be sensitive information exchange, according to the US government, which may be deemed necessary to ensure safety of any ports involved. However, the host countries are not willing to offer any confidential information.

Reformulated Statement

The CSI bilateral system of information exchange requires a host country to conduct a security check on containers shipping to a US port. In return, the host country can send its officers to any US port to target ocean-going containerised cargo being exported to their country. It is somewhat improbable that a security threat to a country originates from the USA, so the reciprocal arrangement does not (today) really add a tangible value to others. Under this system, there can be sensitive information exchange, which is deemed necessary to ensure safety of any ports involved. The USA could cease trading with the export ports if they refuse to provide information. Although the host countries may not be willing to offer any confidential information, most export nations depend upon trade with the USA, so they freely cooperate in varying degrees.

Arguments

The sharing of security information between various countries is not new. There are many global councils such as the UNSC and the WCO, which have existed for many years prior to 9/11. Information sharing adds significant value to the overall supply chain. It is somewhat improbable that a security threat to a country originates from the USA; therefore, the reciprocal arrangement does not really add a tangible value to others. The USA would cease trading with countries that refuse to cooperate, depending upon other circumstances.

S5 Original Statement

There are many ports in Europe. However, there are 'only' about 130 seaports handling containers of which around 40 accommodate intercontinental container services. About 70% of the total container throughput in the EU port system passes through the top 17 load centres. 14 of those have joined the CSI programme. In the short term, small container ports have to stop their US-inbound business and large EU container ports will gain new market share. In the long run, with further CSI implementation, the EU host countries will absorb the extra cost through transferring them to customers. However, the distortion in the competitiveness of large EU container ports will be minor.

Reformulated Statement

There are many ports in Europe. However, there are 'only' about 130 seaports handling containers of which around 40 accommodate intercontinental container services. About 70% of the total container throughput in the EU port system passes through the top 17 load centres. 14 of the top 17 ports have joined the CSI programme. In the short term, small container ports have to stop their US-inbound business and large EU container ports will gain new market share which may be minor. In the long run, with further CSI implementation, the EU host countries will absorb the extra cost through transferring them to customers. However, the distortion among large EU container port competition will be major, which is due primarily to liner network design and costs to the CSI.

Arguments

According to the panellists, the distortion will be major and this has already occurred. As of 15 April 2015, there are 58 ports globally which participate in the CSI. These accounted for 85% of the total inbound US containers shipped. 23 of them are in Europe. Notwithstanding there are several more container ports, many of them are not suited to direct mainline port calls due to their location or scale. Deep-sea lines are instead served through transhipment at one of the 23 main European ports and that is due primarily to liner network design and costs rather than CSI membership or compliance. What is more, the reason why smaller ports lose market share is they lack capacity to handle ever larger container vessels rather than CSI compliance. If smaller ports' main business is not with the USA, the impact of security measures will not be substantial.

Administration of Delphi Round Two

Delphi round two began on 1 December 2015. Seventeen participants who completed Delphi round one received an invitation email to ask them to take part in Delphi round two. The email acknowledged their contribution and an appreciation of their time in Delphi round one. It also contained an explanatory covering letter which presented the aim and context for the research and explained how they were chosen as panel members. It gave a survey link for Delphi round two, utilising the Qualtrics online survey tool. A clear instruction of how to use Qualtrics was included as well. Contact detail was given for further information. Eight weeks were given to the participants to complete the second round considering the Christmas break. Five weeks later, on 5 January 2016, a reminder letter was sent to participants who had not completed their survey, addressing the significance of their contribution to the research. The reminder email also included the original copy of the Delphi round two invitation email.

Response Rate Delphi Round Two

Delphi round two was sent out to 17 panel members based on the first-round responses, and 14 completed the questionnaires, providing an 83% response rate. Table 6.6 shows the size and structure of the participants for the second round Delphi.

Table 6.6   Size and structure of panel participants: Delphi round two

Categories	Response	Percentage (%)
Academic	8	57
Industrial	4	29
Administrative	2	14
Total	14	100

Source The authors

Analysis of the Responses to Delphi Round Two

As with the first-round analysis, the APMO was calculated based on the responses showed in Table 6.7. The actual APMO cut-off rate for consensus in Delphi round two is illustrated in Eq. 6.2. The full results are presented in Table 6.8.

As with Delphi round one, panel members were from the categories of academic, industrial and administrative. Academics formed the largest category, with 57% of the total participants. Industrial-experts remained second, with 29% of the total number of participants. Experts with administrative background formed the smallest category, with only 14% of the total number of participants. In comparison with Table 6.3, two notable changes occurred. Firstly, the total number of participants decreased from 17 to 14. Secondly, two academics and one administrative participant departed from the study. Nevertheless, the panel structure remained the same as the Delphi round one as it still contained three categories.

$$
\begin{aligned}
\text{APMO} &= \frac{\text{Majority Agreements} + \text{Majority Disagreements}}{\sum \text{Opinions Expressed}} \\
&= \frac{86 + 0}{98} = 87.8\%
\end{aligned}
\tag{6.2}
$$

Equation 6.2: APMO cut-off rate for consensus in Delphi round two
Source The authors

Table 6.7 APMO cut-off rate for consensus in Delphi round two

Delphi round two, Average Percentage of Majority Opinions (APMO)	
Majority agreements	86
Majority disagreements	0
Total opinions expressed	98
APMO	87.8%
Number of statements reached consensus	4
Number of statements to be formulated into Delphi round three	3

Source The authors

Table 6.8 Delphi round two analysis

Conceptual category	Statement no.	Agreed No.	Agreed %	Disagreed No.	Disagreed %	U.C No.	U.C %	Total opinion expressed (incl. U.C)	Consensus
Determinants of EU container seaport competitiveness	3	14	100	0	0	0	0	14	Yes Agreed with 100%
The implications of the CSI for EU container seaport competition	4.1	10	71.4	1	7	3	22	14	No
	4.2	11	78.6	0	0	3	21.4	14	No
	4.4	13	92.8	0	0	1	7.2	14	Yes Agreed with 92.8%
	4.5	13	92.8	1	7.2	0	0	14	Yes Agreed with 92.8%
	4.6	14	100	0	0	0	0	14	Yes Agreed with 100%
	5	11	78.6	0	0	3	21.4	14	No
	Majority agreed/disagreed	86		0				98	

Source The authors

Table 6.7 and Eq. 6.2 illustrate the process of calculation for APMO cut-off rate for round two. The calculation differs from round one APMO since it has been adjusted for the second round. As discussed in Chapter 5, there is no unified way to calculate the APMO cut-off rate. Therefore, the formula was adjusted for each round. Since the participants decreased to 14 people, the effect of one expert's opinion is more influential on the final results. One subjective and biased comment could lead to a less inclusive and comprehensive conclusion. Hence, 'unable to comment' was considered in the equation to lower the effect of a biased opinion by increasing the denominator of the APMO equation, which made 'the total opinions expressed' in the second round 98. As Eq. 6.2 shows, 87.8% was the APMO rate that was used in the analysis of the second Delphi round. In other words, if the percentage of either 'agreement' or 'disagreement' for each statement is greater than 87.8%, consensus was reached. Among the seven statements entered into second round, four statements reached 87.8%; therefore, three statements were reformulated into Delphi round three.

Consensus Reached After Delphi Round Two

The results of Eq. 6.2 determined which of the statements from Delphi round two achieved consensus. Four statements—S3, S4.4, S4.5, S4.6—reached a percentage of agreement that was higher than 87.8%, and therefore consensus. Each of the statements will be discussed in Section 'Delphi Round Two: Statements Reaching Consensus Level and Comments' in Chapter 7, making use of the comments made by panellists.

Reformulation of Statements for Delphi Round Three

The statements that did not reach consensus after the second round were reformulated and entered into the third round of Delphi. The reformulated statements were based on the comments made by panellists in round two; therefore, they attempted to reflect panellists' viewpoints. There are three statements which failed to reach consensus. As a result, they were reformulated. The original statements in round two and the reformulated statements for round three are specified in the following sub-sections, based on arguments made by panellists in accordance with the research objectives set out in Chapter 1.

S4.1 Original Statement

To obtain the minimum required level of ISPS compliance, ports need to implement technical and organisational measures. Theoretically, the additional cost brought by security regulations would affect EU container ports, making some small EU ports lose business. Nevertheless, the constraint of handling ever larger container ships effectively is the major reason behind that. The influence of additional cost is minor and it depends on what level of security that the smaller ports are willing to sustain. Moreover, European consumers are contributing to the costs since port/terminals pass them onto shippers/forwarders/3PLs and ultimately to retailers and then consumers. Larger ports may gain new business from smaller ports. A distortion of EU container port market share will arise. However, the positive effect of increasing worldwide maritime security overcomes the negative distortion.

Arguments

This statement was agreed at 71.4% by panellists. Gateway hinterland cargoes are usually exported by only a few ports or terminals. They compete in this business through price and efficiency advantage. The ISPS merely required that all ports and terminals have secure perimeters and access controls. The cost for any infrastructure and superstructure required to meet the minimum standards has been overestimated. The actual incurred costs are low and have been recovered in full through the Container Security Fees which are usually less than US 10 cents per container shipped. The cost of security is extremely minor in the overall scheme of the supply chain. On the other hand, small container ports lose their business largely due to their insufficient capacity of handling mega ships. Therefore, ISPS compliance would not cause financial problems for EU container ports and terminals.

Reformulated Statement

The distortion of the EU container port market is largely caused by mega container ships. Ports and terminals do not bear a financial burden for ISPS compliance. The compliance cost can be overlooked as it is minor in the overall supply chain. Instead, port and terminals create a new revenue stream by charging the Container Security Fees.

S4.2 Original Statement

While port security measures enhance port security, procedural requirements of the new security regime act against operational and logistical efficiency. The proponents of this view list a number of operational inefficiencies ranging from direct functional redundancies such as additional inspections and lengthy procedures to indirect supply chain disruptions stemming from longer lead times and less reliable demand and supply scenarios. However, security inspections cannot be repealed. Better administrative processes and better IT tools can help to mitigate inefficiency. Port operations consist of many factors, and efficiency and security are two of them. If a port is efficient, good security will not cause it not to be.

Arguments

This statement was agreed at 78.6% by panel members; however, 25% was accounted by 'unable to comment' since some of the panellists were confused by the vagueness of 'good security'. Experts who stood for this statement agreed with the importance of security due to the irreversibility of a security incident. Therefore, each player of the supply chain should always make efforts to ensure the security and safety of the process. It is an inevitable responsibility for ports and terminals regardless of the negative influence caused by extra inspection. Moreover, the disruption of container movement has been exaggerated. In practice, the extra procedure is insignificant compared to the 10–14 days of additional transportation time which might result, for example, from slow steaming.

Reformulated Statement

Safe and secured maritime trade is an extremely important issue in the shipping industry that cannot be overlooked. With better administrative processes and IT tools, the container security inspection process can be facilitated without causing supply chain disruptions. The extra inspection time in export ports is insignificant compared to that of total transportation.

S5 Original Statement

There are many ports in Europe. However, there are 'only' about 130 seaports handling containers of which around 40 accommodate intercontinental container services. About 70% of the total container throughput in the EU port system passes through the top 17 load centres. 14 of the top 17 ports have joined the CSI programme. In the short term, small container ports have to stop their US-inbound business and large EU container ports will gain new market share which may be minor. In the long run, with further CSI implementation, the EU host countries will absorb the extra cost through transferring them to customers. However, the distortion among large EU container port competition will be major, which is due primarily to liner network design and costs not CSI compliance.

Arguments

This statement was agreed at 78.6%. Panel members agreed that a change will occur and bigger EU ports will benefit but not in a distorted way. There is no distortion between the competition of main European ports when it comes to security and safety. Joining the CSI is at the national level rather than the port level. Small ports are not affected since cargo will be inspected in the US if necessary. Furthermore, it was pointed out that there are no more than 40 ports in Europe which handle ships which call direct at US ports. The 24-hour rule only applies to those ports.

Reformulated Statement

CSI compliance will not cause container port market distortion in Europe whether in short term or long term since there has been no evidence to show it causes financial burden or logistics disruption. Small ports will be affected by the changing market arising from liner network design which aims at lowering the overall transportation cost.

Administration of Delphi Round Three

On 20 April, an email with the Delphi round three Qualtrics online link was sent out to the 14 participants who completed Delphi round two. The explanatory email acknowledged an appreciation for their engagement and contribution in Delphi round two. A brief introduction of the aim and objectives of this research was also included to remind participants. Three weeks were given to the participants since there are only three statements. What is more, the participants were asked to comment on the research topic as much as they like because their opinions would be extremely helpful for data analysis. On 27 April, a reminder email including the original copy of the Delphi round three invitation was sent to participants who had not replied, addressing the importance of their individual contribution to the research and the importance of this research to EU container port industry.

Response Rates of Delphi Round Three

Of the 14 panel members who were sent Delphi round two, 14 completed the questionnaire, providing a full response rate of 100%.

Table 6.9 Size and structure of the panel participants: Delphi round three

Categories	Response	Percentage (%)
Academic	8	57
Industrial	4	29
Administrative	2	14
Total	14	100

Source The authors

Table 6.9 presents the size and structure of the panel participant response rates of Delphi round three.

As Table 6.9 shows, all Delphi round two participants responded and completed Delphi round three. In Delphi round three, academics formed the largest category, with 57% of the total participants. Industrial-experts remained in-between, with 29% of the total. Experts with administrative background formed the smallest category, with only 14% of the total number of participants.

Analysis of the Responses to Delphi Round Three

In order to analyse Delphi round three, the APMO cut-off rate needed to be calculated and Table 6.10 illustrates the process. As with Delphi round two, the total opinion expressed included 'unable to comment'. Based on Eq. 6.3, the APMO cut-off rate for Delphi round three is 90.5%. Table 6.11 presents the percentage of Delphi round three responses.

Table 6.10 APMO cut-off rate calculation process for Delphi round three

Delphi round two, Average Percentage of Majority Opinions (APMO)	
Majority agreements	38
Majority disagreements	0
Total opinions expressed	42
APMO	90.5%
Number of statements reached consensus	2
Number of statements failed to reach consensus	1

Source The authors

$$\text{APMO} = \frac{\text{Majority Agreements} + \text{Majority Disagreements}}{\sum \text{Opinions Expressed}}$$

$$= \frac{38 + 0}{42} = 90.5\% \tag{6.3}$$

Equation 6.3: APMO cut-off rate for consensus in Delphi round three
Source The authors

Consensus Reached After Delphi Round Three

The results of Eq. 6.3 indicate that the APMO cut-off rate for Delphi round three is 90.5%. This rate determined which of the statements from Delphi round three reached consensus. Three statements entered into round three and two of them—S4.2, S5—reached a percentage of agreement that was higher than 90.5%, and thus reached consensus. Each of the statements will be discussed in Chapter 7, incorporating the panellists' comments.

Statement Does Not Reach Consensus

S4.1 The distortion of the EU container port market is largely caused by mega container ships rather than additional security procedures. Maritime security initiatives compliance does not bring financial burden on ports and terminals. The compliance cost can be overlooked as it is minor in the overall supply chain. Instead, port and terminals create a new revenue stream by charging Container Security Fees.

This statement was agreed at 78.6% by most of the panel members. However, it failed to reach the 90.5% consensus level. Opponents of this statement believed that both mega ships and maritime security and safety issues have a major impact on the market, and therefore would cause distortion. Panellists who agreed with this statement provided certain evidence. They mentioned that financial burden and supply chain disruptions were the initial concerns when the CSI was introduced.

Table 6.11 Delphi round three analysis

Conceptual category	Statement no.	Agreed		Disagreed		U.C		Total opinion expressed (incl. U.C)	Consensus
		No.	%	No.	%	No.	%		
The implications of the CSI for EU container seaport competition	4.1	11	78.6	1	7.1	2	14.3	14	No
	4.2	14	100	0	0	0	0	14	Yes
									Agreed with 100%
	5	13	92.8	1	7.2	0	0	14	Yes
									Agreed with 92.8%
	Majority agreed/ disagreed	38		0				42	

Source The authors

Nevertheless, based on the current container port industry, at which ports the largest vessels call today, there is no difference to the ports at which ships called 20 years ago. They pointed out that Container Security Fees are common at all ports, ranging from US$10 to 20 per container, and have become an additional revenue stream which far outweighs any costs associated with being the CSI compliant.

We can now move on to the analysis of the Delphi results.

References

Abdel-Fattah, N. (1997). *Privatisation of the Road Freight Industry in Egypt and Hungary* (PhD thesis). University of Plymouth, UK.

Baker, T. L. (1994). *Doing Social Research* (2nd ed.). New York: McGraw-Hill.

Cottam, H. (2012). *An Analysis of Eastern European Liner Shipping During the Period of Transition* (PhD thesis). University of Plymouth, UK.

Cottam, H., Roe, M., & Challacombe, J. (2004). Outsourcing of trucking activities by relief organisations. *Journal of Humanitarian Assistance, 1*(1), 1–26.

Denzin, N. K., & Lincoln, Y. S. (2011). *The SAGE Handbook of Qualitative Research*. London: Sage.

Goluchowicz, K., & Blind, K. (2011). Identification of future fields of standardisation: An explorative application of the Delphi methodology. *Technological Forecasting and Social Change, 78*(9), 1526–1541.

Goodman, C. M. (1987). The Delphi technique: A critique. *Journal of Advanced Nursing, 12,* 729–734.

Grix, J. (2004). *The Foundations of Research*. London: Palgrave Macmillan.

Peat, J., Mellis, C., Williams, K., & Xuan, W. (2002). *Health Science Research: A Handbook of Quantitative Methods*. London: Sage.

Rowe, G., & Wright, G. (1999). The Delphi technique as a forecasting tool: Issues and analysis. *International Journal of Forecasting, 15,* 353–375.

Von der Gracht, H. A. (2008). *The Future of Logistics: Scenarios for 2025*. Berlin: Springer Science+Business Media.

7

The Delphi Results

This chapter presents the discussion of Delphi statements which reached consensus after each round, based on the panellists' comments. The conceptual model presented in Chapter 4 will be revised using the results of the Delphi survey. The conceptual assumptions included in the original model are reviewed in the light of the panel members' opinions and the results of the three rounds.

Delphi Round One: Statements Reaching Consensus Level and Comments

S1.1 Maritime security has become a great concern worldwide. The increasing volume of container movements, their relatively high velocity in the international trade and their uniformity have posed formidable security challenges. As the loading and unloading points of a sea transport process, container ports are the most important nodes for maritime safety. However, only around 2–10% of containers are actually inspected. US ports normally inspect roughly 5% of the 17 million containers arriving at the border every year. A great concern about

© The Author(s) 2019
X. Zhang and M. Roe, *Maritime Container Port Security*,
https://doi.org/10.1007/978-3-030-03825-0_7

container security emerged from this low inspection rate. Container security is far more important than efficiency and profit for the port. Therefore, security should be seen as the first priority.

This statement was agreed at 58.8%. Panel members agreed that most, if not all, container shipping has posed security challenges and the security issue is important. Arguments in support stated that many large seaports are situated close to highly populated urban areas, which makes delivery of weapons of mass destruction in a shipping container a reality and risk that needs to be mitigated. Security and safety of container shipping are definitely the key drivers. Supportive comments also advised that there would always be a need for some physical and manual inspections. Nevertheless, as to the low container inspection rate, some disagreed with comments pointing out that inspecting 100% of containers at destination is not a viable solution since it is too far down the supply chain. The rate of inspection is not necessarily a measure of security. There is no evidence to show that security will increase just because the inspection rate increases. Using data, information and applying intelligence are then key tools and resources to enhance supply chain safety. The major disagree comments focused on the priorities between security and efficiency. For shippers and carriers, they considered efficiency more important than security and port efficiency still sits at the very heart of port operations.

S1.2 As the world's largest national economy, USA plays a vital role in global trade. After 9/11, the USA has reacted to the needs for strengthening security measures to enhance maritime transport safety. Some of the maritime security initiatives have influence on some export ports in terms of logistics efficiency and financing. Nevertheless, those export ports should be prepared to comply with the US container port security initiatives for maritime safety.

This statement was agreed at 65%. All panel members acknowledged the importance for strengthening security measures. Comments stated that after 9/11, tightening of security was naturally a high priority. The USA, as the world's largest national economy, plays a vital role within the global supply chain. Export countries need to follow US rules if they trade with the USA. Security has always been a requirement, however, practised to differing levels of quality between ports.

Nevertheless, panel experts disagreed with the significant disadvantages that security measures could bring to logistics efficiency and financing. Measures such as the ISPS/C-TPAT guidelines/regulations which standardised the approach to security post-9/11 are no more than common-sense solutions. The compromise if any is very insignificant compared to the overall benefits derived from them. They also suggested that the responsibility is not only for the export ports, but also includes shippers, carriers and forwarders among others. Security has to be linked to the entire end-to-end journey in order to be more effective and not only depend on inspection at a specific port.

S2.1 The Container Security Initiative (CSI) programme managed by the US Customs and Border Protection (CBP) is an influential voluntary initiative. The CSI was proposed to ensure all containers that pose a potential risk for terrorism are identified and inspected at foreign ports before they are loaded on to vessels imported to the USA. Without a doubt, the CSI has dramatically increased the level of awareness for the need to secure global trade.

At 88%, almost all the panellists agreed with this statement. The purpose behind this statement was to testify the viewpoints of panel experts on the benefits that the CSI brings to maritime security. It can be concluded that the CSI has increased the awareness of relevant stakeholders to secure global trade.

S2.2 Unlike the 24-hour rule, the CSI is a voluntary initiative. However, in order to keep the market share for US-inbound trade, the major exporters have to join the programme. Not joining the programme could make the exports lose competitiveness over their rivals.

This statement was agreed by 58.8% of panel members. Panellists pointed out that fines will be imposed for containers to the USA without have been properly manifested, thus the US government actually makes the declaration compulsory. However, disagreements stated that the 24-hour rule is a primary aspect of the overall CSI. The 24-hour rule has subsequently been adopted in the EU and China. It requires a manifest completed 24 hours prior to loading. This helps to improve the quality of data used in ship and terminal planning processes facilitated earlier. The whole ocean trade has benefited. However, the voluntary aspect, such as mass scanning is largely unadopted, due to the possible efficiency losses. Therefore currently, most export container ports work in similar ways and there are no commercial or operational competitive advantages of any significance as a direct result of the CSI. Not joining the CSI does not create competitive disadvantages.

S4.3 Productivity could improve due to better procedural arrangements. With the reinforcement of security, there is reduced likelihood of security incidents, a probability of fewer incidents being recorded and higher port reliability. Increased reliability which leads to higher trust between a port and its upstream and downstream partners in a container supply chain, contributes to the reduction of cargo processing time and results in reduction of cargo processing cost. This has a positive effect on port selection, thus attracting more container volume. Consequently, improving security level and increasing port reliability can attract more containers. Compliant participants would benefit from access certification and fast-lane treatment as well as reduced insurance costs and risk exposure.

This statement was agreed at 59%. Panellists agreed most with the contribution of efficient security procedural arrangements. They argued their viewpoints from two aspects. In theory, they agreed that productivity and port reliability can be improved; therefore, more containers will be attracted. However, in practice, the results of additional security processes and requirements are probably more neutral than highly beneficial to the overall supply chain, efficiency, productivity and cost. This may be caused by local authorities and customs that lack business awareness. Moreover, it is more difficult to achieve a better procedural arrangement in practice. As a result, the positive effects on productivity improvement would be less significant than the theoretical benefits claimed.

Delphi Round Two: Statements Reaching Consensus Level and Comments

S3 The port environment generally has become increasingly competitive; it varies between regions and places. Ports and terminals no longer enjoy de facto monopolies. Ports need to compete for individual hinterlands and terminals need to compete with other operators within one port. According to prior studies, the components of port competitiveness are: port location, port facilities, overall efficiency, hinterland networks, value-added logistics and port services, safe handling of cargoes, confidence in port schedules, simplification of procedures, operational transparency, and port labour and skills. Among these factors, for EU ports, carriers will use a multitude of tangible criteria such as port efficiency and cost related elements which are still the most important competitiveness components. Port safety and security are considered as intangible criteria. These criteria are also important and ports/terminals as an absolute minimum need to match industry standards and best practices.

This statement achieved 100% agreement. Panellists stated that it is difficult to assign tangible value to security and safety. However, minimum standards need to be met regardless of the CSI. Adequate security and safety measures are a means to ensure benefits to ship operators, shippers and port/terminals. As to ship operators and shippers, vessels and the cargo are protected and maintained at all times against theft and damage. Any port or terminal without adequate safety and security would stand at a huge disadvantage against rivals who are in full compliance.

S4.4 Although the US Customs and Border Protection stated that the CSI can bring benefits to linked ports, those benefits are still controversial. This programme transfers the container examinations from unloading ports in the USA to the loading ports overseas. On the other hand, all the checks are carried out in the host countries which bear the equipment cost. Some research claims that CSI creates competitive disadvantages due to additional investment and running costs. However, in reality, all terminal/port investment is surcharged to direct customers, with the costs ultimately being born by the Beneficial Cargo Owners (BCOs). The real burden falls to the BCOs, and ultimately to US importers/retailers and the end consumers. In fact, security regulation compliance such as ISPS has created new revenue streams.

This statement was agreed at 92.8% with no disagreement. Panellists agreed that the security measures have been looked on as a market benefit. It is cost-efficient to transfer the inspection to export ports out-side the USA due to their high labour cost. On the other hand, there are actually very few containers which are called for inspection in ori-gin ports and those are charged to the container operator and passed to shipper and end consumer as so far, no party in the supply chain incurs unrecoverable costs as a result of improved security.

S4.5 The CSI transfers the container examinations from unloading ports in the USA to the loading ports overseas. Opponents argue that it would slow down loading port efficiency. However, from a security perspective, the best is to intercept suspect containers as early as possible in the logistics chain. Moreover, CSI is merely a documentation pro-cess in which terminals and ports are not directly involved. The process is driven by pre-shipment submission of cargo manifests, from which a few containers require non-obtrusive inspections, and very few of these need actual physical inspections.

This statement was agreed at 92.8% by panel members. All panellists agreed with the necessity of inspecting suspicious containers at the early stages of the supply chain and the CSI does not cause interruption. Panellists pointed out that the manifest needs to be submitted 24 hours before loading which is usually set as the expected date/time when a ves-sel starts to load intake cargo. Any request for inspection is immediate and that will leave ample time for performing inspections. In practice, the number of inspections is a very small percentage, less than 1%. As to the cost side, experts have explained that extra cost will be transferred to shippers and end customers. Therefore, whether conducting the inspections at origin or destination, the results will be the same from cost and time perspectives. Additionally, inspecting containers at origin will prevent potential damage to the vessel caused by hazards. Members also advised that this solution is more applicable to large container ports rather than smaller ones due to their insufficient capability.

S4.6 CSI bilateral system of information exchange requires a host coun-try to conduct a security check on containers shipping to a US port. In return, the host country can send its officers to any US port to tar-get ocean-going containerised cargo being exported to their country. It is somewhat improbable that a security threat to a country originates from the USA, so the reciprocal arrangement does not (today) really add a tangible value to others. Under this system, there can be sensitive information exchange, which is deemed necessary to ensure safety of any ports involved. The USA could cease trading with the export ports if they refuse to provide information. Although the host countries may not be willing to offer any confidential information, most export nations depend upon trade with the USA, so they freely cooperate in varying degrees.

This statement was agreed 100% by panel members. Experts agreed that information exchange is vital for Euro-US maritime trade security where the export ports are willing to provide the information. Under the circumstances, that the USA is a major customer for European shippers, there is not much negotiation power as host countries. The disadvantages from sensitive information exchange are superseded by the benefits of better security and safe trade brings.

Delphi Round Three: Statements Reaching Consensus Level and Comments

S4.2 A safe and secured maritime trade is an extremely important issue in shipping industry that cannot be overlooked. With better administrative processes and IT tools, container security inspection processes can be facilitated without causing supply chain disruptions. The extra inspection time in export ports is insignificant compared to the total transportation.

This statement was agreed 100% by all panel experts. All experts agreed with the necessity for maritime security checks. They also pointed out that safety and security are ensured at multiple levels. The use of intelligence filtering through cargo declaration and manifests is the primary level and does not generate any significant additional costs or delays to the supply chain. Non-obtrusive cargo inspections using scanners are relatively quick when a consignment does not pass the initial checks. In the event that a consignment does not pass the scanning check, some significant costs could be created, potentially resulting in supply chain delays. Nevertheless, in practice, less than 0.1% of all consignments require a physical examination. For a shipper or ship owner, having security and safety checks performed at origin is far more useful than at destination.

S5 CSI compliance will not cause container port market distortion in Europe whether in the short term or long term since there has been no evidence to show it causes financial burden or logistics disruption. Small ports will be affected by the changing market arising from liner network design which aims at lowering the overall transportation cost.

This statement was agreed by 92.8% of the panel experts. Most panellists agreed that the CSI will not cause port market distortion since the industry has matured over the past 20 years and no port has witnessed decline due to maritime security and safety checks. Port call choice is based on primarily cost and secondarily demand volume. Financial burden and logistical disruption used to be the initial concerns when the CSI was introduced in 2002. Since the additional cost of CSI compliance has been set off by the Container Security Fees, from the financial perspective there is no evidence to show that container ports have been significantly affected. What is more, the world over, terminals are moving out of cities and away from urban congestion and that is leading to liner shipping network redesign. Examples can be found in Hamburg, Antwerp and Southampton. However, one expert stood against this statement. It was pointed out that the commencement of the '24-hour rule' which is in conjunction with the CSI alone has resulted in issues such as different time zones, tight documentation deadlines and questions over responsibility. It cannot be denied that operational and financial issues, whether they are significant or not, have affected container ports. As long as there is disruption caused by the CSI, there will be some distortion in the EU container port market.

The Revised Model

The revised assumptions are presented in this section under the main four conceptual categories of maritime safety and security in container shipping.

Conceptual Category 1: The Necessity of Pursuing a Maritime Security Initiative

Original Assumption 1: It is necessary to carry out a maritime security initiative despite the fact that additional inspections may cause supply chain disruption and financial burden.

Revised Assumption 1: It is extremely necessary to carry out a maritime security initiative which needs to be linked to the entire supply chain in order to be effective. Moreover, the supply chain disruption and financial burden are very insignificant compared to the overall benefits derived from effective security measures.

Conceptual Category 2: Introduction of the CSI and Its Controversial Influences

Original Assumption 2: The CSI can facilitate global container seaborne trade safety and security, adding competitiveness to CSI-affiliated ports.

Revised Assumption 2: The CSI has increased the level of awareness for the need to secure global trade dramatically and facilitate global container seaborne trade safety and security. However, there are no commercial or operational competitive advantages of any significance as a direct result of the CSI.

Conceptual Category 3: Determinants of EU Container Seaport Competitiveness

Original Assumption 3: The EU container port industry is highly competitive. Port efficiency, service and cost related elements are still the most important competitiveness components.

Revised Assumption 3: The EU container seaport environment generally has become increasingly competitive. A multitude of tangible criteria that include efficiency and cost are the most important competitiveness components. Port safety and security, as intangible criteria, are an absolute minimum need to match industry standards and best practices.

Conceptual Category 4: Implications of Introduction of the CSI on EU Port Competition

Original Assumption 4: CSI compliance does not cause global supply chain disruption or financial problems for the EU container ports.

Revised Assumption 4: The additional inspection process required by CSI compliance can be facilitated without causing supply chain disruptions. The compliance cost has been overestimated and can be overlooked as it is minor in the overall supply chain. Furthermore, the security requirement has created a new revenue stream for EU export ports.

Original Assumption 5: The introduction of the CSI does not cause small ports to lose market share. EU container port market competition is not disrupted by the CSI introduction.

Revised Assumption 5: There has been no evidence to show that maritime security initiatives such as CSI and ISPS cause EU container ports or terminals lose their competitiveness. Small ports will be affected by the changing market arising from liner network design which aims at lowering the overall transportation cost.

Using the framework of the conceptual model outlined in Chapter 4 and applied throughout the research. Chapter 8 presents the main findings of the literature review synthesis from Chapters 2 and 3 and the Delphi survey.

8

The Implications for Container Port Security

The aim of this chapter is to discuss the findings from the secondary data collected in the literature review and the primary data from the Delphi survey. It starts with a discussion of the Delphi technique and then gives a critical analysis of its implementation. The conceptual model will be discussed to establish if it has succeeded in capturing the complexities and relations among the variables identified in the current maritime security area, namely maritime transport risk; maritime security regimes; implementation of the Container Security Initiative (CSI) and EU container seaport competition, and integrating with the results of the Delphi study. The discussion will make specific reference to the five conceptual assumptions developed in Chapter 4. This chapter also takes into consideration any changes that have continued to occur in maritime security.

© The Author(s) 2019
X. Zhang and M. Roe, *Maritime Container Port Security*,
https://doi.org/10.1007/978-3-030-03825-0_8

Establishing the Methodological Rigour of the Delphi Method

According to Von der Gracht (2008), quality criteria in Delphi should be used to ensure a certain scientific standard. Reliability and validity are two criteria that are usually examined. However, Hasson and Keeney (2011) argued that simply examining reliability and validity is not convincing enough for Delphi research. The reasons include the lack of precise definition of Delphi, indeterminacy in panel formation, various consensus meanings and different types of Delphi. Qualitative research therefore needs to be evaluated in a qualitative manner, on the basis of trust and credibility (Corbin and Strauss 2014). Therefore, Hasson and Keeney (2011) and Bryman and Bell (2011) discussed four more elements of trustworthiness for qualitative research, including the Delphi technique, namely credibility, dependability, confirmability and transferability. Engels and Kennedy (2007) classified confirmability and dependability as auditability.

Reliability

Reliability refers to the accuracy of the actual measuring instrument or procedure (Neuman 2011) and assesses if the instruments would generate the same results at different times. For example, if the same respondent responds to the same questions in the same manner, the data can be considered as highly reliable (Punch 2005). Von der Gracht (2008) explained that Delphi results were reliable if the final statements would be reproduced by other groups of panel members under equal conditions. Drost (2011, p. 108) mentioned several typical methods to test for reliability in behavioural research: '*test-retest reliability, alternative forms, split-halves, inter-rater reliability, and internal consistency*'. For the Delphi research, Hill and Fowles (1975) mentioned two approaches: the variation of internal procedures and the measurement across studies to compare the results of similar Delphi studies. The first approach has been used less frequently. As for the second approach, it is difficult to find two of the same type of studies for comparison. Researchers have agreed that standardisation and pretesting are two alternative approaches to guarantee the reliability of a Delphi survey (Cottam 2012). In relation to this research, group size, number of iterations, design of the questionnaire and contents of the questionnaire for round one were modified based on the four distinct phases of Linstone and Turoff (2002) which have proven to be reliable over the years (Von der Gracht 2008). Moreover, Oksenberg et al. (1991) claimed that pretesting could be utilised to evaluate the statements and ascertain whether they form a cohesive and smoothly flowing questionnaire. Weak points were identified and improved by the pilot survey before the actual survey was sent out. Hence, the reliability of this Delphi survey is considered relatively high.

Validity

Based on Wilson (1990), in order to demonstrate that the research is credible, validity has to be tested. Validity is concerned with the '*meaningfulness of research components*' (Drost 2011, p. 114). Validity has external and internal dimensions (Ritchie and Lewis 2003). External validity refers to the degree to which the research outcomes can be generalised beyond the scope of the sample to the population (Ritchie and Lewis 2003; Von der Gracht 2008). Internal validity is about the evidence of whether a researcher is measuring what should be measured (Sekaran 2003). Validity should always be examined regarding the intended purpose of the measuring instrument since one instrument may be valid for one specific field but invalid for others. In this case, a sufficient number of participants who have academic, industrial or administrative backgrounds were chosen and a three round Delphi survey was designed.

Three main forms of validity will be tested, based on Cottam (2012), namely: content validity, criterion validity and construct validity.

Content Validity

Content validity measures the logical link between research questions and objectives (Kumar 2010). It has three aspects: the completeness of the instrument, the balance of the issues being measured and the degree to which statements represent the issue they are supposed to measure

(Von der Gracht 2008). The researcher is required to specify the content domain related to the topic and then select items related to it (Rowe and Wright 2011). In relation to this research, there are four domains of interests that are associated with the research topic: (1) the necessity of carrying out a maritime security initiative; (2) introduction of the CSI and its controversial influences; (3) determinants of EU container port competitiveness; (4) the implications of the CSI for EU container seaport competition. According to Mitchell (1996) and Saunders et al. (2012), the three aspects of content validity could be assessed by a comprehensive literature view and expert interview. In relation to this research, a series of steps have been completed to ensure content validity for the Delphi method. First of all, a comprehensive literature review associated with the major domains was carried out to specify whether the domain of the content is relevant to the Delphi method. The literature started with developing a good understanding of the history and development of maritime security, including risk factors in seaborne trade and the vulnerability of container shipping. Next, the literature focused on current supply chain and maritime security measures, including the CSI. In addition, a coherent set of arguments on the current and potential implications of maritime security measures for port productivity and financing was formed. Moreover, certain key components of port competitiveness were studied and selected for the Delphi survey. Content validity was also assessed through subjective judgement by means of the Delphi survey pilot study (Bryman 2012). Experts were asked to comment on the questionnaire presented to them, and to judge the appropriateness and give feedback on the instrument regarding ambiguities, length, and completeness, and if it raised their interest.

Criterion Validity

Criterion validity is an indicator to measure to what extent future events are logically related to a construct (Creswell 2014). It includes concurrent and predictive validity. Concurrency can be determined by how well a measurement compares with another assessment concurrently done (Kumar 2010). Predictive validity is judged by the usefulness of the instrument to forecast outcomes (Kumar 2010). The aim of this research is to find out the implications of the CSI for EU container port competition, using the Delphi survey. Certain criteria such as port efficiency and port charges have been selected to investigate the changes of port competition. However, this is not to predict how the criteria might have changed before and after the implementation of the CSI. Moreover, the findings of such a study would be subjective and empirical. Therefore, criterion validity does not apply to this research.

Construct Validity

Von de Gracht (2008, p. 65) defined construct validity as *'the extent to which the items actually measure the presence of those constructs intended to measure'*. The concept developed in this research is that the implementation of maritime security initiatives would have certain effects on ports such as efficiency and financing. Furthermore, these effects could have caused a distortion in container port competition. Several conceptual assumptions were set up based on this concept. In order to test the validity, the Delphi method has been selected to collect appropriate data and its analysis. The validity of the concept will be supported by at least one piece of evidence if the assumptions are accepted. The degree to which the theory investigated in this study is consistent with extant theories also provides an assessment of the validity of the construct.

Qualitative Research Trustworthiness Elements

The Delphi technique contains both positivist/quantitative and interpretative/qualitative traits; therefore, the trustworthiness criteria are more appropriate for enhancing the rigour of the Delphi. As noted, four elements of trustworthiness were mentioned by both Hasson and Keeney (2011) and Bryman and Bell (2011).

Credibility

Credibility relates to whether the data are believable and if the research is carried out based on good research practice (Bryman and Bell 2011).

Regarding the Delphi, according to Engels and Kennedy (2007), central to credibility is member check. Therefore, a researcher can carry out continued iteration and provide feedbacks to the panellists between each round to ensure the Delphi findings match the realities of the participants. They also discussed several practicable guidelines utilised by other researchers to enhance credibility: (1) bias free panel selection and selective dropout; (2) stimulate panellists' commitments and obtain qualitative information in the first round; (3) conduct individual interviews or open-ended questions in the first round; (4) face-to-face meetings with potential participants prior to the formal Delphi; and (5) pilot study comprising individual interviews with potential panel members.

In terms of this Delphi, credibility is enhanced in four ways, as Engels and Kenney (2007) suggested. First of all, the panel is comprised of three groups with different backgrounds. The number of invited participants in each group is almost even (see Table 8.1). The selection process is non-biased and the term 'experts' is the criterion for panel selection, regardless of gender, age and race. The panellists include both knowledgeable academics and practitioners who have expertise and interests in maritime security practice. Given that this research focuses on US-Euro container movement and security, experts whose interests and expertise are close to US-Euro container trade were invited. The participants were offered options to drop out by clicking an opt-out link in the invitation letter. Secondly, the panel members remained committed through three rounds and rich qualitative information were obtained, especially in round one. As Table 8.1 shows, only three experts dropped out over the three rounds and the 17% overall response rate is higher than the average Delphi return rate. Invitation letters with comprehensive explanation of this research and gentle reminders were sent out between each round to keep participants engaged and control the time span. The design of the first round statements also helped to stimulate participant's arguments. In addition, the open-ended question encouraged the experts to provide as much information as possible. Thirdly, a pilot Delphi was conducted to ensure not only the reliability but also credibility. Last but not least, according to Engels and Kennedy (2007) and Dinwoodie et al. (2014), iteration occurred when the results of the first round were fed back to participants before the second round.

Table 8.1 Delphi three rounds response rates

Panel	No. of participants contacted	Round one		Round two		Round three	
		No.	% contacted	No.	% round one	No.	% round two	% contacted
Academics	30	10	33.3	8	80	8	100	27
Industry-users	25	4	16	4	100	4	100	16
Administrative	28	3	11	2	66.7	2	100	7
Total	83	17	21	14	82.4	14	100	17

Overall response rates: Delphi study (Three rounds)

Source The authors

Transferability

Transferability is also called applicability (Engels and Kennedy 2007). It is comparable to the external validity in quantitative research, and it refers to the fittingness of the research findings to real life (Hasson et al. 2000). In terms of this Delphi, transferability is established since the research findings are clearly applicable to real life. First of all, this research aims to analyse a particular industrial initiative and its impacts on the EU port industry. The Delphi statements that contained established theories and historical data were designed for this aim. Furthermore, the Delphi panel includes administrative experts and industrial practitioners and the opinions from them were based on their real-life experience and knowledge. The panel members were also encouraged to give solutions to the issues discovered.

Auditability: Dependability and Confirmability

Engels and Kennedy (2007) explained that auditability refers to the adequacy of the inquiry process and includes dependability and confirmability. Dependability can be achieved by including a range of representative experts in the Delphi panel (Cornick 2006). The considerations of assessing a wide range of expert backgrounds, a good panel size and a robust selection process have been discussed in Chapter 5. To ensure the representativeness of a panel member, the initial Delphi panel included 83 experts with academic, industrial and administrative backgrounds and the number of experts in each category is similar. Although there were 14 experts who completed all three rounds, experts in each category contributed sufficient information in each round. Engels and Kennedy (2007) argued that the Delphi process needs to be sufficiently documented and tracked throughout to enhance dependability. This Delphi research followed the process suggested by Fowles (1978) and Linstone and Turoff (2002) (Fig. 5.2). Moreover, each step of the Delphi research has been recorded and stays trackable using Qualtrics. Therefore, dependability is ensured. Confirmability requires *'all the findings can be traced back to their original sources'* (Engels and Kennedy 2007, p. 436). Regarding this Delphi, as Chapters 6 and 7 presented, the clear record of the selection of panel member, contacts of participants, identification of the consensus level, the construction of the Delphi statements and the administration of each round accords with the practices suggested by Engels and Kennedy (2007). Hence, the confirmability is enhanced.

Critical Analysis of the Implementation of Delphi

Justification of Panel Size and Response Rates

There is no definitive optimal number of participants in a Delphi study (Marchais-Roubelat and Roubelat 2011). Hasson et al. (2000) argued that a larger sample size will generate greater data, which in turn influences the amount and quality of analysis. According to Witkin and Altschuld (1995), the approximate size of a Delphi panel generally ranges from 20 to 50. Some studies employed over 60 participants to gather representative information (Alexander and Kroposki 1999), while others included as few as 15 participants (Fiander and Burns 1998). Ludwig (1994) reported that the panel size for the majority of Delphi studies is between 15 and 20. Therefore, the size of a Delphi panel is variable (Delbecq et al. 1975). According to Hsu and Sandford (2007), for a Delphi study with a very small sample size, the information contributed by the participants is not considered as representative judgements regarding the topic. However, a large sample size often comes with the problems of '*potentially low response rates and the obligation of large blocks of time by the respondents and the researcher(s)*' (Hsu and Sandford 2007, p. 4). Debecq et al. (1975) proposed to employ the minimally sufficient number of respondents. According to Ludwig (1994), a group size of 13 had a correlation coefficient approaching 0.9 for its reliability.

Hasson et al. (2000) mentioned that in addition to the panel size, representativeness of participants also affects the Delphi result. This Delphi panel consisted of three groups of experts with different backgrounds to give a good representation of opinions. Hence, the 14 experts who participated in all three rounds of Delphi made the panel size acceptable. The small number can be explained and interpreted in two ways. First of all, there were only 17 out of 83 experts who responded and completed Delphi round one. The research topic of EU container seaport competition and the sensitive topic of maritime security limited the number of potential participants. Experts needed to have expertise in both EU port competition and the security requirements of trans-Atlantic seaborne trade. Some of the participants contacted did not consider themselves as an expert in the field; therefore, they did not agree to take part. Out of the three categories of Delphi panel, academics formed the largest category since they have more experience and awareness of contributing to academic research than industrial experts and administrative professionals. The non-academics are more actively engaged in business-related activities and less willing to express their opinions on a controversial security topic in which the US government is involved. Furthermore, industrial experts are conservative towards data which tends to be business confidential and administrative professionals are unwilling to reveal the true intention behind a policy. Secondly, the time span of the three round Delphi was 10 months and included Christmas and Easter. Many of the panel members were busy and the time span of the survey did not fit their schedule and their momentum and interests in the survey declined. Based on Hasson and Keeney (2011), participants who rate themselves as less-expert are more likely to leave Delphi rounds early than self-rated experts. As the statements became more specific and in depth, some experts may find their knowledge is insufficient to contribute to the survey. Therefore, they departed from the panel.

Hasson and Keeney (2011) suggested that the overall difference between the number of potential participants contacted and the number of actual participants who complete all rounds was another accurate measure of the response rate. Table 8.1 shows the response rates for the Delphi rounds.

Based on Table 8.1, of the initial 83 potential participants contacted, 17 agreed and completed the survey, representing 21% of the total potential participants. Of the 17 participants that completed round one, 14 went on to round two and completed it, representing 82.4% of the round one participants. From here, all the 14 experts went on to Delphi round three and completed the survey, thus representing 100% of the round two participants. The 82.4% and 100% response rates are higher than the 70% response rate suggested by Sumsion (1998) for each round in order to maintain the rigour of the Delphi technique. What is more, 14 panel members went on to complete all three rounds of the Delphi survey, representing 17% of the total potential participants contacted for the research. According to Cottam (2012), the 17% overall response rate is high, compared with the average Delphi return rate. The response rate for each round and the return rate are both above the suggested rate, thereby, the rigour of this Delphi study is maintained.

Advantages of the Delphi Study

One notable advantage of applying a Delphi technique is inclusiveness. A wide range of responses from different stakeholders and professions was gathered and a wide range of views successfully accommodated. Another advantage is comprehensiveness. The importance of building a comprehensive understanding of the CSI implementation and its implication for the EU port industry is critical. The Delphi technique was considered as a unique approach to gather a holistic response from panel members; therefore, a variety of opinions regarding maritime security regime compliance and its influences was collected. Furthermore, the Delphi method provides a means for prioritisation of key components of EU container seaport competitiveness and how they are affected by the CSI.

Drawbacks of the Delphi Survey

A main disadvantage raised during the Delphi survey is that a small number of participants would have sought group discussion and dialogue regarding their different viewpoints on one issue. Due to the varying backgrounds of multiple stakeholders and their different understanding of the research topic, some participants felt the isolated process of completing questionnaires did not allow them to react to and discuss the grey areas of the study. Participants would have welcomed a seminar or face-to-face meeting to discuss the theoretical and practical context that could lead to a deeper understanding and outcomes.

The Necessity of Pursuing a Maritime Security Initiative

There is no doubt, in the post-9/11 trade environment, the threat posed by seaborne trade should never be overlooked. Making use of shipping networks, terrorists could launch a nuclear attack or other forms of mass destruction. Many seaports are situated close to highly populated urban areas, which makes the delivery of a weapon of mass destruction both a reality and a risk. Among the five major risk factors identified by Organisation for Economic Co-operation and Development (OECD) (2003) (see Fig. 2.1), cargo ships, especially container ships, have caused significant security challenges. Cargo ships, together with vessels, people, financing and logistics support, have been targeted and addressed by a series of compulsory and voluntary maritime security measures.

The Negativities of Maritime Security Measures

With the introduction of several maritime security measures, industry criticism started to get intense (WSC 2007; Bennett and Chin 2008; Miller 2007). The literature review revealed claims that maritime security measures such as the ISPS would hamper international trade and impact negatively on the business results of ports and terminals (Thai 2009). Two major reasons behind that were costly security inspections and potential congestion and delays which would mount up in the global supply chain (Bennett and Chin 2008). A variety of *ex-ante* and *ex-post* cost assessments of ISPS compliance were conducted to express concerns over the capital cost of scanning equipment installation and running costs which placed a heavy burden on ports and terminals (Table 2.10). As to the container scanning required by the USA, analysts believed that each port would have to purchase 1 to 10 scanners and the average initialisation cost for one port to be about US$100 million, which was too large to be justifiable for some smaller ports (Miller 2007). In addition to cost burdens, the possible delay and port congestion caused by additional security inspection also drew the industry's attention.

Maritime Security Measures—Current Implementation

The Delphi results confirmed the necessity of implementing security measures in the shipping industry and suggested that security is an aspect that needs to be ensured throughout the entire supply chain. Experts pointed out that aviation security has been strengthened but ports have not received the same scrutiny and still remain vulnerable to what could be a devastating attack.. In addition, the Delphi results provided a different viewpoint from the literature review in terms of compliance cost issue and supply chain disruption. The Delphi research suggested that over the past few years, the cost estimation and supply chain disruption have been overestimated and exaggerated.

Overestimation of Supply Chain Disruption

First of all, most criticism focused on the 100% container scanning proposed by the USA. The original deadline of full implementation globally was 2012. However, the DHS had delayed the implementation of the scanning requirement three times and the deadline has been extended to 2018 (Congressional Budget Office 2016) and was likely to be extended further. The industry group as well as many foreign governments voiced opposition to the requirement, urging US Congress to repeal it altogether due to the huge expense, inadequate global infrastructure and prohibitive trade volume. The DHS was advised to focus on practical supply chain security solutions and stick to the risk-based strategy such as the CSI rather than the impractical scanning provision which would bring logistical, financial, jurisdictional, diplomatic, economic and technological challenges. Furthermore, increasing scanning rate does not necessarily reduce potential smuggling of nuclear weapons or materials into the USA since the option does not address other paths such as truck and rail at land crossings from Mexico or Canada

(Congressional Budget Office 2016). In fact, terrorists may choose those alternative paths if the USA sharply reinforced container scanning. By 2018, 100% scanning had still not been achieved. The port of Qasim in Pakistan is the only port around the world where 100% scanning is conducted under the SFI. This programme is only feasible because of the low volumes from Qasim to the USA, few logistical challenges, and strong support from a Pakistani government interested in maintaining trade with the USA (American Shipper 2014).

The queuing model created to oppose container screening and scanning assumed that containers were scanned at US ports of entry whereas most maritime security measures require that container scanning is conducted at the point of loading overseas. Non-obtrusive inspections such as scanners are highly efficient in detecting risks in suspected containers. In practical operations, a container can pass through scanners as fast as 60 seconds/TEU which is much quicker than 3 minutes/TEU assumed by Martonosi et al. (2005). Also, under the current CBP's multi-layered defence system (see Fig. 2.2), until recently, few containers go through physical inspection and so cause little port/terminal congestion. The inspection rate is as low as 1% and has already caused the Congress to question the effectiveness of the programme (American Shipper 2014).

Compliance Costs Recuperation

Ensuring a nation's security and preventing a terrorism attack should fall under the scope of government duty. Scanning services are not mandatory to comply with the ISPS. How the capital and human resource investments could be borne depends on the nature of the port. The way in which these costs are covered depends on the body (i.e. port management, national customs authorities and terminal operators) that took on the initial capital cost (Allen 2006). This has direct implications for the surcharges or fees that are passed onto exporters. In practice, a government is responsible for purchasing and providing scanning equipment instead of ports and terminals. For example, the port authority of Buenos Aires established a budget for purchasing and installing four container scanners and upgrading existing infrastructure (Ceriotto 2004). Ports and terminals are unlikely to bear huge costs due to ISPS compliance and it has been pointed out by the industry that the real cost burden falls to the Beneficial Cargo Owners (BCO) and ultimately to importers/retailers and end consumers. To cover the investment, a security fee per container is applied by the terminal to the carrier, which is passed on to the shipper and ultimately retailer and consumer. The new surcharges in many ports/terminals far exceed the actual investments made. Therefore, in contrast to the concept of cost burden, security measures compliance actually generates additional revenues. The Delphi results provide empirical evidence for the argument of Thai (2007) who mentioned security compliance could generate additional revenue for ports. No port or terminal bears the so-called heavy burden estimated by much research and the investment is nowhere close to US$100 million which was proposed by Miller (2007). From the perspective of Return on Invested Capital (ROIC), the Delphi industrial experts confirmed that ports and terminals still remain the most profitable players within the end-to-end supply chain.

Security Measures Compliance in Practice

After 9/11, tightening of security was naturally a high priority. Ports and vessels have since commenced regulated access through perimeter deterrents such as fencing, CCTV, patrols, alarms and scanning devices. Likewise, for security (and also safety) the persons within a terminal or port need to be authorised. Stowaways on ships have been a recurring problem for decades, and also need to be combatted. Therefore, security has always been a requirement, although practised to differing levels of quality between ports, countries and continents. Each entity chooses the most affordable adequate technological enhancements, according to its own specific costs and benefits. The ISPS guidelines/regulations which standardised the approach to security post 9/11 are in fact no more than common-sense solutions which should have been already largely in place for other purposes. For instance, the ISPS Code does not require CCTV or biometrics, but recommends fencing, access control and appropriate lighting of the facility (Donner and Kruk 2009). The new regulations formalised what constitutes a secure area and what is required to achieve that. On the basis that the container supply chain has never been disrupted by terrorism, the measures implemented need to be considered as successful and appropriate. As to the compromise between security, cost and efficiency, if any is needed it is insignificant compared to the overall benefits derived from them, which go way beyond merely US anti-terrorism initiatives.

Determinants of EU Container Seaport Competitiveness

Earlier research pointed out that the port environment generally has become increasingly competitive globally. It is difficult to give an unequivocal definition of port competition since it involves multiple stakeholders with conflicting interests. Van de Voorde and Winkelmans (2002, p.11) explained port competition is influenced by: '*(1) specific demand from consumers, (2) specific factors of production, (3) supporting industries connected with each operator, and (4) the specific competencies of each operator and their rivals. Finally, port competition is also affected by port authorities and other public bodies*'. They suggested three levels of container port competition leading to a major focus on the inter-port competition that can be played out at the national and regional levels or different ports located in different port ranges.

Port Competitiveness Determinants Identified by the Literature Review

Much port competitiveness analysis has studied port selection criteria. The literature reveals a wide range of influential factors of port choice and port competition. Monetary costs (port charges/surcharges/promotion), port efficiency, service-related factors (service quality), as well as geographic location, were identified by Yeo (2007), De Martino and Morvillo (2008) and Parola et al. (2017) and widely discussed as the most important port competitiveness determinants. Port safety and security, as two of the software components related to service quality, are considered influential drivers of port competitiveness. Lehtinen and Lehtinen (1991) and Pantouvakis (2006) also suggested port security is part of port service factors. Tongzon and Heng (2005, p. 408) suggested '*port (terminal) operation efficiency level, port cargo handling charges, reliability, port selection preferences of carriers and shippers, the depth of the navigation channel, adaptability to the changing market environment, landside accessibility and product differentiation*' as key factors that affect a port's competitive position. In addition, certain other port-related issues such as port policy and management identified by Yeo (2007) would indirectly or directly affect port competitiveness. Port competitiveness also varies between locations, affected by how these influential forces influence the nature of the port environment (Tongzon and Heng 2005). Research focused on regional port competition has been undertaken by several researchers, including Kim (1993), Jeon et al. (1993), Fleming and Baird (1999), Fung (2001), Huybrechts et al. (2002), Tiwari et al. (2003), and Song and Yeo (2004).

EU Container Seaport Competition and Influential Factors Suggested by the Delphi Results

The Delphi survey suggested that the features of containerisation make container seaport selection a routing choice. The industrial experts suggested that inter-port competition and the market share of container ports are affected by the routing option for a container flow. '*The growth in the number of intermodal transfer points on the land side, at the sea–land interface in the seaports and at the connecting points of liner services in transhipment ports leads to an increasing number of routing options for a container flow between two regions somewhere on the globe*' (Veldman and Buckmann 2003, p. 3). A container seaport is considered as a node in a container routing network. When making the port choice, shippers, forwarders, shipping companies and terminal operators are the major decision-makers. Some indications are that port authorities and government agencies are affecting port choices of those actors

(Aronietis et al. 2010). The competitive position and port choice of a container seaport are determined by its competitive offering to the host of shippers and carriers (Notteboom and Yap 2012).

According to the Delphi results, historically, there has been little competition between container seaports and terminals in Europe. Seaports enjoyed de facto monopolies and never needed to compete. However, the competition among ports and terminals is becoming increasingly intense, and clear from the literature and Delphi results. At present and in the future, Europe will be served by varying combinations of '*deep-sea shipping lines, seaports and modes of land transport*' (Veldman and Buckmann 2003, p. 4). From a port's perspective, there are great overlaps between the hinterlands of container ports in the EU. For example, the North Sea ports in the Hamburg–Le Havre range also handle the major container flows to and from West Europe. Competition exists among the ports of Hamburg, Bremen, Rotterdam, Antwerp and Le Havre. Major UK container import and export ports include Felixstowe, Southampton, London Gateway and Liverpool. Further, within ports several terminal operators also compete with each other. Rotterdam, as one of the busiest container seaports in the EU, has transformed from relying heavily (80%) on ECT Delta Terminal to decentralise the container flow over APM Terminals, ECT Delta Terminal and DP World Terminals. Therefore, it is essential for ports and terminals to improve their attractiveness and adapt within the current competition environment to prevent themselves from suffering profit losses and ultimately exiting the industry.

'5P' Model Suggested by the Delphi for Port Selection

The results from the Delphi exercise suggest that for EU container ports/terminals, carriers and to an extent shippers will use a multitude of tangible criteria to select the best ports and terminals for their shipping networks. In addition, numerous intangible criteria are becoming more evident. The Delphi experts suggested a '5P' model (passage, price, performance, position, proportion) developed by the EU container seaport industry (Fig. 8.1).

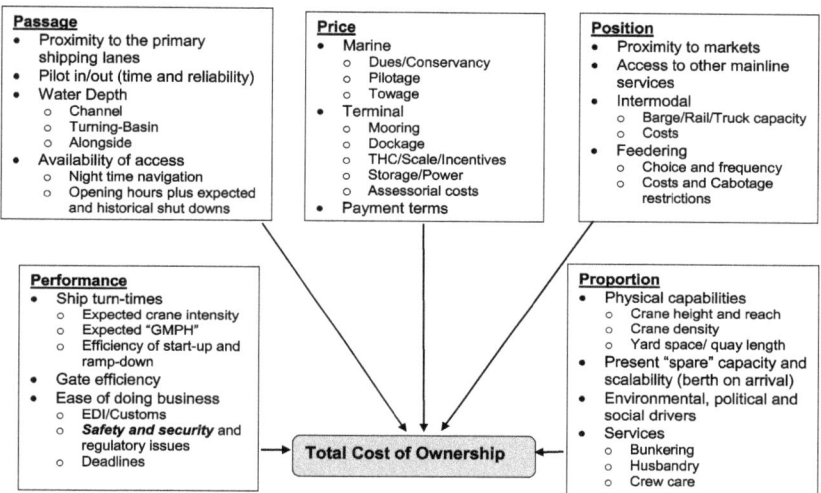

Passage
- Proximity to the primary shipping lanes
- Pilot in/out (time and reliability)
- Water Depth
  - Channel
  - Turning-Basin
  - Alongside
- Availability of access
  - Night time navigation
  - Opening hours plus expected and historical shut downs

Price
- Marine
  - Dues/Conservancy
  - Pilotage
  - Towage
- Terminal
  - Mooring
  - Dockage
  - THC/Scale/Incentives
  - Storage/Power
  - Assessorial costs
- Payment terms

Position
- Proximity to markets
- Access to other mainline services
- Intermodal
  - Barge/Rail/Truck capacity
  - Costs
- Feedering
  - Choice and frequency
  - Costs and Cabotage restrictions

Performance
- Ship turn-times
  - Expected crane intensity
  - Expected "GMPH"
  - Efficiency of start-up and ramp-down
- Gate efficiency
- Ease of doing business
  - EDI/Customs
  - *Safety and security* and regulatory issues
  - Deadlines

Total Cost of Ownership

Proportion
- Physical capabilities
  - Crane height and reach
  - Crane density
  - Yard space/ quay length
- Present "spare" capacity and scalability (berth on arrival)
- Environmental, political and social drivers
- Services
  - Bunkering
  - Husbandry
  - Crew care

Fig. 8.1 5P Port/Terminal Selection Model (THC: Terminal handling cost, GMPH: Gantry moves per hour) (*Source* The authors)

Cost factors and efficiency remain as the major determinants of port competitiveness, which is consistent with the literature review. The port/terminal position which includes proximity to markets, access to other mainline services, inter-model services and feedering is another tangible criterion. In addition to ship turn-times and gate efficiency, safety and security are also considered as port/terminal performance criteria.

Port Security and Safety as Port Selection Intangible Criteria

The Delphi results suggested that security regulations and initiatives can improve port security and service quality. Chang and Thai (2016) stated service quality was an important element for port competitiveness as it improves customer satisfaction, which in turn may positively influence customer loyalty. Security can be seen as part of the quality of service (Lehtinen and Lehtinen 1991; Pantouvakis 2006), as well as software driver (De Martino and Morvillo 2008). The competitive nature of the shipping industry challenges the port industry to increase maritime container security. Delphi experts suggested that service providers within the supply chain such as carriers, ports and terminals compete on not only price and efficiency but also security and safety. These aspects fall within the category of software components mentioned by De Martino and Morvillo (2008). These service providers serve their customers at a desired level through utilising various combinations of production factors. A company that provides higher security levels than their rivals may raise their prices or cut their other existing services, facing the distinct risk of losing customers to their rivals. Therefore, the principle is a trade-off among key determinants which have impacts on customer choice. An overemphasis on any production factors could result in losing competitiveness. Hence, according to the Delphi results, adequate security and safety measures are a means to ensure benefits to carriers, shippers and port/terminals. Improving maritime security positively affects service quality, including '*reliability of service, social responsibility awareness, efficiency in operations and management, and image in the market*' (Chang and Thai 2016, p. 724). Any port or terminal without adequate safety and security would stand at a huge disadvantage against rivals who fully meet standards. The Delphi results also suggested that security cannot be separated from the overall business. Port security should be conducted more than as a reaction to legal and social regulations. Instead, security should be closely integrated and incorporated into business practices since enhanced security is part of the service customers seeking from ports.

The CSI and Its Controversial Influences

Details of the CSI and 24-hour rule which is a primary aspect of the CSI were given in Chapter 2, including the background, aim, arrangements (Table 2.5) and the minimum standard for participation (Table 2.6). The CSI is to identify and inspect all containers that pose a potential terrorism risk at foreign ports before loading on vessels imported to the USA. As discussed in Chapter 2, CSI Phase I (Table 2.7) included nine EU container ports. The number of these EU ports accounts for 45% of the total global initial 'megaports'. During

Phase II (Table 2.8), another 12 EU ports joined the programme, which equates to 52% of the total 23 Phase II ports. Currently, the CSI is under Phase III and 58 ports have joined this programme, including those for North Central, and South America the Caribbean, Europe, Africa, the Middle East and throughout Asia. The participating ports account for 85% of container traffic destined for the USA. There have been 23 EU ports that have joined the CSI that account for 40% of the total 58 CSI ports worldwide and are a greater percentage of the total global CSI ports than the Americas, Caribbean, Asian and African together based on the number of participants.

The advanced information approach under the 24-hour rule amplifies the importance of ensuring security and safety throughout the entire global supply chain. Under the current global safety situation, any node or link within a supply chain could pose a severe terrorism threat to the world. Both the literature review and the Delphi results suggested that using intelligence and automated advance targeting information, and pre-screening at the loading points to identify risks, is much more efficient than traditional inspection at the unloading point.

Improvement of Security Awareness

It has been confirmed by both the literature and the Delphi study that ever since the implementation of the CSI in 2002, the level of awareness of the need to secure global trade has been increased dramatically. Although CSI's initial purpose was to protect the US border, it has participated in developing a world standard. It adds protection for the seaborne trade upon which the worldwide economy depends. Through international collaboration between Customs, the capabilities and the overall effectiveness of the targeting process could be improved. The CSI also brings some significant business benefits. For example, the compliance companies could improve inventory control and reduce administration costs, utilising global logistics management software and other advanced information systems. On the basis that the container supply chain has not encountered disruption by terrorism, the measures implemented should be considered as successful and appropriate for initial purpose.

Container Security Initiative Collaborative Networking and Existing Issues

A collaborative network was formed under a CSI bilateral arrangement, including intelligence sharing and reciprocal service system. As Haynes et al. (2011) noted, modern states could engage in more intensive cooperation to regulate behaviours over varying issues. In the case of container security, this cooperation between Customs under the CSI has been effective. The following sections will discuss the rationale for intelligence sharing and existing issues under such a collaborative network based on the literature review and the Delphi survey.

The Rationale of Information Sharing for the CSI

The literature review and Delphi study showed that current US layered maritime security strategies (Fig. 2.2) are based on a risk-based security management process. Thai (2009) noted that in order to achieve an effective risk-based security management, three phases must be considered: identifying all possible threat scenarios, characterising each scenario and using gained information to adjust the planned risk management controls. Communication and consultation with internal and external stakeholders in the maritime transport industry is the key to the integrated process. It is also believed by the Delphi experts that security information collected and analysed from multiple sources is always better than from a single source (Statement 4.6). Hence, information sharing and exchange runs through the risk-based security management process. Moreover, clear and accountable information should be continuously provided and updated in order to keep security management up with changing security threats and their likelihood of occurrence, and hence, be valid and effective (Thai 2009).

According to the Delphi study, effective security should be prevention from the source rather than inspection. A high inspection rate does not necessarily improve security level and mitigate all risks. In the maritime area, if security is equivalent to final inspection, it has to rely on shipment inspections down the chain at destination ports, which has been proved to be highly costly and inefficient. Prevention from the source philosophy which directs the CSI overseas inspection and advanced manifest is key to ensure security is designed and incorporated right from the beginning of the logistics chain, thereby making everything right from the start. Effective information lays the foundation for a proactive and cost-effective security measure.

The Issues of Inequity Under CSI Bilateral Arrangement

Concerns in terms of competition distortion, sensitive information exchange and sovereignty issues under the collaborative network are commonly brought up. According to the Delphi research, although the competition distortion mentioned caused by the CSI has not emerged, the sovereignty and administration issue and challenges regarding information sharing were brought up by the panel experts when commenting on Statement 4.6.

Challenges Posed by Intelligence Sharing

Information sharing has posed challenges not only for host countries but also on US federal and non-federal stakeholders. Caldwell (2007) summarised several challenges US port security stakeholders encountered, including: obtaining security clearances for port security stakeholders, creating effective working relationships, potential overlapping responsibilities and determining relationships among various centres. Two particular issues brought up by the Delphi experts are sensitive information sharing and the unbalanced information sharing between host countries and the US government.

   Information sharing is the basic requirement of all three regimes (C-TPAT, 24-hour rule and CSI). Countries which are maritime trading partners with the USA have concerns over confidentiality of information they provided. Under the CSI, port authorities of host countries must commit to share critical data, intelligence on potential security threats from within the country and risk management information with the US Customs agents (Allen 2006). For instance, advanced manifest information is required by the 24-hour rule under the CSI and US company's supply chain information, which includes suppliers/manufacturers, freight forwarders, sea and land carriers, and warehouse operators, is needed for C-TPAT certification. Although the host countries are not willing to share intelligence which may include confidential business, most export nations depend upon trade with the USA, so they have to freely cooperate to varying degrees. In fact, the Delphi experts explained that there is little negotiation power for the host countries since the USA could cease trading with the export ports if they refuse to provide information. The host countries' weak positions in this relationship also lead to unbalanced information sharing. The Delphi experts, especially the industrial experts, suggested that the US government is more 'taking' than 'sharing' in practice.

Despite the issues mentioned above, the Delphi results still suggested security information sharing adds huge value overall. Industrial stakeholders including local port authorities and representatives of private companies all agreed that information sharing has increased their awareness for enhancing security at ports and allowed them to identify and handle security issues at their facilities. As to the national level of maritime security stakeholders, information sharing has helped to reduce and mitigate risks without a doubt. National level departments and agencies also rely on information sharing to identify maritime threats and carry out dissemination efforts to support tactical and operational maritime security.

Sovereignty and Administration Problems

Sovereignty and administration problems caused by the US jurisdiction outreach have been observed and brought up by the Delphi experts when they commented on the open-ended question (Q13). One key element of the CSI is transferring the container examinations from unloading ports in the USA to the loading ports overseas. From the industrial perspective solely, it promotes and facilitates security and safety throughout the supply chain efficiently. However, based on the Delphi survey, the pushing out of the US first line of defence and the cooperation between nations claimed by the CBP have triggered stakeholders to suspect the possible unilateralism that lies beneath it. The CSI allows US Customs to screen containers at CSI-designated foreign seaports and place a CSI team overseas to identify high-risk containers prior to their arrival at US ports. This 'outsourcing' made the scope of the programme truly ambitious and costly (Allen 2006). The purpose can be related to the US National Security Strategy by the Bush Administration and the so-called self-defence military action towards Afghanistan after 9/11 (Metaparti 2010). According to the 'Defense Guidance Strategy' White Paper of 1992, the Pentagon-favoured 'no rivals' doctrine pictured US foreign policy as being driven by eliminating all potential challengers to US global hegemony (Bove et al. 2014). On 20 September 2001, the Bush administration announced a change of direction of foreign policy to terrorism focused. However, the Afghanistan and Iraq invasion revealed that the USA was still implementing a 'no rivals' doctrine. Combating terrorism provided a reasonable excuse for taking control over the oil reserves. International security is highly politicised and therefore less transparent. The requirements of the US maritime security regimes such as the CSI and the C-TPAT are actually dominated by their 'no rivals' doctrine. Phase I of the CSI was conducted in the top 20 international 'megaports' which must have '*regular, direct and substantial container traffic*' (CBP 2003a, n.p.). In 2001, approximately 66% of all containers that arrived in US seaports originated from these 'mega ports' which are located in 14 nations, and include Halifax, Rotterdam, Le Havre, Hamburg, Antwerp, Singapore, Hong Kong, Felixstowe, Genoa, Pusan, Algeciras, Tokyo, Shanghai and Shenzhen (Allen 2006). Phase II extended to the 'middle-income' developing countries. Phase III included more ports in 'middle-income' developed countries and theoretically 100% of the containers entering the USA would one day be screened. That implies that the USA will ultimately allocate their officials to every port overseas that ships containers to the USA. According to the CBP (2003b), in the short to medium run, this policy would have significant impacts upon specific players in international shipping and trade and create more obstacles for developing country export-oriented sectors to access the US market.

Furthermore, the Maritime Transportation Security Act (MTSA) developed by the USA required the Coast Guard to help assess a foreign port's security measures under the International Port Security Programme. Under this programme, the Coast Guard makes visits to the ports of foreign nations and reviews security measures implementation with host nations in the host nation ports against established security standards, such as the ISPS Code. Annual visits are also made to host countries to obtain additional observations on implementation. By April 2007, 86 out of 140 countries who are US maritime trading partners have been visited under this programme (Caldwell 2007). Notwithstanding that host countries can make reciprocal visits to US ports, the Coast Guard has occasionally encountered initial reluctance by some countries due to their concerns over sovereignty. As a matter of fact, the Delphi survey, especially the EU port industrial experts, confirmed there are extraterritorial control actions by US CSI teams at foreign ports, such as controlling non-US-inbound container inspection.

As the world's biggest trading nation and consumer market, shipping is vital to the US economy as it moves roughly 75% of trading goods (Thibault et al. 2006). However, although the USA has enacted the Jones Act, 90% of US imports and exports are carried by foreign maritime operators. The USA has no jurisdiction over foreign companies, cargo or vessels until they reach US waters. Key business information of exporters, suppliers and carriers could be very valuable for both political and security purpose for the US government. With information obtained from several maritime security initiatives, the USA could collect intelligence from their extended jurisdiction to those 58 CSI-affiliation foreign ports. Under the current maritime security and safety environment, there is no doubt that these two initiatives have facilitated global trade while improving security. The CSI could help to detect and prevent container-related terrorism at the earliest point along the supply chain, and the C-TPAT helps to address supply chain vulnerabilities (GAO 2003). Nevertheless, the relatively extreme outreach of US jurisdiction in seaborne trade and the potential information safety risks which stem from obtaining intelligence from both many developing and developed nations have been criticised by relevant stakeholders.

The Implications of the CSI for EU Container Seaport Competition

The concern about port competition distortion and discrimination caused by the CSI has been discussed by various public and private stakeholders. Sea carriers would more likely choose CSI ports for shipping to the USA, using non-CSI ports merely for pre-shipment on 'feeder' vessels that would later be loaded to the cargo of other ships at the closest CSI port (Allen 2006). CSI ports would obtain a 'preferred' status, as they would be the only export ports with reduced risk of being delayed at the US port of arrival. However, based on the Delphi survey, at the current stage, most export container ports work in extremely similar ways and there are no significant commercial or operational competitive advantages as a direct result of the CSI. CSI compliance does not cause EU container seaport market distortion whether in the short or long term. Moreover, the Delphi industrial experts claimed that the CSI ports completed a comprehensive and exhaustive list within their respective regions to ensure that the CSI and C-TPAT do not create competitive disadvantages. So long as there is a level-playing field between these ports, which by-and-large there is, none of these ports are suffering in additional costs or burdens. The Delphi survey suggested that there has been no evidence of it causing financial burden or logistics disruption.

Container Security Initiative and 24-Hour Rule Costs Recuperation

Initial Cost: Government and Port Authority Responsibility

Despite the many discussions about the heavy financial burden that the programme may bring for container seaports, the Delphi survey confirmed that the CSI compliance cost and its negative impact on ports/terminals, like other maritime security measures, have been overestimated. The initial compliance costs such as equipment purchase and upgrading are borne by the body that took on the initial capital cost, including governments, local port authorities (governmental or private) and commercial terminal operators, depending on the nature of port management and national customs arrangements (OECD 2003). The EU CSI compliance initial capital cost falls under the responsibility of government, since it is a joint targeting operation with the host government's customs organisation. The labour costs of the USA side fall into the US government budget. As Allen (2006) argued, other costs associated with this initiative such as IT system development and personnel training vary dramatically because of divergent costs of labour in different countries. Private terminal operators are accommodated within the cost-recovery mechanisms such as container surcharges and scanning fees to include all initiative-related costs. This mechanism will be discussed in the following sections.

EU Container Seaport Security Cost Recuperation and Revenue Generation

In most EU container seaports, the Delphi review pointed out that the advanced systems and processes for security and safety already existed prior to the CSI. Due to the high costs of the non-intrusive devices, ports would not make the initial investment unless they were assured to be included in the CSI (Allen 2006). Considering the rigorous requirements of joining, these ports have to make sure they have the financial strength to bear the initial investment in the first place. The Delphi results confirmed that the compliance costs of the CSI and 24-hour rule are passed onto carriers, who in turn recover this cost by charging exporters. The Delphi also revealed that the real cost burden falls onto US importers and ultimately the end consumers. Bichou (2011) suggested that one common approach for calculating the *ex-post* cost of security compliance is looking at how much the market players pass security charges onto final consumers. An average security fee of US$8 per container is charged for the ISPS Code and up to US$40 per bill of lading for the advance manifest fee is related to the 24-hour rule.

Table 8.2 illustrates the security charges of some major container seaports in the EU. In the study of Nijdam et al. (2014) on the level-playing field of seaports, port tariffs between ports within Europe were concluded as largely unimportant. They also revealed that the rates for port dues in the UK were significantly higher than those in the Hamburg–Le Havre range, while the tariffs in Scandinavia and in the Mediterranean were considerably lower. In terms of security charges, a similar pattern can be observed based on Table 8.2. As one of the biggest ports in EU based on handling volume, Rotterdam charged US$10.37, while Antwerp and Le Havre both charged US$10.98 since they share the same hinterland. Among all the CSI ports included in Table 8.2, the port of Gothenburg charges the least at only US$2.6. As to the UK CSI container seaport, Felixstowe charges US$10 for exports.

In addition to recovering the cost, the Delphi study suggested that the CSI and other security initiatives are seen by ports and carriers as a business opportunity and security charges have generated additional revenue for ports and shipping lines. Delphi experts' opinions can be supported by industrial data as well. Take the port of Rotterdam, where every outgoing container is charged an average rate of US$10. According to statistics provided by the port, their container traffic volume between 2011 and 2015 are presented in Table 8.3.

Table 8.2 EU Port/Terminal Security Charges

Port or Terminal	US$/TEU
Antwerp	10.98
Aarhus	0.7
Rotterdam	10.37
Le Havre	10.98
Gioia Tauro	9.76
Valencia	6.1
Dublin	8.54
Gothenburg	2.6
Felixstowe and Harwich (HPH)	17 for import and 10 for export
Tilbury	12

Source The authors adapted from Bichou (2011)

Table 8.3 Port of Rotterdam container traffic volumes (by sea) 2011–2015

	2015	2014	2013	2012	2011
Outgoing TEU	5,882,941	5,882,161	5,583,631	5,787,561	5,777,314
Security surcharges based on the rate of US$10 (million)	59	59	56	58	58
Outgoing TEU grouped to USA	784,000	833,000	Unknown	777,000	745,000
Security surcharges based on the rate of US$10 (million)	7.8	8.3	Unknown	7.8	7.5
Per cent of total outgoing TEU security charges	13.2%	14.1%	Unknown	13.4%	12.9%

Source The authors adapted from Port of Rotterdam (2015)

From this, in general, the port of Rotterdam generates US$58 million from security surcharges alone each year, not to mention other categories of fees. The security charges of US-inbound containers account for 13.4% of the total outgoing containers' security charges on average. The port also charges extra for container scanning when needed. It is the importer to a US port who bears the cost of unloading and emptying any potential threat posed by a dangerous container. The port at host country decides the cost for handling such cargo. For the port of Felixstowe, the Delphi experts claimed at least US$22 million are collected each year in additional costs. Referring back to the earlier *ex-ante* and *ex-post* cost assessment presented in Chapter 2, the revenue generated from security charges can definitely offset the compliance cost and other security-related costs. The additional revenues derived from security requirements are used to pay for any additional equipment such as CCTV and sensors. So far, none of these EU CSI ports are suffering uncovered costs or burdens as estimated, and as the industry claimed, security measurements have created a substantial revenue stream for ports.

As to small container ports, the Delphi study explained that the initial investment would be decreased, corresponding to their business scale and container traffic volume, to avoid an unbearable financial situation. It was also pointed out by the port industry that the actual investment, procedural costs and operational costs are much less than estimated previously since the advanced systems and processes for security and safety already existed prior to the CSI in most EU container seaports.

The difference with estimations can be explained by two reasons. Firstly, as Bichou (2004) and Bosk (2006) explained, there are different interpretations of the regulations across global ports and terminals. For instance, the ISPS Code only provides general security provisions in ports without exact compliance instructions. Furthermore, a variety of methods were used to estimate *ex-ante* and *ex-post* costs. Bichou (2008, p. 23) commented that '*ex-ante assessments of the compliance cost of maritime and port security are largely based on data and methods from national regulatory risk assessment models such as the US National Risk Assessment Tool (N-RAT) and the UK Risk Assessment Exercise (RAE). These are ad hoc programmes undertaken by governmental agencies in order to assess the costs and benefits of new regulatory initiatives*'.

Secondly, a survey was commonly adopted for the ex-post cost assessment. As noted by Bichou (2008), when a survey investigates a single security programme, their results can show inconsistent cost outcomes either over time or between participants. For instance, the figure of US$200,000 initial costs and US$113,000 annual operating costs were widely quoted by the industry as the average compliance cost of C-TPAT for a multinational company in 2004 (Bichou 2008). Nevertheless, Diop et al. (2007) reported that C-TPAT implementation and operating costs were lower at US$38,471 and US$69,000. In the same survey, 33% of respondents agreed that C-TPAT benefits outweighed the compliance costs but an additional 25% thought the C-TPAT costs and benefits were about the same. This is because the case-specific survey is generalised to all stakeholders, and different viewpoints stem from respondents' various interests and backgrounds. Last but not least, as Thai (2007) and the Delphi experts argued, these ports see security measures as a business opportunity to generate extra revenue. Their commercial operation makes sure the security measures are implemented cost-effectively.

Carrier's 24-Hour Rule Cost Recuperation

Sea carriers are the stakeholders that bear the costs of 24-hour rule compliance. The Delphi experts admitted that the 24-hour requirement caused shock waves among players in the global container shipping industry. It was the shipping company who has traditionally controlled the submission of documentation. Companies must provide detailed data about each container shipment, including the origins and the contents. Trading businesses started to worry about gathering the required information in such a tight time frame (Holmes 2004). These companies—both trading and shipping—needed to significantly improve and manage their information flow to ensure consistency in their reporting for planning and auditing back along the supply chain.

As a result, they were required to invest in new IT systems, personal training and working hours. In a similar vein to how ports recover costs, carriers passed these costs onto exporters as documentation fees (Table 8.4). Most carriers started to charge between US$25 and US$35

Table 8.4 Trans-Atlantic sea carrier security surcharges

Name of surcharge	Code	Definition/application	Scope/rate (approximate)
Port Security Fee	ISPS SEC SED ISPS SEO	Charge to cover ISPS Code compliance costs	SEC: Russia–US$20 Greece–US$6
AMS charge—For all countries with advance manifesting requirements USA, China, etc.	AMS	Covers costs associated with the preparation and submission of advance manifest declarations to US, Canadian and Mexican customs authorities for cargo loaded on a vessel at a non-US port is chargeable per Master B/L and each House B/L	UK—£30 per B/L Ireland/Switzerland/Spain/Portugal/Italy/Germany/France/Finland/Denmark/the Netherlands/Belgium—€25
AAM Security charge	AAM	Covers administration costs when SI change requests are received after the Advance Manifesting SI cut-off	UK—£40 per amendment request Ireland/Switzerland/Spain/Portugal/Italy/Germany/France/Finland/Denmark/the Netherlands/Belgium—€30

Source The authors adapted from Orient Overseas Container Line (2016)

SEC—Security Charge in Europe, SED—Security Charge at Destination, SEO—Security Charge at Origin, ISPS—International Ship and Port Facility Security, AMS—Advance Manifest Security, B/L—Bill of Lading, AAM—Amendment for Advanced Manifest, SI—Shipping Instruction per bill of lading to recover administrative expenses of programme compliance (Allen 2006). As a matter of fact, all imports to the USA face this documentation fee whether or not they originated from a CSI port since the 24-hour rule targets all US-bound containers. Due to the fact that shipping charges only account for 3% of the market price of goods in the USA (Limao and Venables 2001), the total/average cost passed onto US end consumers due to CSI/security screening is no more than a few cents per item of goods in the US market. The Delphi experts claimed that the costs for having improved maritime and supply chain security accounts for no more than 1% of shippers' total costs that can be overlooked as it is minor in the overall supply chain.

Hence, it is suggested by both earlier research and the Delphi study that the CSI and 24-hour rule do not bring a financial burden to participating ports and terminals, and instead, CSI affiliation and security compliance provide them with new business opportunities.

Container Security Initiative Compliance and Port Productivity

The Delphi research suggested that operational disruption is inevitable since safety and security measures act against operational and logistical efficiency since they require additional procedures, but the same experts also claimed that security regulation could improve port infrastructure and good infrastructure can positively affect efficiency. In the case of maritime security measures, the investments required are productive expenditures to attain efficiency improvements. Nevertheless, they also pointed out that in most cases, it is more difficult to achieve an effective arrangement from this expenditure since the relevant authorities' lack business awareness.

Clark et al. (2004) suggested that having some level of regulations such as security measures could increase port efficiency; however, an excess of it can start to reverse these gains. Banomyong (2005), Altiok (2011), and Yang (2011) mentioned that a balance between trade facilitation and security needs to be achieved. Therefore, a moderate level of security practice has a positive effect on port/terminal efficiency.

In 2013, US ports handled 18 million TEUs and about 1% of containers were inspected overseas under CSI (American Shipper 2014). The Congressional Budget Office (2016) reported that under the current container inspection regime (Fig. 2.2), the CBP identified about 5% of all seaborne containers entering the USA at high risk, although only a small proportion of them are flagged for national security reasons. This small fraction of total US-inbound containers scanned is consistent with what the EU port industry confirmed in the Delphi study. They claimed that in fact, in practice, using the NII devices required by the CSI can lower the chance of a container being physically inspected. Very few containers would experience a physical check and consequently would not cause any operational disruptions.

What is more, all three categories of panel experts agreed that if a port/terminal has efficient and effective operational arrangements, additional security procedures would have minor negative effects on them. Port efficiency '*varies widely from country to country and specially, from region to region*' (Clark et al. 2004, p. 17). Clark et al. (2004) studied port efficiency in various locations and presented some estimates of port efficiency by geographic region.

Table 8.5 shows that EU ports ranked as the second most efficient port ranges. Although these regional efficiency variables

Table 8.5 Port Efficiency in Various Regions

Geographic region	Port efficiency 7 = the best 1 = the worst	Custom clearance (days)	Container handling charges in ports (US$/TEU)
North America	6.35	3.50	261.7
Europe (excl. East)	5.29	4.00	166.7
Middle East	4.93	NA	NA
East Asia and the Pacific	4.66	5.57	150.5
East and South Africa	4.63	12.00	NA
North Africa	3.72	5.50	NA
East Europe	3.28	2.38	NA
Latin America and the Caribbean	2.90	7.08	251.4
South Asia	2.79	–	NA
West Africa	NA	11.70	NA

Source The authors adapted from Clark et al. (2004)

cannot be directly compared with each other, it gives a general picture of the EU port efficiency level. Moreover, the EU container seaports included in the CSI are among the busiest container ports in the EU, which indicates that their existing operations and logistics are efficient. The Delphi experts suggested with better IT arrangements, most of the operational obstructions could be minimised. Additionally, the EU CSI ports' increase in communication among terminal operators, liner companies and customs helps reduce delays to the time that containers depart ports (Allen 2006). With the assistance of the US team, the negative consequences of additional procedures could be minimised.

The CSI—Positive Effects on Trade Facilitation

It has been suggested by the literature review and the Delphi study that the CSI has both direct and indirect positive effects on trade facilitation. The most significant direct impact stems from its better procedural arrangement, such as container pre-screening prior to loading. The Delphi study mentioned that previous scholars who criticised the negative influences of the CSI on member ports in fact neglected the role of a container seaport in a global logistics chain. Although container examinations from unloading ports in the USA have been transferred to the loading ports overseas, routing through a CSI port represents less time when it clears US Customs due to the 'Green Lane' benefits. It would lower the risks that containers may be delayed due to US custom clearance and shorten the total transit time from its origin to destination, hence enhancing trade facilitation. On the other hand, efforts in terms of simplifying paperwork, modernising procedures and harmonising customs requirements can positively affect trade facilitation. A number of supply chain benefits are available to CSI compliant participants, including lower insurance costs, fewer penalties and less risk exposure, reduction in fraud and theft, and better predictability through advanced cargo processing procedures as Bichou (2008) mentioned. All of the advantages meet the criteria of trade facilitation efforts.

Container Security Initiative—Implications for Small Ports

It has been estimated that small ports would suffer from security measures such as the ISPS due to compliance cost estimation and market share loss. Due to the financial and operational constraints of small container seaports, meeting the requirements of security measures and joining the CSI would be difficult. Losing US-inbound container traffic volumes seemed to be inevitable as a result of being a less 'preferred' export container seaport compared with large CSI seaports. Hence, one major concern about introducing the CSI focused on its negative influence on small ports and the possibility of market share distortion.

Nevertheless, over a decade since the introduction and implementation of the ISPS and CSI, substantial profits have been gained by large and small container seaports. Additional security charges are not only applied to US-inbound containers but also all other containers. These costs from ports/terminals are levied to carriers who in turn pass them onto shippers, forwarders and third-party logistics, and ultimately to retailers and end consumers, which normally amount to a few cents per consumable purchased. The Delphi experts explained that small container ports would make a security plan and initial investment proportional to the size of their assets and the operations to be covered to avoid the unbearable financial situation and overcome operational constraints. Their efforts also depend on the level of security which the smaller ports are willing to accommodate, as a result of a sound risk assessment. Furthermore, US-related trade is not their major business; therefore, they are less affected by US maritime security requirements. The industrial, academics and administrative experts of the Delphi panel all agreed that there could be a slight shift of market share from small to large CSI ports in the EU; however, this would be a natural consequence of service differentiation. McCalla (1999) argued that many ports were facing global issues and the consequential local responses in terms of port service. The increasing vessel size is one of these global issues. The Delphi experts explained that smaller ports are more likely to lose business due to being unable to efficiently handle the ever-larger container ships rather than security measure compliances.

In the next chapter, we move on to examine the governance and policy implications of changes in security for ports.

References

Alexander, J., & Kroposki, M. (1999). Outcomes for community health nursing practice. *Journal of Nursing Administration, 29,* 49–56.

Allen, N. H. (2006). The container security initiative costs, implications and relevance to developing countries. *Public Administration and Development, 26*(5), 439–447.

Altiok, T. (2011). Port security/safety, risk analysis, and modelling. *Annals of Operations Research, 187,* 1–3.

American Shipper. (2014). *CSI's Evolution.* Available at http://www.americanshipper.com/main/news/csis-evolution57536.aspx?taxonomy=Security. Accessed 10 December 2016.

Aronietis, R., Van de Voorde, E., & Vanelslander, T. (2010). *Port Competitiveness Determinants of Selected European Ports in the Containerised Cargo Market.* International Association of Maritime Economists Conference IAME (Vol. 10), Lisbon, Portugal.

Banomyong, R. (2005). The impact of port and trade security initiatives on maritime supply chain management. *Maritime Policy and Management, 32*(1), 3–13.

Bennett, A. C., & Chin, Y. Z. (2008). *100% Container Scanning: Security Policy Implications for Global Supply Chains* (Master of Science Dissertation). Massachusetts Institute of Technology.

Bichou, K. (2004). The Isps Code and the cost of port compliance: An initial logistics and supply chain framework for port security assessment and management. *Maritime Economics and Logistics, 6,* 322–348.

Bichou, K. (2008). Security and risk-based models in shipping and ports: Review and critical analysis. In *ITF, Terrorism and International Transport: Towards Risk-Based Security Policy.* Paris: OECD Publishing.

Bichou, K. (2011). Assessing the impact of procedural security on container port efficiency. *Maritime Economics and Logistics, 13*(1), 1–28.

Bosk, L. B. (2006). Port and supply chain security initiatives in the United States and Abroad. *The University of Texas at Austin Policy Research Report, 150,* 1–192.

Bove, V., Elia, L., & Sekeris, P. (2014). US security strategy and the gains from bilateral trade. *Review of International Economics, 22*(5), 863–885.

Bryman, A. (2012). *Social Research Methods.* Buckingham: Open University Press.

Bryman, A., & Bell, E. (2011). *Business Research Methods* (3rd ed.). Oxford: Oxford University Press.

Caldwell, S. L. (2007). *Maritime Security: Observations on Selected Aspects of the SAFE Port Act: GAO-07-754T* (GAO Reports), p. 1.

CBP. (2003a). *Container Security Initiative: Update. United States Department of Homeland Security 2003.* Available at http://www.whitehouse.gov/homeland/. Accessed 17 October 2014.

CBP. (2003b). *Enforcement of 24 Hour Rule Begins February 2.* Available at http://www.cbp.gov/xp/cgov/newsroom/news_releases/archives/cbp_press_releases/012003/01302003.xml. Accessed 30 July 2013.

Ceriotto, L. (2004). *Buscantecnologia china para la aduana.* Available at www.clarin.com. Accessed 30 October 2014.

Chang, C., & Thai, V. (2016). Do port security quality and service quality influence customer satisfaction and loyalty? *Maritime Policy and Management, 43*(6), 720–736.

Clark, X., Dollar, D., & Micco, D. (2004). *Port efficiency, maritime transport costs and bilateral trade* (NBER Working Paper No. 10353). Available at http://www.nber.org/papers/w10353.pdf. Accessed 4 January 2017.

Congressional Budget Office. (2016). *Scanning and Imaging Shipping Containers Overseas: Costs and Alternatives.* Available at http://www.cbo.gov/sites/default/files/114th-congress-2015-2016/reports/51478-Shipping-Containers.pdf. Accessed 10 March 2017.

Corbin, J., & Strauss, A. (2014). *Basics of Qualitative Research* (4th ed.). London: Sage.

Cornick, P. (2006). Nitric oxide education survey—Use of a Delphi survey to produce guidelines for training neonatal nurses to work with inhaled nitric oxide. *Journal of Neonatal Nursing, 12*(2), 62–68.

Cottam, H. (2012). *An Analysis of Eastern European Liner Shipping During the Period of Transition* (PhD thesis). Plymouth University, UK.

Creswell, J. W. (2014). *Research Design Qualitative, Quantitative, and Mixed Methods Approaches.* London: Sage.

De Martino, M., & Morvillo, A. (2008). Activities, resources and inter-organisational relationships: Key factors in port competitiveness. *Maritime Policy and Management, 35*(6), 571–589.

Delbecq, A. L., Van de Ven, A. H., & Gustafson, D. H. (1975). *Group Techniques for Program Planning: A Guide to Nominal Group and Delphi Processes*. Glenview, Ill.: Scott, Foresman.

Dinwoodie, J., Landamore, M., & Rigot-Muller, P. (2014). Dry bulk shipping flows to 2050: Delphi perceptions of early career specialists. *Technological Forecasting and Social Change, 88,* 64–75.

Diop, A., Hartman, D., & Rexrode, D. (2007). *C-TPAT Partners Cost/Benefit Survey*. Washington, DC: CBP.

Donner, M., & Kruk, C. (2009). *Supply Chain Security Guide*. The World Bank/DFID, 1, pp. 1–107. Available at http://siteresources.worldbank.org/INTPRAL/Resources/SCS_Guide_Final.pdf. Accessed 20 April 2016.

Drost, E. A. (2011). Validity and reliability in social science research. *Education Research and Perspectives, 38*(1), 105–123.

Engels, T. C. E., & Kennedy, H. P. (2007). Enhancing a Delphi study on family-focused prevention. *Technological Forecasting and Social Change, 74*(4), 433–451.

Fiander, M., & Burns, T. P. (1998). Essential components of schizophrenia care: A Delphi approach. *Acta Psychiatrica Scandinavica, 98,* 400–405.

Fleming, D. K., & Baird, A. J. (1999). Some reflections on port competition in the United States and Western Europe. *Maritime Policy and Management, 26*(4), 383–394.

Fowles, J. (1978). *Handbook of Futures Research*. Westport, CO: Greenwood Press.

Fung, K. F. (2001). Competition between the ports of Hong Kong and Singapore: A structural vector error correction model to forecast the demand for container handling services. *Maritime Policy and Management, 27*(1), 3–22.

GAO. (2003). *Container Security: Expansion of Key Customs Programs Will Require Greater Attention to Critical Success Factors 2003* (United States Government Accountability Office (GAO) Reports), p. 1. Accessed 28 October 2016.

Hasson, F., & Keeney, S. (2011). Enhancing rigour in the Delphi technique research. *Technological Forecasting and Social Change, 78*(9), 1695–1704.

Hasson, F., Keeney, S., & McKenna, H. (2000). Research guidelines for the Delphi survey technique. *Journal of Advanced Nursing, 32*(4), 1008–1015.

Haynes, J., Hough, P., Malik, S., & Pettiford, L. (2011). *World Politics*. London: Pearson Education Limited.

Hill, K. Q., & Fowles, J. (1975). The methodological worth of the Delphi fore-casting technique. *Technological Forecasting and Social Change, 7,* 179–192.

Holmes, J. L. (2004). The container security initiative. *Fleet Equipment, 30,* 15.

Hsu, C. C., & Sandford, B. A. (2007). The Delphi technique: Making sense of consensus. *Practical Assessment Research and Evaluation, 12*(10), 2.

Huybrechts, M., Meersman, H., Van de Voorde, E., Van Hooydonk, E., Verbeke, A., & Winkelmans, W. (Eds.). (2002). *Port Competitiveness: An Economic and Legal Analysis of the Factors Determining the Competitiveness of Seaports.* Antwerp: De Boeck Ltd.

Jeon, I.-S., Kim, H.-S., & Kim, B.-J. (1993). *Strategy for Improvement of Competitive Power in Korea Container Port.* Seoul: Korea Maritime Institute.

Kim, H.-S. (1993). *Decision Components of Shippers' Port Choice in Korea.* Seoul: Korea Maritime Institute.

Kumar, R. (2010). *Research Methodology: A Step-By-Step Guide for Beginners* (3rd ed.). London: Sage.

Lehtinen, U., & Lehtinen, J. R. (1991). Two approaches to service quality dimensions. *The Service Industries Journal, 11*(3), 287–303.

Limao, N., & Venables, A. J. (2001). Infrastructure, geographical disadvantage, transport costs and trade. *The World Bank Economic Review, 15*(3), 451–479.

Linstone, H. A., & Turoff, M. (2002). *The Delphi Method: Techniques and Applications.* Available at http://is.njit.edu/pubs/delphibook/delphibook.pdf. Accessed 7 July 2013.

Ludwig, B. G. (1994). *Internationalizing Extension: An Exploration of the Characteristics Evident in a State University Extension System That Achieves Internationalization* (PhD thesis). The Ohio State University, Columbus.

Marchais-Roubelat, A., & Roubelat, F. (2011). The Delphi method as a ritual: Inquiring the Delphic Oracle. *Technological Forecasting and Social Change, 78*(9), 1491–1499.

Martonosi, S. E., Ortiz, D. S., & Willis, H. H. (2005). Evaluating the via-bility of 100 percent container inspections at America's ports. In H. W. Richardson, P. Gordon, & J. E. Moore (Eds.), *The Economic Impacts of Terrorist Attacks.* Cheltenham: Edward Elgar Publishing Ltd.

McCalla, R. (1999). Global change, local pain: Intermodal seaport terminals and their service areas. *Journal of Transport Geography, 7,* 247–254.

Metaparti, P. (2010). Rhetoric, rationality and reality in post-9/11 maritime security. *Maritime Policy and Management, 37*(7), 723–736.

Miller, J. (2007, October 25). New shipping law makes big waves in foreign ports. *Wall Street Journal*.

Mitchell, V. (1996). Assessing the reliability and validity of questionnaires: An empirical example. *Journal of Applied Management Studies, 5*(2), 199–207.

Neuman, W. L. (2011). *Social Research Methods: Qualitative and Quantitative Approaches*. Boston: Allyn & Baker.

Nijdam, M., de Jong, O., van der Horst, M., van den Bossche, M., de Swart, L., & Buckmann, E. (2014). *Level Playing Field: Study on Distorted Cross-Border Competition Between Seaports*, RHV-Erasmus University/Ecorys, Available at https://www.government.nl/binaries/government/documents/reports/2014/02/01/level-playing-field/level-playing-field-eindrapport-engels.pdf+&cd=1&hl=zh-CN&ct=clnk&gl=uk. Accessed 4 March 2016.

Notteboom, T., & Yap, W. Y. (2012). Port competition and competitiveness. In W. Talley (Ed.), *The Blackwell Companion to Maritime Economics* (pp. 549–570). Blackwell: Oxford.

OECD. (2003). *Maritime Transport Committee Security in Maritime Transport: Risk Factors and Economic Impact*. Available at https://www.oecd.org/newsroom/4375896.pdf.

Oksenberg, L., Cannell, C., & Kalton, G. (1991). New strategies for presenting survey questions. *Journal of Official Statistics, 7*(3), 349–365.

Orient Overseas Container Line. (2016). *Local Surcharges*. Available at http://www.oocl.com/netherlands/eng/localinformation/localsurcharges/Pages/default.aspx. Accessed 15 September 2016.

Pantouvakis, A. (2006). Port-service quality dimensions and passenger profiles: An exploratory examination and analysis. *Maritime Economics and Logistics, 8*(4), 402–418.

Parola, F., Risitano, M., Ferretti, M., & Panetti, E. (2017). The drivers of port competitiveness: A critical review. *Transport Reviews, 37*(1), 116–138.

Port of Rotterdam. (2015). *Port of Rotterdam Statistics*. Available at https://www.portofrotterdam.com/en/downloads/factsheets-brochures/port-statistics-2015. Accessed 14 February 2017.

Punch, K. (2005). *Introduction to Social Research: Quantitative and Qualitative Approaches*. London: Sage.

Ritchie, J., & Lewis, J. (2003). *Qualitative Research Practice: A Guide for Social Science Students and Researchers*. London: Sage.

Rowe, G., & Wright, G. (2011). The Delphi technique: Past, present and future prospects. *Technological Forecasting and Social Change, 78*(9), 1487–1490.

Saunders, M., Thornhill, A., & Lewis, P. (2012). *Research Methods for Business Students* (6th ed.). London: Prentice Hall Publishing.

Sekaran, U. (2003). *Research Methods for Business* (4th ed.). Hoboken, NJ: Wiley.

Song, D. W., & Yeo, K.-T. (2004). A competitive analysis of Chinese container ports using the analytic hierarchy process. *Maritime Economics and Logistics, 6,* 34–52.

Sumsion, T. (1998). The Delphi technique: An adaptive research tool. *British Journal of Occupational Therapy, 61*(4), 153–156.

Thai, V. V. (2007). Impacts of security improvements on service quality in maritime transport: An empirical study of Vietnam. *Maritime Economics and Logistics, 9*(4), 335–356.

Thai, V. V. (2009). Effective maritime security: Conceptual model and empirical evidence. *Maritime Policy and Management, 36*(2), 147–163.

Thibault, M., Brooks, M., & Button, K. (2006). The response of the US maritime industry to the new container security initiatives. *Transportation Journal, 45*(1), 5–15.

Tiwari, P., Itoh, H., & Doi, M. (2003). Shippers' port and carrier selection behaviour in China: A discrete choice analysis. *Maritime Economics and Logistics, 5*(1), 23–39.

Tongzon, J., & Heng, W. (2005). Port privatisation, efficiency and competitiveness: Some empirical evidence from container ports (terminals). *Transportation Research Part A, 39*(5), 405–424.

Van de Voorde, E., & Winkelmans, W. (2002). A general introduction to port competition and management. In M. Huybrechts, H. Meersman, E. Van de Voorde, E. Van Hooydonk, A. Verbeke, & W. Winkelmans (Eds.), *Port Competitiveness* (pp. 1–15). De Boeck: Antwerp.

Veldman, S., & Buckmann, E. H. (2003). A model on container port competition: An application for the West European container hub-ports. *Maritime Economics and Logistics, 5,* 3–22.

Von der Gracht, H. A. (2008). *The Future of Logistics: Scenarios for 2025.* Berlin: Springer Science & Business Media.

Wilson, B. (1990). *Systems: Concepts, Methodologies and Applications* (2nd ed.). New York: Wiley.

Witkin, B. R., & Altschuld, J. W. (1995). *Planning and Conducting Needs Assessment: A Practical Guide.* Thousand Oaks, CA: Sage.

WSC. (2007). *Statement Regarding Legislation to Require 100% Container Scanning.* http://www.worldshipping.org/pdf/wsc_legislation_statement.pdf.

Yang, Y. C. (2011). Risk management of Taiwan's maritime supply chain security. *Safety Science, 49*(3), 382–393.

Yeo, G. T. (2007). *Port Competitiveness in North East Asia: An Integrated Fuzzy Approach to Expert Evaluations* (PhD thesis). Plymouth University, UK.

9

Maritime Governance, Security Measures and Port Competition in the EU

The impacts of the Container Security Initiative (CSI) on EU container seaport competition have been discussed in Chapter 8 through analysing the conceptual assumptions developed in Chapter 4. The analyses were based on the secondary data collected from the literature review and primary data from the Delphi survey. The Delphi results suggested that the CSI has not caused competition distortion in the EU container seaport industry and no evidence has shown that ports are suffering an unrecoverable burden from CSI compliance in terms of costs and efficiency within the EU. The findings are quite different from those suggested by previous research. There is a lack of existing theories or models to explain such differences. As this research is shaped through adopting an abductive approach, a model (Fig. 9.1) is developed and will be explained in this chapter to interpret the findings from this Delphi survey. Although this model is built upon existing knowledge and theories, it provides a new perspective which originates from the political and economic environment to investigate how maritime security measures affect the port industry, rather than looking at individual determinants. The model classifies the factors into four groups, which are: (1) economic liberalism rationality; (2) EU port management

© The Author(s) 2019
X. Zhang and M. Roe, *Maritime Container Port Security*,
https://doi.org/10.1007/978-3-030-03825-0_9

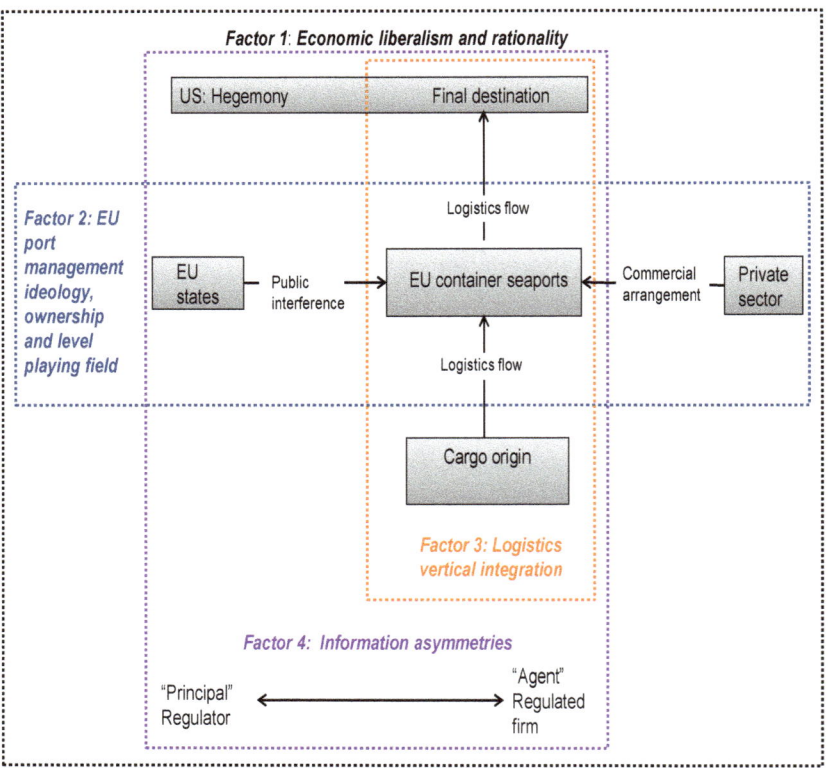

Fig. 9.1 Maritime Security and the EU Container Seaport System (*Source* The authors)

ideology, ownership structure and level-playing field; (3) logistics vertical integration; and (4) principal–agent (PA) relation and information asymmetries.

This research follows an abductive approach. Kovács and Spens (2005) reviewed the adoption of such approaches in the logistics and supply chain fields. Abduction was seen by researchers as systematised creativity to develop new theory or knowledge when an unexpected observation cannot be explained by existing theories (Kovács and Spens 2005). In terms of this research, the results of the Delphi survey are in opposition to what have been argued by many current scholars noted in Chapter 2. The key conclusions from the Delphi in Chapter 8 suggested the industrial stakeholders generally hold an active and optimistic view towards CSI implementation; and EU container seaport competition is not distorted unlike the suggestions by the Parliament of Australia (2003), Banomyong (2005), Dallimore (2008), and Donner and Kruk (2009) noted in Chapter 2. These unexpected results cannot be fully explained by established theories; therefore, a new conceptual framework is needed for further interpretation. Abduction allows the researcher to examine and interpret existing phenomena from a new perspective, and 'new' knowledge is created in this way (Kovács and Spens 2005). During this theory building process which was described by Dubois and Gadde (2002) as 'theory matching' or 'systematic combining', additional data are collected simultaneously. This creates an interactive learning loop that connects theory and empirical study. In most of the cases, the research goes back and forth between established theories, attempting to develop a new conceptual framework. Kirkeby (1990) explained that a 'creative' or 'surprising' element is normally introduced. Kovács and Spens (2005, p. 139) summarised abduction as '*to understand the new phenomenon (Alvesson and Sköldberg 1994) and to suggest new theory (Kirkeby 1990) in the form of new hypotheses or propositions (Andreewsky and Bourcier 2000)*'.

In terms of this abductive research, the theory matching process follows the interactive learning process described by Kovács and Spens (2005). A framework which seeks the cause of the industrial stakeholders' behaviour and attitudes towards CSI compliance at a deeper level was intended to be built. Danermark et al. (2001) interpreted abduction as a new framework that provides supposition to the new phenomena rather than a logically necessary conclusion. Therefore, rules can be suggested based on perception of the phenomena. Regarding this research, it started with relevant political economic theories as the fundamental presupposition on which the maritime players perceive maritime security regulations and act. EU port management ideology and ownership are believed to be the second premise as a derivate of the literature review, Delphi panellists' comments, particularly on Statement 3, 4.1, 4.4, 5, and the discussion in Chapter 8. Logistics integration is developed based on the synthesis of the literature review (Chapter 3), and Delphi experts' comments on Statement 4.5. Information asymmetries were added as another fundamental precondition of how the maritime practitioners cope with security measures' implementation. The information asymmetries and PA relationships exist in modern commercial activities; therefore, it is considered to be applicable to this case. Additional secondary data were collected to examine these four factors, mainly from existing theories in the field of international trade, political economics, maritime governance, logistics and supply chain management, and historical port data.

Economic Liberalism and Rationality

Maritime activities are closely linked to globalisation. It is the shipping industry that makes global trade possible. Roe (2013) noted that the shipping industry reflects and promotes a broader globalised world economy. Economic liberalism, on the other hand, is considered as the dominant ideology of globalisation (Usher 2003) and therefore, it is rational to believe that maritime activities and governance can be interpreted from an economic liberalism perspective. 'Rationality' can be seen as an explanation of human beings' propensity to maximise their own interest in the economic sphere. Jeremy Bentham, a 'utilitarian' thinker, believed that people who behave rationally would always act to maximise their own 'utility' and a collective of this behaviour could produce beneficial outcomes to balance between consumers' demand and producers' supply. According to this ideology, all actors within a global trading system act to maximise their own interest and the overall result will create the greatest happiness of the greatest number. In the case of the shipping industry, all stakeholders of the maritime security initiative including both public and private sectors are acting to seek maximisation of their own interest, dominated by the ideology of 'rationality'.

Liberals still acknowledge the role of the state in the economy. Public goods such as clean air and security should be provided by governments since the market would not necessarily produce them (Smith 1910). Moreover, governments are also necessary in terms of providing a regulatory framework to enforce contracts and protect fair competition.

However, classical liberalism argued that the role of government should be limited to a minimum, although there remains some dispute about the necessary extent of state intervention.

Maritime Governance and Security Measures

In modern society, large public works are still needed and contemporary government must provide a mechanism for the purposes of: resolution of private disputes, specifying the rights and obligations of corporations, imposing taxes or regulations upon externalities and reducing the gap between rich and poor by progressive income taxation, welfare and other measures (Usher 2003). Due to the very nature of the shipping industry, administration is necessary not only for industrial competition but also various externalities. The framework of maritime governance is a hierarchical model that is characterised by formal structures with a set of rules to govern the process by which decisions are taken and imposed (Roe 2013). This hierarchical framework can be viewed as international, supranational, national, regional and local, comprising of various NGOs (e.g. International Organisation for Standardisation) and intergovernmental organisations (IGO) (e.g. IMO and OECD). The process is shaped with top-down authority, beginning with broad policies developing at higher levels (e.g. IGOs and NGOs) and then passing down the hierarchy to lower jurisdictions (national and regional level). Lower levels then operate the broad policies derived from upper levels. The whole system relies on coordination between jurisdictions and regulatory bodies to minimise conflicts between them (Roe 2013).

Hegemony in Maritime Governance and Maritime Security

Maritime governance and the international trade system illustrate the importance of a hegemon and the phenomenon of hegemony. A hegemon refers to a great power with sufficient political influence and motivation to dominate international affairs in ways that create rules and institutions which serve to further their interests (Haynes et al. 2011). Gilpin (1987) explained that Neo-Realists saw hegemony as a more sophisticated way of understanding how governments could impose power over others by using institutions and rules. Liberals considered hegemony as a means of achieving free trade by overcoming the collective goods problem (Haynes et al. 2011). Dominant trading states such as the USA at the end of the Second World War and Great Britain in the nineteenth century saw liberalisation playing an entrepreneurial role in developing and enforcing international rules that promote trade.

The USA, which relies heavily on global trade, has been a leader in the Liberal International Economic Order (Bove et al. 2014). Security has become an important aspect in the current international trade system in which a logistics chain connects the cargo origin to its destination. As to maritime regulation and policy regarding security and safety, the USA plays a leading role in establishing and projecting its power worldwide by developing and conducting various maritime security regimes and measures (see Chapter 2). The CSI can be seen as an example of how the USA exerts its power, owing to the fact that it transfers container inspection from the traditional unloading point at the US borders to the loading point at the export ports overseas. Despite improvement of the total efficiency of the logistics chain, it triggered discussions on costs, operational disruption, information sharing, administrative issues and sovereignty when it was first introduced in 2002 (Allen 2006; Donner and Kruk 2009; Parliament of Australia 2003; OECD 2003; Dekker and Stevens 2007; Metaparti 2010). Yet, by January 2003, US Customs had reached bilateral arrangements with 15 foreign customs to place Customs officials at 24 seaports (GAO 2003). Despite all the negativities suggested by varying scholars (see Chapter 2), as the CSI progressed, more countries started joining it. So far there are 58 foreign ports participating in the CSI, which account for 85% of container traffic destined to the USA (CBP 2014). In fact, due to the hegemon of the USA coming from its military and economic power (Metaparti 2010; Bove et al. 2014), foreign nations and ports joined this programme to maintain their current position and status in the international trade system. According to the Delphi results, from the perspective of improving global trade security, the US hegemony has proved to be effective in spite of inequity issues. The public entities and private players who are subject to this hegemony have developed their own mechanisms to cope with the negativities. The process of maritime security compliance cost recuperation suggested by the Delphi experts can be seen as such a mechanism.

EU Port Governance and Management

According to McConville (1999), in the ports industry, there are two most common and extreme managerial ideologies, namely the European or Continental, and the Anglo-Saxon or Peninsular. European philosophies see the ports as a public service and there is a comprehensive port authority instructing the whole operation (Bennathan and Walters 1979). The Anglo-Saxon approach sees the port as a commercial activity, and management control of the port is a private undertaking. Although both approaches are useful, there are no pure examples of these philosophies to be found. Based on an examination of the position of port services undertaken by UNCTAD in the mid-1970s, the Anglo-Saxon approach is mainly found in developed country ports and the ports of developing countries mainly seem to be managed under European ideologies (McConville 1999). Within the EU, the Delphi results and the literature review indicated that most ports are managed and operated under the Anglo-Saxon ideology, particularly in the UK and Northern Europe. The primary objective is to earn appropriate profits and avoid unnecessary commercial losses. According to this approach, public intervention needs to be severely curtailed, and limited to general duties such as land planning permission, safety, environmental problems, pilotage and navigation. Furthermore, privatisation, commercialisation, cooperation and some forms of deregulation give ports' management the ability to function in a liberalised environment.

EU Port Ownership and Governance

A number of European examples reflect recent trends in port ownership. In the 1980s, public ports in the UK went through asset privatisation, i.e. selling assets (including land) to the private sector. Baird and Valentine (2007) noted that the UK port industry was more concentrated than ever before, and 15 of the 20 largest ports were privately owned, handling 85% of all UK port traffic in 2003. In Greece, the ports of Piraeus and Thessaloniki were listed on the Athens Stock Exchange in 1999 when the Greek government undertook port reform. The Greek state retained 75% of their ownership. In 2003, they transferred to limited companies to operate as private business, having only one share owned by the state (Talley 2009). The remaining Greek ports were managed by local authorities. In order to overcome port inefficiencies, Greek port reform was still developing. China's COSCO Shipping took a 67% stake in Piraeus Port Authority in August 2016 and became the controlling shareholder (Xinhua News Agency 2016).

One of the major tasks of contemporary government is providing public services, and ports fall into this category (Usher 2003). A strong and efficient seaport is an important asset for a nation or region that could generate added value and employment. Belgium has a decentralised port governance structure and ports are publicly owned and managed due to their national economic importance. Hence, port services are ruled by municipal regulation and regional governments provide primary funds for port investment (Talley 2009). The ports of Rotterdam, Amsterdam and Zeeland are the three largest ports in the Netherlands and are under public management of port authorities. There is no direct involvement of the national government in port management. Rotterdam was a municipal port, but, in 2004, the port authority changed to a public corporation (Talley 2009). The municipality of Rotterdam became a major shareholder and the national government became the minor shareholder and the financier of port expansion projects (De Langen and van der Lugt 2007).

Italian Law no.85/94 divided Italy's commercial ports into three categories (Brooks and Cullinane 2007). These three categories are: Class I, ports of international economic relevance; Class II, ports of national economic relevance; and Class III, ports of regional and interregional economic relevance (Valleri et al. 2007). Public port authorities own 24 ports of Class I and Class II and have the legal rights to lease the port or its terminals to private investors (Talley 2009). The competitive private operators perform port operations and entrepreneurial activities, and port authorities can only provide ancillary activities.

Public–Private Ownership and Maritime Security

Although early empirical research shows that there was a lack of clear-cut relationship between ownership and port efficiency, there are some studies that have argued that decentralisation and privatisation could improve port performance (Estache et al. 2002; Song 2003; Tongzon and Heng 2005). In the study of Wang et al. (2004), the government's 'hands-off' mode could create an effective commercial operation to achieve better port performance. Table 9.1 shows the ownership of all EU CSI ports. The level of privatisation varies among these CSI ports, ranging from fully privatised UK container ports to partially privatised landlord ports. A landlord port has the mixed public–private feature and is the mainstream model for larger- and medium-sized ports, and especially for EU ports. Under this model, the port authority is the regulatory body and the landlord, and private companies conduct port operations (Dholakia et al. 2009). The landlord port model encourages efficiency and accountability within the private sector and creates competitive market dynamics (Brooks and Cullinane 2007). Additionally, investment made by the private sector can ensure a strong market leadership and achieve financial stability. On the other hand, a seaport could attract a broad range of industries. In order to avoid impractical investment and strengthen the control over port externalities, the public sector retains infrastructural investment and regulatory laws. Legal restraints are instituted. An essential element in economic modelling is that all participants seek the maximisation of something. In the shipping industry, for instance, a shipping company will operate to achieve profit maximisation or lowest cost possible. Firms or individuals will

Table 9.1 EU CSI ports and their ownership

Country	CSI ports	Ownership, management and operations
The Netherlands	Rotterdam	Landlord port (public–private): municipality (major) and national government (minor)+private operators
Italy	La Spezia, Genoa, Naples, Gioia Tauro and Livorno	Landlord port (public–private): public port authorities and private operators
Germany	Bremerhaven, Hamburg	Landlord port (public–private): local public authority+private operators
UK	Felixstowe, Liverpool, Thamesport, Tilbury and Southampton	Fully private ownership
Belgium	Antwerp and Zeebrugge	Landlord port (public–private): national government and regional government+private operators
Greece	Piraeus	Limited company: national government (major shareholders) and minor shareholders
France	Le Havre and Marseille	Landlord port (public–private): national government+private operators
Spain	Algeciras, Barcelona and Valencia	Landlord port (public–private): local port authority+private operators
Sweden	Gothenburg	Landlord port (public–private): local port authority+private operators
Portugal	Lisbon	Public–private: local port authority+publicly owned limited company (management)+private operators

Source The authors adapted from relevant ports' official websites, Brooks and Cullinane (2007) and Valleri et al. (2007)

never deliberately make a decision or take an action knowing in advance it is against self-interest (McConville 1999). In terms of maritime security, the involvement of both the private and public sectors could help to maximise the positive effect of security measures and minimise the negative impacts on port operations and financing. The responsibility of ensuring and investing in maritime security and safety falls onto the port authority and government as public goods, while the stakeholders in commercial and private sectors such as terminal operators seek the way of cost recovery, process facilitation and profit maximisation. Therefore, despite the objections and suggested negative influences of maritime security measures such as the CSI on port operations, in fact, the port authorities or other private sector parties have seen solution to any possible negative effects prior to implementation.

Container Security Initiative Participation in EU Port Ranges

The European container port system is one of the busiest worldwide and features large as well as medium-sized to smaller ports each with specific characteristics regarding hinterland markets and geographic locations (Notteboom 2012). According to Meersman et al. (2010), due to different economic, legal, social and fiscal environments, and the features of liner networking, it is difficult to compare the competition environment across different container port ranges. Although the Delphi survey suggested that the EU container seaport competition is not distorted by the CSI, it is more realistic to analyse the competition within a specific port range that serves the same economic hinterland and foreland.

On the one hand, EU container seaports that have regular US-inbound container flows have seen and realised the opportunities and benefits of CSI, hence joined the programme in different phases to prevent them from being a less preferred choice by port users (Table 9.2). Based on Lloyd's List (2014), 16 EU container seaports which rank as the busiest European container seaports have joined the CSI. In the Hamburg–Le Havre (HLH) range which handles almost half of the total European container flows, ports are involved in fierce competition. Of the 11 major deep-seaports in the HLH range, six ports which are included in Top 20 European container seaports have joined the CSI within four years, handling almost 98% of the total TEU flow in the range. In terms of ports within each port range, the total annual TEU throughput (outgoing) of non-CSI ports only accounts for approximately 1%, which means that the non-CSI ports have a small fraction of market share in their range. What is more, for

Table 9.2 CSI ports in different port ranges at different phases

EU container seaport range	Phase I (2002–2003)	Phase II (2003–2006)	Phase III (by 2018)	Non-CSI ports and Total Annual TEU Throughput. % of Total Range Throughput (Outgoing—2013)
Hamburg–Le Havre	Germany: Hamburg, Bremerhaven; The Netherlands: Rotterdam; France: Le Havre; Belgium: Antwerp	Belgium: Zeebrugge	None	Wilhelmshaven Amsterdam Zeeland Seaports Ghent Dunkirk 1.31%
Mediterranean	Italy: Genoa, La Spezia; Spain: Algeciras	Italy: Livorno, Gioia Tauro, Naples; Spain: Barcelona, Valencia; France: Marseilles; Greece: Piraeus; Turkey: Izmir	None	Not available
UK (east and south coast)	Felixstowe	Southampton, Thamesport	Liverpool, Tilbury	Not available
Atlantic	None	Portugal: Lisbon	None	Not available
North Sea	None	Sweden: Gothenburg	None	Not available
Black Sea	None	None	None	Not available

Source The authors adapted from CBP (2014), Port of Rotterdam (2015), and Notteboom (2012)

these non-CSI small container seaports, US-related container traffic is not their major business. Therefore, although CSI was introduced to the EU as a voluntary programme to individual ports, the participation of all the major players in one port range at early stage to gain a 'preferred' status implies that the CSI in fact works at major EU container seaports as a 'must have' programme. On the other hand, there are a few national and regional authorities that artificially protect their seaports by partially or fully subsiding port infrastructure. Meersman et al. (2010) pointed out that by doing so, a mutual accusation of distortion of competition arises. Dekker and Stevens (2007) also suggested that subsidies for security measures would affect the price mechanism and in turn the seaport's competitive position. Hence, different ports within the same range have similar investment plans and are competing for the same goods flows. Nijdam et al. (2014) stated that the security rules are also defined at the European level and that they are equal for all EU member states. The Delphi survey has confirmed that there have been rare subsidies from government to ports/terminals regarding CSI compliance besides the occasional loan of portable scanning units which are designed to identify radioactive emissions. So long as there is a level-playing field between these ports regarding security enforcement, which by-and-large there is, there will be no competition distortion caused by CSI affiliation.

Additionally, the security charges at EU container seaports are on a range basis. The survey conducted by Drewry (1998) indicated that port tariff diversification was greater among different port ranges/clusters than within each range. The existence of tariff diversification on a range basis is not only caused by the different degree of competition existing in the different markets and port management but also by the different monopolistic power of ports regarding their hinterlands (i.e. traffic is less footloose). For instance, the security charges within the EU container seaports vary from US$11 per TEU in Aarhus to US$2.6 per TEU in Gothenburg (Bichou 2011). In 2011, the ports of Rotterdam, Antwerp and Le Havre all charged approximately US$11 since they shared the same hinterland. This range basis of security charges ensures a fair competition for prices for ports that serve the same economic hinterland.

Vertical Integration of Logistics and Port Function

Phenomena such as globalisation and liberalisation have fostered international trade. There is a process of mutual influence between international trade and the transport sector. This mutual influence implies a substantial degree of dynamism, especially in the maritime sector (Meersman et al. 2010). Competition is no longer seen at the level of individual ports or shipping companies, but at the more complex level of logistical relationships between origins and destinations (Meersman et al. 2010). Port competition would '*shift from the institutional, functional and spatial levels to channel management*' (Bichou and Gray 2005, p. 89). The strength of a logistics and supply chain depends on the quality of each individual node and link. The success of the entire chain depends on the competitive strength of incorporated seaports and the success of a seaport depends on the competitive strength of the logistics chain of which it is a part. In other words, whether a seaport policy or strategy is successful should be aligned with the international logistics context. Therefore, to what extent the trade and commodity flow can be facilitated from cargo origin to destination remains a crucial factor to port policy and strategy. Meersman (2005) suggested that the ability of the port to be one key player of the entire supply chain to minimise the generalised costs would determine the profitability of an investment in port infrastructure.

This research suggested that previous scholars who criticised the negative influences of the CSI on member ports neglected the role of a container seaport in a global logistics chain. As noted in the discussion regarding trade facilitation, routing through a CSI port would lower the risks of container delay caused by US Custom clearance and shorten the time from its origin to destination, hence, enhancing trade facilitation. The Delphi research also confirmed that the CSI decreases total cargo processing costs and improves port reliability, thus attracting more container volumes. In addition, industrial experts claimed that the provisions of the new security regulations make the security check process more cost-effective and less time-consuming than the traditional random inspections, as Bichou (2008) suggested. In addition to the direct benefits such as more reliable cargo movement, other benefits include lower insurance costs, fewer penalties and less risk exposure, advantages that go beyond the security benefits.

Principal–Agent Relation and Asymmetric Information

Cvitanić and Zhang (2013) described a PA problem as a problem of optimal contracting between two parties (principal and agent). The agent could act to influence the value of the outcome process. A typical example of a PA problem is in investment where the principal is an investor and the agent is a portfolio manager who manages the investor's money. In finance, a company is the principal and its chief executive is the agent. In broader terms, the principal offers a contract to the agent who performs a certain task on behalf of the principal.

Tirole (1986) developed a model that regarded regulation as a PA problem, with the government or 'regulator' as the principal, and the regulated company as the agent. In the basic Laffont–Tirole model of regulation, the government procures an indivisible public good from a privately owned firm. In this case, the regulator observes realised production costs without knowing how much effort the company has put into cost reduction (Tirole 2014). The regulated company knows more about its cost-reducing technology or means than the regulator. Hence, the regulator encounters hidden information as well as hidden action. The manager of the regulated company can reduce the production cost by working hard. This is caused by the information asymmetries in a PA problem.

As aforementioned, the governance framework in the shipping sector is a multilevel governance system which consists of international, supranational, national, regional and local entities. A multilevel governance system has to face the problem of how to ensure policy outcomes are in line with the original objectives when there exists asymmetric information, different capacity and resources of actors, and priorities and values at different levels (Kassim and Menon 2003; Elgie 2002; Bauer 2006). In the context of economic liberalism in which rationality and a seeking for self-interest have become a dominant ideology, *operating public policy/regulation in a multilevel governance system requires shared understanding and commitment to policy goals, trust and resource interdependence'* (Bachtler and Ferry 2013, p. 1259).

The CSI was introduced as a voluntary initiative between US Customs and overseas exporting container seaports. The US Customs imposed the CSI as a regulation on CSI-affiliation ports overseas. Based on the Laffont and Tirole model of regulation, the PA relation can be applied in this case. By joining the CSI, a contractual relationship is formed between the US Customs and CSI-affiliation ports, where the CSI port (the agent) is authorised to act on behalf of the US Customs (the principal) to carry out container inspections at the CSI ports. However, according to the PA problem, the US Customs cannot assume that the CSI ports will always act for the best interest of the principal, particularly if CSI compliance will be costly to the agent. Moreover, the asymmetric information between the principal and the agent will enable the CSI port to use the US Customs' resources to pursue goals that benefit their own business. This is because the agent's actions are normally unobservable to the principal. The CSI ports, as the agent, have the advantage of greater knowledge and specialised abilities in port operation to maximise their own interests and minimise negative effects. Hence, CSI ports recuperate relevant compliance costs by charging the carriers security fees which are ultimately transferred to US importers and final consumers. Under such a mechanism, CSI ports and carriers who are subjected to the 24-hour rule not only achieve cost recovery, but also create a new revenue stream.

In the next and final chapter, we draw together the issues, discussion and arguments that have been presented in the earlier chapters before moving on to look at the future.

References

Allen, N. H. (2006). The container security initiative costs, implications and relevance to developing countries. *Public Administration and Development, 26*(5), 439–447.

Alvesson, M., & Sköldberg, K. (1994). *Tolkning och Reflektion. Vetenskapsfilosofi och Kvalitativ Metod.* Lund: Studentlitteratur.

Andreewsky, E., & Bourcier, D. (2000). Abduction in language interpretation and law making. *Kybernetes, 29*(7/8), 836–845.

Bachtler, J., & Ferry, F. (2013). Conditionalities and the performance of european structural funds: A principal–agent analysis of control mechanisms in european union cohesion policy. *Regional Studies, 49*(8), 1258–1273.

Baird, A. J., & Valentine, V. F. (2007). Port privatisation in the United Kingdom. In M. R. Brooks & K. Cullinane (Eds.). *Devolution, Port Governance and Port Performance: Research in Transportation Economics* (Vol. 17, pp. 55–84). Amsterdam: Elsevier.

Banomyong, R. (2005). The impact of port and trade security initiatives on maritime supply chain management. *Maritime Policy and Management, 32*(1), 3–13.

Bauer, M. W. (2006). Co-managing programme implementation: Conceptualizing the European Commission's role in policy execution. *Journal of European Public Policy, 13*(5), 717–735.

Bennathan, E., & Walters, A. A. (1979). *Port Pricing and Investment Policy for Developing Countries.* Oxford: Oxford University Press.

Bichou, K. (2008). Security and risk-based models in shipping and ports: Review and critical analysis. In *ITF, Terrorism and International Transport: Towards Risk-Based Security Policy.* Paris: OECD Publishing.

Bichou, K. (2011). Assessing the impact of procedural security on container port efficiency. *Maritime Economics and Logistics, 13*(1), 1–28.

Bichou, K., & Gray, R. (2005). A critical review of conventional terminology for classifying seaports. *Transportation Research A, 39,* 75–92.

Bove, V., Elia, L., & Sekeris, P. (2014). Us security strategy and the gains from bilateral trade. *Review of International Economics, 22*(5), 863–885.

Brooks, M. R., & Cullinane, K. (2007). *Devolution, Port Governance and Port Performance.* London: Elsevier.

CBP. (2014). *CSI: Container Security Initiatives.* Available at https://www.cbp.gov/border-security/ports-entry/cargo-security/csi/csi-brief. Accessed 27 August 2016.

Cvitanić, J., & Zhang, J. (2013). *Principal–Agent Problem, in Contract Theory in Continuous-Time Models* (pp. 3–6). Berlin Heidelberg: Springer.

Dallimore, C. (2008). *Securing the Supply Chain: Does the Container Security Initiative Comply with WTO Law?* (Dissertation, University of Muenster). Available at https://www.wwu-customs.de/fileadmin/downloads/pdfs/diss_dallimore.PDF. Accessed 30 January 2016.

Danermark, B., Ekstrom, M., Jakobsen, L., & Karlsson, J. C. (2001). *Explaining Society: An Introduction to Critical Realism in the Social Sciences.* London and New York: Routledge.

De Langen, P. W., & van der Lugt, L. M. (2007). Governance structures of port authorities in the Netherlands. *Research in Transportation Economics, 17,* 109–137.

Dekker, S., & Stevens, H. (2007). Maritime security in the European Union-empirical findings on financial implications for port facilities. *Maritime Policy and Management, 34*(5), 458–499.

Dholakia, N., Hales, D. N., & Lee, S. W. (2009). *Competitiveness of Asian and American Ports: Implications for Global Supply Chains* (University of Rhode Island Working Paper Series 2009. No. 24). College of Business Administration.

Donner, M., & Kruk, C. (2009). *Supply Chain Security Guide.* The World Bank/DFID, 1, pp. 1–107. Available at http://siteresources.worldbank.org/INTPRAL/Resources/SCS_Guide_Final.pdf. Accessed 20 April 2016.

Drewry. (1998, April). *World Container Terminals: Global Growth and Private Profit.* London: Drewry.

Dubois, A., & Gadde, L. E. (2002). Systematic combining: An abductive approach to case research. *Journal of Business Research, 42*(1), 553–560.

Elgie, R. (2002). The politics of the European central bank: Principal–agent theory and the democratic deficit. *Journal of European Public Policy, 9*(2), 186–200.

Estache, A., Gonza'lez, M., & Trujillo, L. (2002). Efficiency gains from port reform and the potential for yardstick competition: Lessons from Mexico. *World Development, 30*(4), 545–560.

GAO. (2003). *Container Security: Expansion of Key Customs Programs Will Require Greater Attention to Critical Success Factors 2003* (United States Government Accountability Office (GAO) Reports), p. 1.

Gilpin, R. (1987). *The Political Economy of International Relations.* Princeton, NJ: Princeton University.

Haynes, J., Hough, P., Malik, S., & Pettiford, L. (2011). *World Politics*. London: Pearson Education Limited.

Kassim, H., & Menon, A. (2003). The principal-agent approach and the study of the European Union: Promise unfulfilled? *Journal of European Public Policy, 10*(1), 121–139.

Kirkeby, O. F. (1990). Abduction. In H. Andersen (Ed.), *Vetenskapsteori och metodläˊra. Introduktion* (C. G. Liungman, Trans.). Lund: Studentlitteratur.

Kovács, G., & Spens, K. M. (2005). Abductive reasoning in logistics research. *International Journal of Physical Distribution and Logistics Management, 35*(2), 132–144.

Lloyd's List. (2014). *Top 20 European Ports*. Available at https://www.lloydslist.com/ll/incoming/article431990.ece. Accessed 25 May 2015.

McConville, J. (1999). *Economics of Maritime Transport Theory and Practice* (1st ed.). London: Witherby & Co. Ltd.

Meersman, H. M. A. (2005). Port investments in an uncertain environment. *Research in Transportation Economics, 13,* 279–298.

Meersman, H., Van de Voorde, E., & Vanelslander, T. (2010). Port competition revisited. *Review of Business Economic Literature, 55*(2), 210–232.

Metaparti, P. (2010). Rhetoric, rationality and reality in post-9/11 maritime security. *Maritime Policy and Management, 37*(7), 723–736.

Nijdam, M., de Jong, O., van der Horst, M., van den Bossche, M., de Swart, L., & Buckmann, E. (2014). *Level Playing Field: Study on Distorted Cross-Border Competition Between Seaports*, RHV-Erasmus University/Ecorys. Available at https://www.government.nl/binaries/government/documents/reports/2014/02/01/level-playing-field/level-playing-field-eindrapport-engels.pdf+&cd=1&hl=zh-CN&ct=clnk&gl=uk. Accessed 4 March 2016.

Notteboom, T. (2012, April 18). Dynamics in port competition in Europe: Implications for North Italian ports. *Workshop 'I porti del Nord'-Milan*.

OECD. (2003). *Maritime Transport Committee Security in Maritime Transport: Risk Factors and Economic Impact*. Available at https://www.oecd.org/newsroom/4375896.pdf.

Parliament of Australia. (2003). *The US Container Security Initiative and Its Implications for Australia*. Available at http://www.aph.gov.au/About_Parliament/Parliamentary_Departments/Parliamentary_Library/Publications_Archive/CIB/cib0203/03cib27.

Port of Rotterdam. (2015). *Port of Rotterdam Statistics*. Available at https://www.portofrotterdam.com/en/downloads/factsheets-brochures/port-statistics-2015. Accessed 14 February 2017.

Roe, M. (2013). *Maritime Governance and Policy-Making*. London: Springer.

Smith, A. (1910). *An Inquiry into the Nature and Causes of the Wealth of Nations*. London: J. M. Dent.

Song, D. W. (2003). Port co-opetition in concept and practice. *Maritime Policy and Management, 30*(1), 29–44.

Talley, W. K. (2009). *Port Economics*. New York: Taylor and Francis Group.

Tirole, J. (1986). Hierarchies and bureaucracies: On the role of collusion in organisations. *Journal of Law, Economics, and Organisation, 2*(2), 181–214.

Tirole, J. (2014). Market Power and Regulation. *Scientific Background on the Sveriges Riksbank Prize in Economic Sciences in Memory of Alfred Nobel 2014*. Stockholm: The Economic Sciences Prize Committee of the Royal Swedish Academy of Sciences.

Tongzon, J., & Heng, W. (2005). Port privatisation, efficiency and competitiveness: Some empirical evidence from container ports (terminals). *Transportation Research Part A: Policy and Practice, 39*(5), 405–424.

Usher, D. (2003). *Political Economy*. Oxford: Blackwell Publishing Ltd.

Valleri, M. A., Lamonarca, M., & Papa, P. (2007). Port governance in Italy. In M. R. Brooks & K. Cullinane (Eds.), *Devolution, Port Governance and Port Performance: Research in Transportation Economics* (Vol. 17, pp. 139–153). Amsterdam: Elsevier.

Wang, J., Ng, A. K. Y., & Olivier, D. (2004). Port governance in China: A review of policies in an era of internationalising port management practices. *Transport Policy, 11*(3), 237–250.

Xinhua News Agency. (2016, July). *China, Greece Pin Great Hopes on Piraeus Port*.

10

Conclusions for Container Port Security

Realisation of the Research Aim and Objectives

The aim of this book was to analyse the impacts of the CSI programme on EU container seaport competition. In order to achieve this aim, five objectives were developed in Chapter 1. Research Objectives 1 and 2 and partial Objectives 3 and 4 were addressed in the literature reviews (Chapters 2 and 3) and conceptual model development process (Chapter 4). In order to fully achieve Objectives 3, 4, and 5, a Delphi survey was conducted to collect primary data to test the conceptual model and a further model was developed based on the Delphi findings and secondary data. The following sections will explain each objective in detail.

Objective 1: To Review Earlier Work on Maritime Security and EU Container Seaport Competition

This objective has been addressed in Chapter 2 by reviewing published research regarding maritime security, port competition and the EU port industry. The review reveals the risk factors exposed in maritime

© The Author(s) 2019

X. Zhang and M. Roe, *Maritime Container Port Security*,
https://doi.org/10.1007/978-3-030-03825-0_10

transport and the necessity of carrying out maritime security measures, particularly in container shipping due to its high velocity and uniformity. However, it has been argued that the compliance of maritime security measures brings negative influences to the port industry including cost and logistics disruption. Port competitiveness and competitive position would be affected accordingly. The focus has been on the EU container seaport; therefore, the characteristics of container port competitiveness, port selection criteria and determinants of port competitiveness have been critically reviewed in Chapter 3. In addition to geographical location and port charges, port efficiency, port service, port performance and port policy were reviewed as key aspects regarding port competitiveness based on the model developed by Yeo (2007).

Objective 2: To Review the Various Port Security Regulations of the USA, Focusing on the CSI Programme and the Existing Debate Over Implications

Several compulsory and voluntary frameworks have been introduced at international, supranational, national and regional level in order to enhance maritime and port security (Tables 2.1 and 2.2). The ISPS Code, the IMO/ILO code of practice on security in ports and the WCO 'SAFE Framework' have been implemented and endorsed at the international level. The USA, as the hegemon, has been playing a leading role in establishing and projecting maritime security regimes and measures at national level (Metaparti 2010). In order to keep terrorism out of the USA and ensure supply chain security, the DHS is adopting a multi-layer approach, which includes the 24-hour rule, the C-TPAT, the CSI, the SFI and using of ATS and NII. The voluntary CSI has been criticised as bringing negative effects to the port industry in terms of operational efficiency and financing. Transferring container inspection from the US unloading point to the CSI ports overseas has been argued as damaging the interests of the CSI-affiliation ports. Some advocates of the CSI argued that its implementation was commercially rewarding and improves productivity of the logistics chain since it was more cost-effective and less time-consuming than conventional inspections. Nevertheless, there is little empirical analysis to support both arguments. Moreover, trade and transport operators may operate at a competitive disadvantage without joining in one of those voluntary programmes (Donner and Kruk 2009). The EC raised their concerns about the possible erosion of fair and genuine competition between the EU ports when the CSI was firstly introduced in 2002 since the CSI is between the USA and individual EU ports rather than the EU as a whole. The topic of long-term analysis on the effects of security initiatives on the competitive position of EU seaports has been highlighted as one of three research gaps mentioned in Dekker and Stevens (2007) in the field of maritime security costs and measures implementation. This research was developed to fill this gap, and Delphi was chosen as a qualitative research method to identify the CSI implications for the EU container seaports.

Objective 3: To Identify the Determinants of EU Container Port Competitiveness

The Delphi results suggested that the container seaport environment in the EU generally has become increasingly competitive. A multitude of tangible criteria that include efficiency and cost have been identified as the most important competitiveness components (Fig. 8.1). Port safety and security, as intangible criteria, are an absolute minimum needed to match industry standards and best practices. The implementation of security measures can improve port security and service quality. Security should be closely integrated and incorporated into business practices since the outcomes of security are part of the service that customers seek from ports. Any port or terminal without adequate safety and security would stand at a huge disadvantage against rivals who fully meet standards. It is suggested that security cannot be separated from the overall business. Port security should not be conducted merely as a reaction to legal and social regulations.

Research Objective 4: To Investigate the Effects of the CSI on EU Container Seaport Competition

The research aims to analyse the impacts of the CSI programme on EU container seaport competition. In order to fulfil this aim, the Delphi technique was adopted as the qualitative method to collect primary data. The research design, process and implementation were described and discussed in Chapter 5. Data collection and analysis of all three rounds were presented in Chapters 6 and 7. Thirteen Delphi questions which consisted of twelve Delphi statements and one open-ended question were designed based on the five conceptual assumptions (Chapter 4) under five categories. The five categories were: (1) the necessity of carrying out a maritime security initiative; (2) introduction of the CSI and the its controversial influences; (3) determinants of EU container seaport competitiveness; (4) the implications of the CSI for EU port competition; and (5) open-ended question for experts to express their comments.

Both the literature and the Delphi study advocated the necessity of implementing maritime security measures which need to be integrated into the entire supply chain to be effective. Additional cost and operational obstructions are inevitable due to additional inspections and administration. However, they are insignificant compared to the overall benefits derived from a secure supply chain. Moreover, utilising production factors and IT systems rationally could minimise the negative influences.

Both the literature review and the Delphi survey confirmed that the CSI has dramatically increased stakeholders' awareness for strengthening and facilitating global container trade security. On the basis that the container supply chain has not experienced disruption by terrorism, the measures implemented should be considered as successful and appropriate for purpose.

CSI Compliance Cost

In terms of CSI financing, the port industry pointed out that the actual investment, procedural costs and operational costs are much less than estimated previously. The Delphi research suggested that the CSI and other security initiatives have been treated by ports and carriers as a business opportunity and security charges have generated additional revenue for ports and shipping lines. None of these CSI ports are suffering uncovered costs or burdens as estimated. There are two reasons behind that. Firstly, the ownership of the EU CSI ports comes from both the public and private sectors. The responsibility of providing appropriate security and safety falls within the scope of government. Many security facilities existed prior to the CSI. Secondly, the most important reason is that the CSI ports and related carriers have formed a cost recuperation mechanism such as charging security-related fees. The real cost burden falls to the Beneficial Cargo Owners (BCO) and ultimately to importers/retailers and end consumers. Under such a mechanism, not only is the initial cost recovered, but also a new revenue stream has been created. The additional revenues are used to pay for any additional equipment such as CCTV and sensors. As to non-CSI small ports, the initial investment for security regulations compliance corresponds to their business scale and container traffic volume and so could avoid an unbearable financial situation. From the perspective of Return on Invested Capital (ROIC), ports and terminals still remain the most profitable players within the end-to-end supply chain.

Port Productivity and Logistics Efficiency

Theoretically, security inspection acts against operational and logistical efficiency owing to the fact that additional procedures are required. Nevertheless, the Delphi experts confirmed that there has been no evidence to show that CSI affiliation has caused severe operational obstruction. In fact, CSI has improved the efficiency and productivity of the entire supply chain from cargo origin to destination. Security regulation compliance could improve port infrastructure which in turn could positively affect efficiency. The investments required by security measures are productive expenditures to attain efficiency improvements. In addition, using NII devices suggested by the CSI has lowered the chance of a container being physically inspected. Very few containers (less than 1%) would undergo a physical check. On the other hand, EU ports rank as one of the most efficient port ranges around the world and EU CSI ports are among the busiest container ports, which implies that CSI implementation has been achieved on an effective and efficient operational basis. With a better IT arrangement and US team assistance, the negative consequences of additional procedures could be minimised.

What is more, competition in the maritime sector is no longer seen at the level of individual ports or carriers, but at a more complex level of logistical relationships between origins and destinations. The CSI could shorten the time from cargo origin to destinations with better procedural arrangements and enhanced trade facilitation.

Implications for EU Container Port Competition

The introduction of the CSI has not distorted competition between EU container seaports. According to the key EU port competitiveness determinants identified by the Delphi, it has no significant direct negativities on operational cost and efficiency. Port service, as one of the identified port selection criteria, is levelled up as a result of improving port security and safety. CSI participation also brings other commercial advantages beyond intended security benefits such as increased supply chain reliability. CSI ports obtain a more preferred status than non-CSI ports. Hence, port competitiveness is improved. With regard to the non-CSI small ports, US-related trade only counts for a very small fraction of their total container traffic volume. There are no commercial or operational competitive disadvantages of any significance as a direct result of not joining the CSI. The competitive position among EU container seaports is not altered by CSI implementation since the CSI is implemented at most of the ports that have a level-playing field within a port range. It is the changing market arising from liner network design aimed at lowering the overall transportation cost that would cause the market share to shift from small to megaports.

A model was developed to interpret the findings of this Delphi research. The model contains four factors, namely (1) economic liberalism and 'rationality'; (2) EU port management ideology, ownership structure and level-playing; (3) logistics vertical integration; and (4) information asymmetries. These four factors underlie the global trade system that affects how the EU container seaport industry manages CSI compliance.

The 'rationality' existing in the current economic liberalism system is the basis of individuals' seeking profit and interest maximisation. The Anglo-Saxon ideology, as the dominant port management approach within the EU, together with port privatisation, directs ports to take action to avoid the loss of self-interests. Regarding maritime security, the involvement of both the private and public sector could help to maximise the positive effect of security measures and minimise the negative implications for port operations and financing. Additionally, so long as there is a level-playing field between these ports regarding security enforcement, which by-and-large there is, there will be no distortion of competition caused by CSI affiliation. Competition within the transportation industry is seen at a more complex level due to logistical integration. Whether a seaport policy or strategy is successful should be aligned with the international logistics context. From this context, the CSI has been beneficial to trade facilitation. The CSI was introduced as a security initiative between the US Customs and commercial ports overseas and a principal–agent relationship is formed in this case. Due to the information asymmetries between the principal and the agent, CSI ports are able to pursue goals and approaches that benefit their own business. Therefore, efficiency issues and cost recuperation are managed effectively to make sure their interests are maximised.

Objective 5: To Propose a Sustainable Solution to Existing Issues Discovered on Maritime Security

The CSI adds additional layers of protection through increasing stakeholders' awareness of security and chances of detection; however, it does not guarantee to prevent terrorists from using sea transportation. The CSI can be seen as a successful initiative in terms of fitness for purpose owing to the fact that there has been no terrorism-related material discovered so far; however, some issues are revealed by this research.

Issue 1: Substantial Liability Issue

The substantial liability issue under the CSI in the event of a terrorist attack utilising container shipping remains unaddressed in a fully CSI compliant cooperative work. Container movement involves a large number of actors globally, including business companies, customs authorities and international organisations. Nonetheless, the transport chain is not fully transparent, and no single authority or industry has the full responsibility for security from origin to destination. With the 100% scanning measures postponed, under current container inspection regimes, the CBP identified about 5% of all seaborne containers entering the USA at high risk (Congressional Budget Office 2016). Moreover, less than 1% of containers are inspected physically overseas under the CSI, which has caused its effectiveness to be questioned. The large percentage of uninspected containers and the possibility of tampering a sealed container during transportation pose potential security risks and vulnerability.

Issue 2: Collaboration Network Under Current Bilateral Regimes

A collaborative working relationship has been fostered between the US government and participating foreign governments to share intelligence and best practice. However, the inequity issue was brought up by the Delphi experts. First of all, since the USA is playing a leading role in establishing a collaborative network based on the bilateral agreement, the partnership between member states and the US government is not balanced. In terms of information sharing and exchange, it has been pointed out that the USA takes more information than sharing their own intelligence to others. The second inequity issue originated from the jurisdiction problem and the reciprocal agreement. Under the CSI, the US Customs officers are sent to the host states' ports for assistance and the host states have the opportunity to send their customs officers to major US ports. However, if all countries reciprocated in the CSI by sending their officers to each others' ports, an overabundance of officials in container operation would occur and create chaos. In fact, so far, very few host countries have sent their officials to the USA; therefore, the implementation of this reciprocity arrangement has diverged from its original plan. Last but not least, the jurisdiction and administration issue arising from the CSI bilateral agreement has been a major criticism. Generally speaking, a nation's jurisdiction is limited to its sovereign territory (Dallimore 2008). Nevertheless, the CSI provisions make the host ports under US jurisdiction outreach. Although the objective of the US Customs team is to assess goods entering the USA, the port industry revealed that there are extraterritorial control actions by US CSI teams at foreign ports, such as controlling the non-US-inbound container inspection process. Both the literature review and the Delphi results revealed that there has been some resentment over the US authorities imposing their will and methods regarding the security issue upon the port industry to solely achieve their own goals and aims.

Solution: Supply Chain Security Integration and Multilateral Regimes

Both of the issues revealed in this research indicate that the reason behind the central deficiency in the CSI is a result of the bilateral agreement rather than a global arrangement. A feasible and effective solution to the vulnerability in container movement and the issues discussed above is to form a comprehensive multilateral regime between all supply chain actors and integrate security into the entire supply chain, as suggested by the Delphi panellists. A multilateral agreement is different from the current bilateral agreement such as the CSI, and a multilateral regime will provide security accountability standards and improve traceability for all elements of container operations. Under a multilateral regime, all supply chain actors will commit themselves into providing more secure and fair global trade. Moreover, SCS stakeholders are currently facing a mosaic of measures and regulations that are overlapping and confusing (Fig. 2.2). A multilateral regime would lead to a harmonisation of security requirements and a collaborative network that is applicable to container transportation operations throughout the supply chain downstream and upstream.

Implementation Considerations

Certain issues need to be taken into consideration during planning and implementation of the proposed multilateral regime.

Stakeholder Participation and Commitment

To make sure all actors are fully committed to such a multilateral regime, all stakeholders and their interests should be considered. Currently, global maritime governance is formed as a hierarchical model. In the case of developing a multilateral security regime, a strong push from the national level is essential to make sure realisation of such a regime is enforced effectively between all parties, especially the private actors and relevant authorities. Furthermore, security, as a public good, should be provided by the government. A strong continuing oversight of a security regime is needed from the government. Secondly, shipping companies, port authorities and other companies will play a major role in implementing such a regime. Hence, industries should be consulted and brought into the process at a very early stage to gain their support and assure their efforts are effective and realistic. Taking the 100% scanning measure as an example, the industries' self-interest should take a leading role in formulating effective procedures, rather than letting them be imposed by governments since the industries are more concerned about costs, effectiveness, substantial responsibilities and possible competition inequities. This multilateral regime not only should have full-scale horizontal coverage which includes all public and private stakeholders within a global supply chain, but also forms a vertical integrated cooperation network which includes participation from all governance levels. In a nutshell, two dimensions are needed in this regime—vertical and horizontal.

Cost Issue

Implementation of a multilateral regime would cause not only monetary cost, but also economic loss due to logistical interruption. Although it is difficult to estimate and measure accurately, the economic cost could be offset by a more secure and reliable supply chain if the revenue loss from theft and smuggling are significantly reduced. Three different levels of costs will occur in establishing and implementing such a multilateral agreement, which are (1) the national cost of establishing and conducting the multilateral agreement; (2) the maritime industrial cost of compliance and operating the regime; and (3) the cost of forming and coordinating the multilateral regime at international level. States should provide suitable equipment at participating transit points such as scanning sensors and subsidise private sectors as incentives. In addition, installation costs, operation and maintenance of equipment and relevant technical support should be covered by relevant authorities at national and regional level. Moreover, participating private actors should work with public actors to process and recuperate the compliance cost. However, the cooperation of all stakeholders should make sure there is a level-playing field and avoid inequities of competition. The last category of cost is for forming and enhancing an international coordination mechanism. A forum at the international and supranational level should be set up for preliminary negotiation and increase engagement of all parties. A protocol or Memorandum of Understanding (MOU) could be generated from such a forum. The cost should be shared among all member states based on the agreement.

The Future

This book was designed to analyse how the CSI will affect EU container seaport competition in the long run and has focused on the most important EU container seaport competitiveness determinants. Moreover, it provides empirical evidence to the controversial port operational and logistical efficiency issues caused by security initiative compliance. In addition, the results of the Delphi survey also support the arguments by McCalla (1999), Wang et al. (2004) and Bichou and Gray (2005). The literature review revealed that most previous researches regarding the implications of maritime security measures for ports are quantitative studies, using methods such as conceptual work, modelling techniques, economic analysis and efficiency measurement. Very limited and abstracted input factors were used and major obstacles occurred in attempts to obtain quantitative data. This Delphi research is a qualitative approach that enabled a more in-depth response than a quantitative survey in terms of ideological issues as well as obtaining attitudes from various experts in relevant fields. The primary data collected from the Delphi survey provides insights from stakeholders so that it helps policy-makers and regulatory bodies to form better policy about developing an effective and efficient maritime multilateral security regime. In addition, this research also interpreted the results of the Delphi survey from economic political, logistics, and port management and ideology perspectives, and developed a comprehensive model to illustrate the underlying factors. To resolve further issues which have emerged, a multilateral agreement among all stakeholders involved in the entire supply chain could be derived. This multilateral agreement should be more industry based than administration based to incentivise all stakeholders' participation to ensure its effectiveness.

This work needs to be taken much further. Clearly, much is going on in the port security world and in the container sector in particular as the political games played by major trading nations have their inevitable (and commonly unforeseen and unwanted) ramifications. Issues such as automation (Grillot and Cruise 2016), the role of blockchains, emerging regional trading bloc policies (Banomyong 2005) and the implications of major transport projects such as the Chinese One Belt One Road proposals (Len 2015; Yu 2017) need to be accommodated. It would be beneficial to consider the implications of the CSI at the global level and form a comparative study between developed and developing country ports. Maritime security is closely linked to politics and remains opaque. There will be more government intervention in the shipping industry in less developed regions. Therefore, the action and attitude from public sectors towards implementation of maritime security measures should be included as a key ambition. However, there could be obstacles in obtaining data since the shipping sector in developing countries is less privatised and relevant stakeholders may be less willing to reveal their true opinions on a political matter.

Although there is no definitive size for a Delphi survey, 20–50 participants would be an appropriate size to provide a representative pooling of judgements regarding this research topic (Witkin and Altschuld 1995). In addition to larger panel size, a wider variety of stakeholders should be taken into consideration as potential participants.

In terms of research method, more than one approach can be adopted to generate more comprehensive data. Interviews or group discussion could be carried out. Moreover, both quantitative (port operational data, financial performances) and qualitative data (comprehensive comments from a wider stakeholder range) should be collected to develop a model to have a sound understanding of how maritime security policy affects the port sector.

In summary, future research should be based on a global level and the development of a multilateral security agreement throughout the entire supply chain. Therefore, a wider variety of stakeholders, larger sample size, a mix of quantitative and qualitative data analysis and adoption of various research methods should be taken into consideration for future research.

References

Banomyong, R. (2005). The impact of port and trade security initiatives on maritime supply-chain management. *Maritime Policy and Management, 32*(1), 3–13.

Bichou, K., & Gray, R. (2005). A critical review of conventional terminology for classifying seaports. *Transportation Research A, 39,* 75–92.

Congressional Budget Office. (2016). *Scanning and Imaging Shipping Containers Overseas: Costs and Alternatives.* Available at http://www.cbo.gov/sites/default/files/114th-congress-2015-2016/reports/51478-Shipping-Containers.pdf. Accessed 10 March 2017.

Dallimore, C. (2008). *Securing the Supply Chain: Does the Container Security Initiative Comply with WTO Law?* (Dissertation). University of Muenster. Available at https://www.wwu-customs.de/fileadmin/downloads/pdfs/diss_dallimore.PDF. Accessed 30 January 2016.

Dekker, S., & Stevens, H. (2007). Maritime security in the European Union-empirical findings on financial implications for port facilities. *Maritime Policy and Management, 34*(5), 458–499.

Donner, M., & Kruk, C. (2009). *Supply Chain Security Guide.* (The World Bank and DFID, 1), pp. 1–107. Available at http://siteresources.worldbank.org/INTPRAL/Resources/SCS_Guide_Final.pdf. Accessed 20 April 2016.

Grillot, S. R., & Cruise, R. J. (2016). *Protecting Our Ports: Domestic and International Politics of Containerized Freight Security.* London: Routledge.

Len, C. (2015). China's 21st century maritime silk road initiative, energy security and SLOC access. *Maritime Affairs: Journal of the National Maritime Foundation of India, 11,* 1–18.

McCalla, R. (1999). Global change, local pain: Intermodal seaport terminals and their service areas. *Journal of Transport Geography, 7,* 247–254.

Metaparti, P. (2010). Rhetoric, rationality and reality in post-9/11 maritime security. *Maritime Policy and Management, 37*(7), 723–736.

Wang, J., Ng, A. K. Y., & Olivier, D. (2004). Port governance in China: A review of policies in an era of internationalising port management practices. *Transport Policy, 11*(3), 237–250.

Witkin, B. R., & Altschuld, J. W. (1995). *Planning and Conducting Needs Assessment: A Practical Guide.* Thousand Oaks, CA: Sage.

Yeo, G. T. (2007). *Port Competitiveness in North East Asia: An Integrated Fuzzy Approach to Expert Evaluations* (PhD thesis). Plymouth University, UK.

Yu, H. (2017). Motivation behind China's 'One Belt, One Road' initiatives and establishment of the Asian Infrastructure Investment Bank. *Journal of Contemporary China, 26*(105), 353–368.

Index

© The Editor(s) (if applicable) and The Author(s), under exclusive license
to Springer Nature Switzerland AG, part of Springer Nature 2019
X. Zhang and M. Roe, *Maritime Container Port Security*,
https://doi.org/10.1007/978-3-030-03825-0

Lightning Source UK Ltd.
Milton Keynes UK
UKHW022254231219
355898UK00002B/17/P